DigiMarketing

The Essential Guide to
New Media & Digital Marketing

Kent Wertime
and
Ian Fenwick

WILEY

John Wiley & Sons (Asia) Pte., Ltd

This publication is designed to provide accurate and authoritative information in regard to the subject matter covered. It is sold with the understanding that the publisher is not engaged in rendering professional services. If professional advice or other expert assistance is required, the services of a competent professional person should be sought.

Other Wiley Editorial Offices

John Wiley & Sons, 111 River Street, Hoboken, NJ 07030, US
John Wiley & Sons, The Atrium Southern Gate, Chichester PO19 8SQ, England
John Wiley & Sons (Canada) Ltd., 5353 Dundas Street West, Suite 400, Toronto Ontario M9B 6HB, Canada
John Wiley & Sons Australia Ltd., 42 McDougall Street, Milton, Queensland 4064, Australia
Wiley-VCH, Boschl strasse 12, D-69469 Weinheim, Germany

Library of Congress Cataloging-in-Publication Data

ISBN 978-0470-822319

Typeset in 11/14 Points Rotis Serif by JC Ruxpin Pte. Ltd.
Printed in Singapore by Saik Wah Press Pte. Ltd.
10 9 8 7 6 5 4 3 2

Dedication

To Toby, Sasha, and Nok with my love and appreciation. You are everything to me.

Kent

For Somjit, Virginia, Vitoon, and Phanita and countless students, colleagues and helpful friends too numerous to name. You know who you are!

Ian

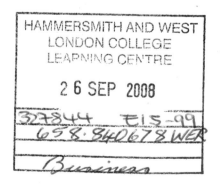

Contents

Acknowledgments

We'd like to acknowledge a number of people who provided their assistance as we wrote *DigiMarketing*. Thank you to Yuranan (Pim) Suwanagul and Surapa (Tik) Chattanont for assistance throughout the process of writing this book. Thanks to Saharath (Chy) Sawadatikom for putting together all of the visuals included in the book and for his help in developing the website that accompanies the book. Thanks to Asmat Yousri and the team at Ring Zero (www.rznet.com) for their help and assistance in producing the website. A special thanks for reviews, comments and advice from Roy Tomizawa, Roy Chapin, Aung Kyaw Moe, and Dr. Krittinee Nuttavuthisit. The use of QR codes in this book and website are thanks to Martin N. Copus and 3G Vision Inc.; we would like to take this opportunity to acknowledge their valuable input.

And we would like to recognize Starbucks Thailand for their excellent coffee, ambiance, and internet connections: invaluable for author meetings and in writing this book.

Errors and omissions, of course, are solely the fault of the authors!

Preface

A NEW ERA

Wei Wei and Huang Yixin are two consumers every marketer needs to know. That may seem odd, since neither of these two university students from Guangzhou possesses talents that would normally make them worthy of note. However, as the Back Dorm Boyz (http://twochineseboys.blogspot.com), Wei Wei and Huang Yixin have become internet stars in China and emblems of a new era in media and marketing.

Their rise to fame began with a simple web posting of their lip sync rendition of the Back Street Boys' *As Long As You Love Me*. Interest in their videos quickly grew, given the instant distribution power of the internet, boosted by viral pass-on from web surfing fans. This was followed by more home-made videos, and then appearances to endorse the likes of Motorola, Pepsi-Cola, and Cisco.[1] Today, their lip sync videos have been seen by an estimated 60 million people across China and Asia.[2]

New media has rapidly brought the power for anyone to create and share content with everyone. But this is only part of a much bigger sea change brought about by digital technology. Massive social networks are becoming digital watering holes that connect people globally. Virtual worlds such as *Second Life* are attracting millions of users to parallel, digital metaverses. New types of digital signage are popping up on roadsides, in malls, and at the end of grocery store aisles, making digital media a street-level reality.

These and other developments in the media landscape are having a big impact on marketers. The multi-channel world of new media presents companies with enormous opportunities and challenges. Marketers have an unprecedented array of channel options through which to reach and interact with consumers. Yet many feel overwhelmed by the speed of change and don't know how to take full advantage of the new options.

As a result, some marketers continue to sit on the sidelines or under-invest in their digital plans. However, in the future, digital channels will play the primary role in marketers' media options. All marketers must build a deep proficiency in new media channels and digital marketing. In fact, our contention throughout this book is that digital marketing – DigiMarketing – is the long-term future of marketing, not a niche part of a marketing plan. It will become part of the mainstream of what marketers will do to sell their products and build their brands.

Therefore, we've written this book as a comprehensive guide on the topic of new media and digital marketing. Our aim is to help you better understand the new media and the digital marketing options available, so you can harness the power of DigiMarketing to grow your business.

Introduction

As we start out, it is useful to address some of the key features of this book. First, this book is divided into three, primary sections:

Section 1: New Media and Marketing in the 21st Century addresses the big picture changes in media and in marketing that are driving companies to transform their marketing. We also outline the 12 Tenets of DigiMarketing.

Section 2: Digital Channels provides an explanation of channel options and examples of how marketers are using those channels. We outline key trends and share best practice learning from digital marketers. Plus, we provide brief analyses of how these trends are likely to evolve in the future.

Section 3: A DigiMarketing Planning Framework covers the key issues a DigiMarketer should address in putting together a digital media and marketing plan. This is to ensure that you have a clear roadmap for success.

Since digital developments are truly global, this book incorporates examples from around the world. While it's true that countries are at different points in the technology development curve (Japan, for example, has mobile technologies that you don't readily find yet in many other countries), our focus is on the universal aspects of digital rather than on specific technologies by geography. We want to help you understand the long-term trends and their underlying implications, not simply highlight the latest technology.

This leads to the next point. It's also worth addressing briefly at the start what this book is *not* about. This book is *not* a how-to guide to website design or a deep-dive on infrastructure or technology issues. We will cover the basics of various digital technologies only as an introduction to how companies can use them for effective marketing solutions. And while e-commerce is no doubt an increasingly important topic for many companies, our focus is on the use of digital channels in all aspects of the marketing mix, not e-commerce-enabling your company.

Lastly, we'd be remiss if this book itself didn't use a digital form. Therefore, throughout each chapter we've noted links to web pages where you can view examples of the material covered in this book. We also urge you to visit this book's own website, www.DigiMarketingNow.com, where you can learn more about DigiMarketing and share your feedback with other readers. After all, in our digital world, we are all connected.

For a personal introduction to the authors, go to www.DigiMarketingNow.com/authors.

END NOTES
1   The campaigns for Motorola and Cisco were created by Ogilvy & Mather China.
2   Estimates from Ogilvy & Mather China.

New Media and Marketing in the 21st Century

Chapter 1

The Media Game-Changers

I n some US cities, the lines at the Apple stores started to form a few days in advance of the new iPhone going on sale. The people who queued up were a diverse bunch. There were gadget freaks eager to trump their friends; Apple die-hards keen to add to their collection of stuff; and regular consumers who wanted to be sure they didn't have to wait months to get a new phone. There were even a few, such as Greg Packer (see his blog at firstinline.wordpress.com), who have made a hobby of waiting in lines, simply to be the first. However, all of them had one thing in common: they were participating in the latest phase of an ongoing, multi-trillion-dollar revolution in the media business.

Blogs

The name "blog" originates from "web log," being an online daily or near daily diary. Free blogging software has brought blog creation within the capabilities of almost any web user. Blogs are now effectively personal websites.

In the last ten years, mobile phones have morphed into mobile computers, offering users a variety of text, music, and video functions. And consumers have responded. Research firm Gartner estimates that spending worldwide on music received on mobile handsets will exceed US$30 billion by 2010, up from less than US$14 billion in 2007.[1] In fact, it's estimated that by 2015, mobile content could be worth in excess of $1 trillion, with voice comprising only a 10% share of the market.[2] No wonder there is such intense competition to bring advanced devices to this rapidly evolving market.

But these substantial changes in the mobile industry are about more than devices and amusing content. Fundamentally, mobile phones are now media. They have become another powerful channel through which marketers can reach consumers, and through which consumers can reach marketers.

As we will see in chapter 6, the growth of mobile is one of the main digital marketing trends. But there are others too. In fact, several tectonic shifts are changing the media and marketing business. These shifts have already made an enormous impact over the past ten years, and they promise even greater change in the decade ahead. Therefore, as a foundation for the remainder of this book, we will start by outlining the media trends that are the major game-changers of the future.

Game-Changer: Proliferation and Invasiveness

Not so long ago, Television and Print were the mainstays of most marketers' media plans, with Radio, Outdoor, and a few other things filling in the gaps where appropriate. Even with the emergence of the internet in the late nineties, television commercials were heavily favored by the dotcoms as the way to build their brands.

What a difference a few years make. Digital technology has spawned a dizzying array of channels. Some channels have developed in response to marketers' craving to get closer to the point of sale. For example, media companies have deployed digital signage in innovative ways in stores and sales environments to help marketers activate sales. Digital paper being introduced in Japan could eventually turn every billboard, pillar or hanging mobile into a digital screen, to which different material can be served, just like today's websites.

Global Positioning Standard(GPS) Receivers

These are included on many mobile phones, bringing the capability to monitor and report a user's location. When integrated with mapping software, GPS makes the mobile a navigational device. This may also allow highly localized and targeted marketing. This is discussed in chapter 6.

Other channels help marketers try to reach captive audiences as they wait in bank lines or on railroad platforms. Games, an enormous growth area that has surpassed Hollywood in size, provide a variety of options for in-game sponsorships, tie-ins, and product placements (see chapter 7). Technology is enabling internet and GPS connections in cars. Even packaging, using radio frequency identity tags (RFIDS) and QR codes (see below), has become a channel via which to communicate with consumers. The ecosystem of channels is indeed vast.

> ## QR (Quick Response) Codes
>
> QR codes are two-dimensional bar codes, already widely used in South Korea and Japan. Although the same size as regular barcodes, QR codes can convey 200 to 300 times as much information. When a consumer photographs the code using his or her mobile phone camera, the code is immediately interpreted and can open a website in the phone's browser.
>
> QR codes effectively turn any "flat" space, such as a billboard or print ad, into a direct response mechanism that can automatically link a viewer or reader to the web. We'll also look at QR codes and similar tools in chapter 6.

However, it's not just the *breadth* of media choices that is driving change: channels are becoming a more *invasive*, as well as pervasive, part of people's lives. Mobile devices, for example, are in pockets or purses on a constant basis. So messaging, and video messaging, can touch people wherever they go, including places that have traditionally been unreached by advertising.

You may not be familiar with all of these channels. If you're not, don't worry. We will highlight many of them in section 2 of this book, when we cover channels in detail.

television	podcasts	viral
print	mobile	blogs
digital media	teleweb	live events
radio/satellite radio	email	sponsorship
branded content	direct mail	telematics
gaming	PVR/DVRs	video on demand
iPod	outdoor	digital signage
packaging	search	instant messaging
digital video	point-of-sale	street theatre
3G phone video	QR codes	guerilla marketing

Marketers are increasingly eager to consider these pervasive/invasive options because they doubt the impact of traditional media channels. And the evidence is mounting that more passive traditional channels are indeed declining in effectiveness.[4] However, there is also mounting tension between marketers and the public, with people increasingly blocking and weeding out unwanted messages. Plus, there is the emotionally charged issue of data privacy. Recent mergers mean that marketers have unprecedented powers to cross-reference different types of information about consumers. While this composite picture of consumers will help marketing become more targeted and so more relevant, many people are nervous about the degree to which they are being tracked and analyzed.

Key Implications for the Future: Media proliferation will continue. As it does, media will be more pervasive and invasive. There will be increasing tension between marketers and consumers over the issues of intrusion, personal data, and privacy.

Game-Changer: The New Mass Media of One

The internet is now over a decade old. It certainly isn't new. In fact, any product that advertised itself as *new* ten years on would be laughed at or even sued by the authorities. However, we use the term *new media* throughout the book since it is commonly used to describe the many digital media options that have come into existence in the last several years. However, we do so with one big caveat about the term: too often, people think that new equates with niche, which is certainly not the case.

Today, digital channels are mass and mainstream, reaching vast national and global audiences. For example, the social networking site MySpace (www.MySpace.com) had an estimated 110 million monthly viewers as of mid-2007.[5] This far exceeds even the most popular newspapers, radio stations, and magazines. Even *Time* magazine, long considered one of America's most popular magazines, has an estimated US circulation of less than 3.5 million readers per week.[6]

Social Networking

Social networking sites are built around the needs and interests of like-minded individuals, and are built by those individuals. Users create a profile for themselves and can join or create "groups." Social networks usually have privacy controls that allow users to choose who can view their profiles or contact them.

In some national markets, a popular website can reach a staggeringly large percentage of the population. In Korea, Cyworld (you can see the English language version at us.cyworld.com) – a social networking site akin to MySpace – reaches an estimated 40% of the total population and 90% of internet users in their twenties.

It's not just the big portals or social networking sites that command large audiences. Perez Hilton, the web gossip king, reaches an estimated 5 million people daily via his blog.[7] Again, this audience tops most newspapers and magazines. Plus the power of these new media is not just passive reach. Some of the most popular online games, such as *World of Warcraft* (www.worldofwarcraft.com), can have a few hundred thousand people playing together online at any given moment.

All business people today need to be fully literate in the world of new media. Games, blogs, and websites are not obscure destinations visited only by teenagers with a lot of free time on their hands. Instead, these channels have enormous audiences that include both genders, all age groups, and (increasingly) rural populations. Admittedly, there is still a gap between rich and poor – the so-called "digital divide." However, even in places such as rural India there are programs underway to bring digital access to the populace. Already, non-metros and small towns in India account for nearly 40% of the nation's internet users.[8] No marketers should dismiss digital channels as being irrelevant to them.

While digital channels are now mass, they can also be extremely targeted, allowing for singular interactions with consumers. This is one of the defining benefits of new media. Marketing through new media can be personalized in many ways. Emails or SMSes might be tailored to individuals based on their preferences, usage histories, and account specifics. Or different content might be sent to different individuals based upon their behavior or actions (in chapter 4 we'll see that this is called *behavioral targeting*). Or an individual's preferences in an online game might be tracked, and offers within the game itself tailored to the individual (we look at games in chapter 7). In later chapters, we will show you many examples of how marketers are tailoring digital marketing today. At this stage, the key point is that large-scale usage of these new media doesn't mean one-size-fits-all. Digital channels are perfect for personalization.

Key Implications for the Future: New media, including social networks, games, mobile, and other digital formats, will continue to attract ever larger audiences. Consequently, marketers will shift more of their activities to these channels. However, marketers will use them as one-to-one channels, not as "mass" media.

Game-Changer: Traditional Media Digitizing

As we consider digital channels, it's important to note that we are not talking solely about new-fangled devices. Traditional media – Television, Print, Radio, and Outdoor – are in the process of going from analogue to digital; they are becoming digital media too. Over the next 20 years, the majority of all media will be digital.

This shift has been happening for years now. As anyone in the newspaper business can attest, there has been a large migration of print publications to digital formats. Today, most newspapers can be read in the traditional paper format or online, or both. Plus, the digital format of newspapers, and even television, is being used to provide additional coverage not shown in the non-digital editions. News alerts delivered to mobile phones extend the interaction between the news media and readers.

Addressable Media

Addressable media are any channels where devices have unique return addresses. Each mobile phone, for example, has a unique number. Each web browser does too (that identifier may even be the same over time, as a so-called fixed IP address). Even an iPod is addressable. And as television becomes digital too, each set-top box or personal digital recorder will be addressable. Addressable devices can be sent unique messages, and generate unique data – digital DNA – that can be tracked.

Radio, which has been around since the early part of the 20th century, is in the process of shifting to digital too. Digital radio allows new types of targeted services, with users enjoying more specific media genres brought to them via satellite. As traditional forms of media move from atoms to bytes, they are gaining all the associated features of interactivity and addressability. This will dramatically alter the relationship between consumers and the media.

Perhaps the most profound impact will be seen in the most venerable of traditional media: television. Television has already gone through major changes over the years, such as the development of cable, and the resulting explosion of targeted channels. But while cable lets people watch more tailored programming, they are still passive viewers. Internet protocol television (IPTV) will take television into the digital world. Television will evolve to have all the goodies that come along with digitalization.

Content can be time-shifted to whenever the user wants it rather than being scheduled. All content will be searchable. Viewers will be able to share blog comments or other material with each other as they watch. They will be able to vote and text chat to see what other people think of particular programs. Look at Current TV (www.currenttv.com), which bills itself as a "global television network that gives you the opportunity to create and influence what airs on TV."[9] On Current TV, people can submit their own videos and vote on which get shown.

Or look at Joost (www.joost.com), currently a beta service from the founders of Skype, promising television with the functionality and participation of the internet. Chapter 10 looks at the impact of these new, digital, interactive versions of television.

As traditional media become digital, they become addressable, and so measurable. Each individual's actions – every click, stop, or interaction – with the digital channel can be tracked and user profiles can be built. The more consumers interact with the media, the better effectiveness can be measured. The guesswork of broadcast media will be replaced by the precision of digital media and the core disciplines of direct marketing.

Key Implications for the Future: Soon, as traditional media become digital, digital media will be the norm. Marketers will have to rethink how they use media, moving from a broadcast model to addressable media. Marketers will leverage the benefits of addressability to personalize, delivering customized messaging and content, and performing analytics.

Game-Changer: Digital Devices Become Media

A complicating factor in understanding the rapidly changing digital ecosystem is that digital devices aren't static: they are gaining new functions. In some cases, the added functionality enhances their use. In other cases, added functionality fundamentally changes their purpose.

We already noted the dramatic transformation of the mobile phone into a mobile computer, complete with web surfing, music, and even sophisticated photography and video functionality. So, when you stand in Heathrow watching a news clip or video commercial on your mobile, is that still a phone or has it become a "media" device?

The mobile phone is only one example of a device having new functionality and new roles in people's lives. There are others too. Wifi-enabled mp3 players are used today to enjoy a wide variety of digital content. Old-style video cassette recorders have morphed into digital video recorders, such as TiVo, dramatically changing consumers' control of media content. Networked game consoles connect to a wide variety of dynamic material. All of these can be considered *media* in the sense of being channels in which both content and marketing are now commonplace.

It's important to note that the impact of digital technology goes far beyond devices. Increasingly, digital will provide functionality you can't see, but from which you definitely benefit. For example, digital sensors built into a car could automatically connect with global positioning technology and local area search services to alert the nearest hospital if you have a car crash.

Lastly, the long-term promise of Web 3.0 is more functionality via background processing. The notion of Web 3.0 (which we will cover in detail in chapter 3) is that the web will do more on users' behalf. Instead of you spending hours in front of the computer searching travel sites to decide where to go for your holiday, digital agents will do the work. Starting with some basic inputs from you, smart agents will scour the web and come back with all the elements of your perfect holiday package already configured. In this manner, technology will be deployed to deal with technology.

Key Implications for the Future: Myriad digital devices will have new functionalities and, as a result, play very different roles in people's lives. More devices will become "media." At the same time, more digital functionality and processing will be embedded and will therefore happen behind the scenes.

Game-Changer: Video Richness and Direct Response

Over time, more screens in our lives will be filled with video. Plus, digital technology allows consumers to reply – direct response – turning every channel into a direct marketing medium.

In chapter 3, we will see that the web is going video – so-called "media richness." This is partly a reflection of faster connection speeds. In countries across Asia and Europe, 100 megabit connections are increasingly common.[10] Without getting into the technicalities of bandwidth, a 100 megabit connection allows for a two-hour movie to be downloaded in about a minute.[11] At these speeds, it's not hard to imagine a video world.

Looking to the future, there will be more broadband and more media richness. The costs of telecommunication will continue to go down, and bandwidth will go up because there are so many players in the game driving that growth. Plus, video is rapidly expanding on what many call the *third screen* – mobile devices.

The reality is that mobile devices are more ubiquitous than internet connections. Mobile penetration is growing at a fast clip in the Middle East, Asia, and Africa. In India, for example, there are six to seven million new mobile phone users per month.[12] What's more, mobile screens around the world are increasingly able to receive rich video content. In Korea, digital media broadcasting (DMB) technology is enabling the re-broadcasting of dozens of channels of terrestrial television to mobile phones. In the US, companies such as MobiTV (www.mobitv.com) offer over 100 channels that can be seen on your mobile phone or Palm device. In Europe, 3G technology is making video on mobiles more commonplace. In the UK, 3, a unit of Hutchison Whampoa, delivers free news, sports and entertainment videos. The content is free but follows the old television advertising model of advertising sponsorship, with each video clip beginning and ending with a 30-second commercial.[13]

In addition to video richness, another feature of the future will be direct response, even from in-market locations. This may use codes, such as QR codes (see Box Insert, QR Codes), or radio frequency identification (RFID) chips or other technologies. For example, digital point-of-sale displays will be able to interact with your mobile phone and alert you to special promotions. If you're carrying a loyalty card, the display could read the card, identify you, and personalize the offers it sends.

A Bluetooth reader (Bluetooth allows digital devices to connect wirelessly over short ranges) at the entrance to a football stadium could automatically interact with your mobile phone to alert you to the team's line-up for the match. As noted earlier, this type of interactivity is transforming devices into media. We'll see more of these possibilities in chapter 9.

These small examples actually have profound implications, particularly when you factor in the critical dimension of location-specific technology. More objects and locations will become direct response vehicles. When any logo, billboard, bus shelter, print ad or other object can instantly connect you to some form of offer or digital content, the game will definitely change.

Key Implications for the Future: Video will be standard through all digital channels, including mobile and in-market media. Plus, new technology will increase interactivity through new media touch points. Effectively, all new media will be used for direct response activity.

Game-Changer: New Channel Connections

The next game-changer extends from the last. As myriad media channels and devices become digital, they can connect in new and inventive ways.

Digital technology provides an underlying standard for a wide variety of different devices. As channels become digital, they will effectively be on the same "gauge of railroad track." Anything digital can easily link to anything else digital. An email or video clip can be displayed on a mobile phone, an in-market digital screen, or an iPod with (almost) equal ease.

For example, Slingbox (www.slingmedia.com) solves the problem of television content being stuck on the television. Using Slingbox, people can port television content via the internet to a variety of devices, anywhere around the world. The common digital platform allows digital content to be place-shifted and time-shifted to the device and schedule that people choose. Goodbye mister television scheduler.

Often, marketing and entertainment drive innovative uses of channels. A wonderful example of this is the advertising being done for Unilever's Dove brand. A program called "The Campaign for Real Beauty," developed by advertising agency Ogilvy & Mather, challenges traditional notions of beauty. Consumers were encouraged to share opinions and cast their votes on different issues. Interactive billboards were used to allow people to vote via mobile phones, with results showing up "live" as a running tally on the billboard. This campaign is discussed in more detail in chapter 8.

Today, networked games include clickable objects. When you click on the courtside billboards in a virtual basketball game you go directly to the advertiser's website. The in-game billboard acts as a live link for e-commerce. A fast food company with delivery services can buy billboards in the game, which consumers can then click to get food at their door – without ever leaving the game!

Wearable computing will have an impact on our lives too. For example, when a micro-chip in clothing links with global positioning, parents will be able to monitor the whereabouts of their children, or hospitals the whereabouts of aged, forgetful adults.

Connectivity of digital devices is also changing the way people pay for things. In Japan, the introduction of smart card chips into mobile phone handsets has enabled millions of Japanese consumers to use their mobiles as digital wallets for a variety of payments. The digital wallet can even be used as a paperless boarding pass on certain domestic air flights. It can also connect to other digital units such as vending machines, allowing cash-less transactions at traditional points of purchase and enabling the marketer to share offers and digital content.

Key Implications for the Future: Digital technology will act as a standard, enabling a wide variety of devices to connect seamlessly. In the future, you can expect more devices to be connected in innovative ways.

Game-Changer: Social Networking, Virtual, and Viral

The next game-changer is a grouping of three dynamics that are at the heart of new media: social networking, virtual realities, and viral pass-on.

New media are essentially social. Everything in digital format can be easily replied to, commented on, tagged, or passed to others. Even the simplest digital formats, SMS and instant messaging, connect people more easily and continuously than ever before. Anybody with a teenager in the house will be able to tell you that! However, there are also a growing number of more sophisticated social networking sites, such as Facebook (www.facebook.com), which serve as ways for people to connect virtually.

At the same time, networked games and sites that act as virtual worlds (see chapter 7) are creating enormous platforms within which people interact. This social connectivity of digital media is a central point that marketers habituated to traditional, one-way media must grasp.

Viral Marketing

Viral marketing works by persuading customers to pass along your message, or product, to others. A virus (think influenza) stimulates its host to actions (sneezing) which enable the virus to infect other susceptible hosts. Similarly, successful viral marketing provides something (perhaps a quirky video clip) – almost always free – that consumers want to share. They pass it on to whoever they feel would be most appreciative, causing it to spread rapidly, provided it's good content. We look at viral in more detail in chapter 5.

The proliferation of digital devices and digital destinations means people spend more of their time today in virtual spaces. People who check email, send SMSes, and surf the web repeatedly leave the physical world for virtual worlds. As a result, the boundaries between the physical and the virtual begin to blur. This leads to a second, central point that traditional marketers must grasp: virtual spaces are not poor facsimiles of reality.

Virtual spaces are often extensions of reality, or even heightened, improved versions of reality. In a virtual world, people can have powers they may not possess in the physical world. They can create virtual characters (known as avatars) to become their virtual selves, often in a way that releases them from their repressions and the constraints of the physical world. People spend physical world money to own virtual wardrobes, virtual real estate, and other virtual items. So, a virtual experience is not a second-rate experience. It can be both truly engrossing and emotionally rewarding. Internet game addiction clinics are a perverse affirmation of the powerful influence that new media are having.

The new media are handy enablers, letting people, who are innately social, share things that they find interesting, funny, or useful. Most readers will nod their head in agreement as they recall how they have forwarded different types of material to friends, colleagues, and family members. As a result, news and information spreads faster than ever before. We live in an increasingly connected society where it's harder and harder to monopolize information. Even countries with repressive governments are finding it difficult, if not impossible, to control people on the internet. As we look to the future, it's clear that news and information will increasingly zip around the world, fuelled by viral pass-on.

Key Implications for the Future: The physical and virtual worlds will increasingly overlap and intermesh. People will interact in new ways as they participate in social networks that permeate their lives, and they will share more information virally.

Game-Changer: Consumer Paid and Created Content

The nature of content is changing dramatically too. Over several decades, marketers and consumers have had a symbiotic relationship, the essence of which was that marketers would indirectly bankroll the production of content, via the purchase of advertising space, so that consumers could watch that entertainment for free (or at subsidized prices). The only hitch was that people had to see a bit of advertising between the content. This model is still the way traditional television works.

But this old arrangement has been coming undone for years as consumers have tired of what seems like ever more advertising clutter and many other entertainment options have become available. Today, the media business is continuing a migration to entertainment material that consumers pay for directly or have created themselves.

The ascendancy of consumer-paid content was highlighted in a 2004 issue of *Advertising Age* under the banner

"A MAJOR MEDIA REVOLUTION HAS JUST OCCURRED... Consumers Spent More to Reach Media Than Marketers Spent to Reach Them."[14] This major crossover in the market has been fuelled by many things, including DVD sales, subscription cable television, and pay-per-view. But digital entertainment in a variety of formats has been a major contributor too. As traditional media goes digital, the content and advertising models change. For example, digital radio, from companies such as Sirius (www.sirius.com), provides commercial-free programming that consumers are willing to pay for by subscription.

The biggest game-changer in content, however, is the essence of what is generally referred to as Web 2.0 – namely, the trend towards co-created content. In the traditional media model, content was scarce and used to attract a large audience, on which advertisers thrived. But the growth of social networking sites, blogs, podcasts, and now video blogs has fuelled a massive upswing in consumer-created content. As a result, the world is awash in content. Consumers are as likely to opt to see free material created by another consumer as they are to look for "professionally" produced content.

As we look to the future, there are some key content trends that will bring further changes. First, more content will be dynamic. The large multiplayer game platforms and virtual universes (highlighted in chapter 7) are filled with dynamic content that is in perpetual creation by participants. Consumers are increasingly testing the boundaries of existing content. They are creating new types of mash-ups, covers, and remixes of music, films, and other popular content, often irrespective of copyrights. They are also taking advertising materials and creating new things with existing logos, mascots, and commercials, sometimes as brand fans and sometimes as anti-brand activists.

Mash-Ups

A mash-up is an application that integrates complementary elements from two or more (usually) internet sources to create something interesting. Mash-ups are a remixing of content. As we will see in chapter 3, they are becoming easier and easier for non-experts to make.

Second, more content will be pulled by consumers, using RSS (see Box Insert below) and other technologies. Consumers choose which feeds of headlines or summaries they are interested in receiving. Then, if they want to know more, they click on the headline. Consumers are in control. Consumers pull the information, identifying what they want and what they will omit. Consumers decide when they want to know more. We look at RSS further later in the book.

Real Simple Syndication...really!

Real Simple Syndication[15] is a set of web-feed formats that allow frequently updated materials – such as blogs, or news, or even podcasts – to be distributed over the web. Consumers choose to subscribe to feeds of headlines or summaries from sources in which they are interested. This means that consumers get your information and material without having to go to your site.

Third, as content becomes more liquid, it will become device independent and scale to more channels. Content will move freely across multiple devices and gadgets in the home and outdoors. People will become multi-modal nomads, connected constantly with their favorite content. Many of the big, sophisticated media companies have been diversifying their content for years; this is why you can easily get Mickey Mouse on multiple screens. In the future, even consumer-created content will scale to multiple devices.

Consumer-created content is becoming richer as it goes to more devices. There is still plenty of text-based content, however a consumer with a modern digital camera (perhaps in their phone) and a computer can do incredible things. Over the years, video cameras have captured countless weddings, little league games, and adult fun. But while the means of production have been there for some time, the means of distribution haven't. Today, the internet serves as the most effective and egalitarian distribution system ever. Consumer-created content and its possibilities for marketing are the topic of chapter 8.

Key Implications for the Future: Consumers will have an expanding wealth of content options. Consequently, companies will have to focus more than ever on content that attracts consumers. At the same time, consumers will use technology to create increasingly varied, sophisticated, and rich materials. With almost no barriers to entry, and the easy global distribution power of the internet, everyone will be in the media business.

Game-Changer: Consumers Organize Information

Consumers are actually doing more than just creating content. They are now helping each other screen, filter and organize that content. Traditionally, content was screened and filtered by professional publishers, editors and reviewers. Content was then organized by librarians using detailed, arcane classification systems. This screening and organization was the domain of trained experts. The layperson probably needed assistance to find what they wanted.

Interestingly enough, on the web, faced with massive information overload, people are dealing with screening and organization themselves! We see two major customer-driven activities: collaborative filtering and tagging (also known as creating folksonomies). Both are great examples of people helping people.

Collaborative filtering, which we'll look at in chapter 3, helps customers help each other by pooling information about our behavior. When you choose a book at Amazon (www.amazon.com), the site automatically tells you that "Customers who bought this item also bought…," and provides a list of books. The idea is that customers who have one purchase in common with you will be likely to lead you to other things you will like. Collaborative filtering is consumers pooling information to make better decisions.

Tagging means attaching a few descriptive words to an item (a photo, web page, article, person, book) to make it easier to find in the future. Tags are not new. What is new is that today tagging is not left to expert librarians and indexers. Anyone can do it. And (usually) there is no controlled list of tags that must be used. Consumers can spontaneously tag with words they feel are most descriptive. Some call this creating a folksonomy.[16] The idea is it's like taxonomy but created by folks! By relying on consumers' own language, rather than arcane cataloging terms, retrieval should be easier. Folksonomies promise to play the editing and filtering role previously played by publishers, and temper the tsunami of consumer-created content.

Key Implications for the Future: Consumers want to participate actively in the co-creation of content. They have their own ideas of how things should be tagged and organized. The DigiMarketer needs to leave room for consumers to express these ideas and actively participate in organizing information.

Game-Changer: Search

The final media game-changer is search. John Battelle, a leading web guru and founder of Federated Media (http://federated media.net), has called search the "database of intentions."[17] This statement neatly summarizes search's expanding role as the initiation point in the consumer–marketer relationship.

It's true that there has long been an analogue version of search in the form of classified advertising and the *Yellow Pages*, both substantial businesses in their prime. However, digital search has implications well beyond a person simply locating a phone number or piece of information.

Search is the statement of consumer intent or interest. It's the digital equivalent of "hand raising" to show when the consumer is interested in something. Once that intent is known, by virtue of the person's search, relevant marketing material can be instantly matched to that individual. Some searches reflect temporary needs or desires (for example, to find some last-minute birthday flowers); other searches reflect longer term consumer interests (such as researching one's genealogy). However, *all* of a customer's searches can be collected in a database. Over time, this provides the search company with a very powerful composite picture of an individual's habits and patterns – the database of intentions.

Search, the fastest growing part of digital media, is now enormous. One website estimates there were 14,400,000,000 searches made globally during the month of February 2007, which works out to over 514 million searches per day, or almost 6,000 per second.[18] As we look to the future, this number is set to grow even further. There are a number of reasons for this. First, as we've already noted, there is simply more and more digital content that people must search through to find what they want. Second, search is rapidly extending to all types of digital material, including photographs (remember the tagging discussed above) and video. Given the future growth of IPTV (which we mentioned before), video search promises to be huge. Third, search is moving beyond the desktop to localized search conducted on mobile phones. The in-market use of search will make search even more of a workhorse in everyday life.

To appreciate the future impact of search, you've got to factor in some of the game-changers we've already covered. Imagine that you're standing on a street corner in Dublin and want to find some good Italian food. A local area search on your mobile will yield a selection of nearby restaurants. But the result on your 3G phone will be a selection of video introductions from each restaurant, highlighting their specials for the evening. Perhaps your smart agent – loaded into your phone – will have learned from your past behavior (and searches) that you're a big fan of tortellini. Your smart agent will spot that one restaurant has a video highlighting the tortellini of their resident chef from Bologna, Italy. Your smart agent will put that video in first place on your playlist – having first checked with the restaurant's online reservation system that there is space for you tonight. While you are watching the tortellini video, the smart agent will be using the GPS built into your mobile to develop your route to the restaurant. Once you confirm that tortellini is it for tonight, the agent will confirm your reservation and guide you through the nearby streets to the restaurant, while checking with your credit card companies to see if any of them have special dining promotions for that restaurant on this night. This is not far-fetched. Most of the technology needed to accomplish this is available today.

A positive outlook for search is not a blank cheque for Google, currently the largest of the search engines. While Google enjoys a dominant position in some large markets, there are a host of local search engines across the world, including local language search engines.[19] And, as we'll see in chapter 4, there will be new pressure on the mass search players from vertical search providers. Vertical search engines – sometimes called *specialty search* or *vortals* – are growing in response to the frustration many feel with the driftnet-style results they get when they use the most popular search engines. Instead of the millions of results returned for a basic query, people often want fewer, more relevant matches. So, vertical search services are growing around specific topics or industries such as law, medicine, and marketing to facilitate more focused results.

In later chapters, we'll detail how search works, and the need to develop a search strategy for your business. At this stage, it's important simply to register why search is growing so rapidly as an important part of the new media landscape.

Key Implications for the Future: Web search will evolve from general search to more "vertical" search, or contextual search. Mobility will drive local area search. As this happens, the role of search as the way people find all things will grow further.

SUMMARY: DIGITAL MEDIA BECOMES THE MAINSTREAM

While it's impossible to say exactly what the future will look like, a few things are certain. First, we will eventually reach an inflection point when the majority of channels become digital; digital will be the mainstream and mainstay of media. Second, content created by companies and consumers alike will proliferate, particularly video content, and will be viewed on the multiple screens and devices in people's lives. People will increasingly search for the content they want among an ever-expanding mound of digital media. Third, as channels and content proliferate, the virtual and physical worlds will intertwine, with consumers crossing back and forth constantly between the two.

These major changes in media can best be summarized as a shift from traditional mass media to an era of personalized and participatory media. Although revenues from traditional media currently exceed those from new media by more than

10:1, the growth of new media revenues is almost four times that of traditional media.[20] No doubt traditional media will play an important role for years to come. However, the shift to new media is not a fad or short-term trend; it is the inevitable result of a series of deep, long-term, structural changes. Consumers' personal preferences and configurations will be known to marketers at a variety of touchpoints. This will make marketing more useful and personalized, but, at the same time, tracking personal data and habits will potentially put marketers on a collision course with consumers over privacy and security.

The new media world will have a profound impact on consumers and marketers alike for decades to come. For consumers, new media will provide easy access to more options, but may also leave them more befuddled by those options. Stress and information overload are likely to increase. Indeed, for many consumers they already have. Hopefully, smart agents will be there to help.

Perhaps this isn't far off from how marketers feel too! Many companies are uncertain which digital route is the right one for them. Particularly given the pace of change, they wonder where they should jump in. But to be successful in this environment, you will have to be ready to make a step-change; small experiments will no longer suffice. You must be ready to take a transformational view of your marketing. This means making a shift to DigiMarketing.

END NOTES
1   www.gartner.com/it/page.jsp?id=500295
2   www.budde.com.au/Reports/Contents/Global-Mobile-Content-Statistics-and-Services-3561.html
3   Usually, but not always, attributed to Benjamin Disraeli, en.wikipedia.org/wiki/Lies,_damned_lies,_and_statistics
4   mckinsey.com/practices/retail/knowledge/articles/Boostingreturnsonmarketinginvestment.pdf
5   Brad Stone, "MySpace Ready to Challenge Lead of You Tube", *International Herald Tribune*, June 28, 2007, page 13.
6   www.forbes.com/business/2007/08/13/magazines-audit-circ-biz-cx_lh_0813mags.html?feed=rss_business
7   Jac Chebatoris, "A Gossip's Golden Touch", *Newsweek*, June 4, 2007, page 53.
8   Internet and Mobile Association of India, eTechnology Group@IMRB presentation.
9   www.currenttv.com/about
10 www.convergedigest.com/Daily/daily.asp?vn=vl4n45&fecha=3%2F8%2F2007

11 www.divxmovies.com/video/
12 www.cellular-news.com/story/24839.php
13 Aaron O Patrick, "TV Ads Find a Spot on Smallest Screens", *The Asian Wall Street Journal*, July 6–8, 2007, pages 26–27.
14 August 23, 2004, adage.com, Scott Donaton.
15 Sometimes said to stand for Rich Site Summary, or even (an acronym within an acronym) RDF Site Summary – RDF being Resource Description Framework.
16 The term was invented by information architect Thomas Vander Wal; see www.vanderwal.net/about.php
17 John Battelle, *The Search: How Google and Its Rivals Rewrote the Rules of Business and Transformed Our Culture*, Penguin Group, New York, 2005.
18 firsthit.com.au/2007/04/number-of-searches-every-day/
19 www.cryer.co.uk/resources/searchengines
20 *Navigating the Media Divide*, IBM Global Business Services, 2007, p3.

Chapter 2

DigiMarketing: The New Imperative

DigiMarketing: The Future of Marketing

The media game-changers we have just outlined will alter forever the physics of marketing. In particular, the shift from mass broadcast to digital, one-to-one media means that the traditional advertising algorithm of building brand image primarily through paid reach and frequency must be re-thought. When the majority of media is digital, participatory, two-way, and potentially viral, it doesn't make sense to still execute marketing as if it were a one-way world.

To be successful, marketers can't simply add a few digital activities to their traditional marketing plans. Instead, they must fundamentally re-craft their approach to marketing around the features of the new media and digital marketing. This will bring about a renovation of marketing. While basic marketing principles – such as positioning and segmentation – will remain, digital channels will extend and accelerate how marketers engage consumers. The pressures of digital Darwinism will force this marketing evolution as consumers will favor brands that engage them continuously through digital channels.

The interconnection of people through digital channels means that news, information and content spread with breathtaking speed. Plus, the material distinction between products has become more short-lived. In this environment, set-piece marketing is becoming an anachronism. It's a bit like 18th century British redcoats trying to fight a modern guerilla strike force. What's needed is a more dynamic approach to brand management, with marketers continuing to guide their brands, but ready to do so at the speed of the market conversation, and with much, much, more consumer participation. Digital marketing plans will be constantly evolving and improving, based on real-time data about what consumers are actually doing. This is where new media channels offer such an advantage.

DigiMarketing Defined

DigiMarketing is the future evolution of marketing. It happens when the majority, or totality, of a company's marketing uses digital channels. Digital channels are addressable, enabling marketers to have a continuous, two-way, personalized dialogue with each consumer. This dialogue leverages data from every customer interaction to inform the next, much like a neural network. Additionally, marketers use real-time behavioral information and direct consumer feedback continuously to improve and optimize interactions.

DigiMarketing is not prescriptive. As with traditional marketing, there are numerous roads to success. One marketer might create a website-centric program, while others might have success using games or viral videos. Although there's no one *right* way to do DigiMarketing, there are a number of interrelated shifts in your planning, thinking, and approach that are required to transform your traditional marketing to DigiMarketing. What follows is a brief overview of 12 tenets that guide DigiMarketing. In section 3, we will come back to these tenets as we outline the decisions you will face as you develop your own DigiMarketing plans.

From Viewers to Participants

Consumers are no longer docile media targets or viewers. Today, consumers are more likely to be participating than watching. Through the web, podcasting, and blogging, they actively express their opinions. While some marketers are still trying to sort out their digital plans, consumers are actively using digital channels to compare, critique, and sometimes condemn the products and services of those marketers.

People's use of new media is about more than simply selecting a new set of gadgets. New media channels today allow more consumer control and so gain greater relevancy to consumers. Plus, the dimension of mobility means they can participate from virtually anywhere.

These are critical points for marketers to grasp. What's needed from the beginning is a reframing of your view of consumers as active participants. To truly transform your marketing, you will need to expand your planning process to incorporate contemporary insights about how your consumers are changing, particularly in relation to digital media channels.

DigiMarketing Tenet 1: Consumers and customers must be actively engaged as participants – creators, contributors, and commentators – not treated as passive viewers or targets.

From Impressions to Involvement

Given the more participatory role of consumers, marketers need to shift their focus from impressions to creating ongoing engagement.

Share of voice (SOV) has traditionally been a key measure for marketers. However, as channels proliferate, SOV is much harder to determine accurately. Plus, it is arguably becoming less relevant. Marketing tonnage – outspending the competition in media – is no longer a viable route to success. Simply comparing your spending levels to others is not an accurate gauge of brand impact.

New media is often not measured, or even paid for, on a cost-per-thousand (cpm) basis. What's more, given the viral nature of new media, the actual reach of effective digital marketing can far exceed its spending. For example, the award-winning *Evolution* viral video for Unilever's Dove brand (see Boxed Insert, "The Campaign for Real Beauty," in chapter 8), created by Ogilvy & Mather in Toronto, has been seen by an estimated 500 million people globally, creating enormous value.[1]

The effectiveness of new media channels is not directly correlated with media spending. Other measures relating to performance need to be applied. Effectiveness is a function of consumer interaction and involvement, not simply the extent of awareness. This is not to say that reaching a sufficiently large audience is not relevant; it will always be important for certain types of mass products. However, marketers must relinquish the safety blanket of cost-per-thousand thinking and look more deeply at what each channel is generating in terms of participant engagement. Today, the companies with the best customer relationships are the ones who win.

Engagement isn't just people logging a lot of time in a channel. Rather, engagement happens when participants are interested and emotionally involved so that they want to respond and interact. Engagement implies mutuality. DigiMarketers must take part in a constant conversation *with* their customers. DigiMarketers must learn to learn from consumers, not talk *at* them. Successful DigiMarketers will require new, dynamic engagement strategies to encourage participant involvement. They will also need to have a clear proposition if they expect participants to give them their time and attention.

DigiMarketing Tenet 2: Marketers must move beyond the traditional metrics of reach and frequency. Successful DigiMarketing engages people on a sustained basis. This requires better planning and a clear proposition.

From Broadcast to Addressable

The change from broadcast media to addressable channels requires a big change of mindset, the essence of which is to shift from thinking about a mass audience to focusing on individual consumers.

Digital media is addressable, which means that even if there are millions (or billions) of people with that same type of device, you can still connect with each of them as individuals. Moreover, each user will connect with you as an individual, displaying his or her particular usage habits and preferences.

Addressable media have the potential for two-way communication, for interactivity. And experience shows that when interactivity is possible, people do what comes naturally to them: they interact! Consumers are quick to assert their views and desires. In the early days of digital marketing, many companies were completely unprepared to handle the flood of responses they got on the web. Even today, digital marketing novices are often surprised by the amount of feedback they can get from consumers. Unfortunately, many companies still don't make sufficient use of consumer feedback. Even worse, a lot of digital marketing is still not geared to individual participants.

A mass approach is simply insufficient in new media. DigiMarketing requires that you leverage the essential benefits of addressable channels: individuality and interactivity. A key part of your planning will be to figure out which addressable channels – or mix of channels – is right for you. Then, you must design engaging creative that encourages customer response and participation. If you do this right, customers will help tailor your creative content according to their individual preferences. Then you will really be positioned to fully exploit the potential of addressable channels.

DigiMarketing Tenet 3: Marketers need to determine which mix of channels is right for their marketing needs. Engaging digital creative should encourage participants to adapt your digital marketing around their personal preferences and desires.

From Schedule-Driven and Location-Bound Content to Time-Shifted and Borderless

For years, most marketers' content creation was limited to a bit of advertising, some sales literature and perhaps some customer relations materials. Digital media makes new content demands. As you develop your digital marketing, you will have to shape your plans around some major content changes. These changes can best be summarized as five freedoms, four of which we'll mention here, with the fifth one coming up shortly.

Freedom from Scheduling. The starting point is to recognize the implications of time-shifting. When people have the technology that allows it, they free themselves from a schedule, preferring to enjoy content when they feel like it. After all, why shouldn't they? Increasingly we are seeing entertainment, sports, and information being time-shifted. Devices such as personal video recorders and iPods facilitate this liberation of content from a schedule. Many owners of digital video recorders (like TiVo) *never* watch programs at their scheduled time. What's more, many digital media are always-on, on-demand, and unscheduled.

Freedom from Geographic Boundaries. As we've already noted, digital content today is instantly global. One click can take you across national borders to a website in Tokyo as easily as to one in Oslo. Any website is effectively a global outpost for your brand and all web material is potentially global content.

Freedom to Scale. Digital media presents the most scaleable form of marketing ever. Digital content can be scaled from global to very specific audiences. So, if you want to engage a highly focused audience, such as funeral directors, you can do that. In fact, check out www.funeraldirector.com for an example of this point.

Scalability

DigiMarketing is not solely the domain of large companies. Businesses of every size, down to the local pet shop or trinket store, can take advantage of it. As we will see in chapter 4, text advertising keyed to search words can be purchased in a very focused and affordable manner. Plus this advertising is usually sold on a cost-per-click (cpc) basis. If no-one clicks your ads, you don't pay. The scalability of DigiMarketing means we can access what is generally called the "long tail." (You can read more about that in chapter 3.)

Freedom from Formats. Content is increasingly freed from specific formats. Standard units such as 30-second television commercials, half-page ads, and static billboards have been the mainstay of marketing for decades. However, a viral video can be as long as people are willing to watch; nobody tells you how deep, involving, or long your podcast can be; and nobody (except for irate parents) forces participants to stop interacting with a game or website after a set amount of time.

These four freedoms have significant implications for marketers. Most importantly, companies will need to become much more proficient in developing content that consumers truly want. We can no longer simply rely on a media buy to deliver a mass audience. Instead, marketers will have to create content that succeeds or fails by virtue of its appeal to individual consumers, who will increasingly select what content they want, and on what terms.

Companies will need to innovate in their content creation, in particular to shift from hard-selling to creating branded material that entertains and informs audiences. A good example of innovative content creation is BMW, who produced a number of short, exciting web videos (www.bmwfilms.com) with BMW cars embedded throughout each video. Other marketers are experimenting with advertising in webisodes and mobisodes – short episodes of television shows that are specially created for viewing on (respectively) a computer screen or a mobile phone. This freedom from formats should be seen as a boon to inventive marketers who aren't afraid to take advantage of a vastly different creative canvas for building their brands.

In order to make sense of this exciting but challenging new era, marketers will require clear content plans. These plans could include a spectrum of options from videos to embedded content to consumer co-created content. We will address this in chapter 12.

DigiMarketing Tenet 4: In DigiMarketing, content will increasingly be freed from specific delivery mechanisms, the limitations of media units, and physical boundaries. All DigiMarketers will need to make relevant, quality content their focus in order to generate sustained participant interest.

From Marketer-Driven to Consumer-Initiated, Created and Controlled

The fifth content freedom is the ability for anyone to create content. We've touched upon this major trend already. And given its importance, we've dedicated an entire chapter (chapter 8) to the subject. However, it's worth noting here since consumer content creation reflects a key shift of power to consumers.

For a long time, marketers have led the dance. So while there's plenty of industry jabber about consumer-centricity, the behavior of most marketers suggests a reluctance to relinquish the reins. However, the genie is out of the bottle. Media companies no longer have the lock on distribution that they used to have. Engrossing content in blogs, video-blogs (vlogs), You Tube videos, and mash-ups can come from anywhere, as the Back Dorm Boyz showed in our preface. Production and distribution is increasingly easy. Everyone can be in the media business.

> ### Vlogs
>
> "Vlog" is short for "video blog," or a blog which uses video extensively. Because the video is often shot using the vlogger's mobile phone, these are sometimes called "moblogs" or "mobile vlogging." Vlogs are the real reality television!

People are using the open forum of digital media for a wide variety of purposes, ranging from frivolous fun to serious issues involving public health, safety, politics and the environment. The emergence of citizen media is a key trend, creating greater transparency and vexing repressive governments. Blogs have become a mechanism for sharing views on all types of topics, or blowing the whistle on things that otherwise would have been suppressed. By mid-2007, the number of blogs tracked by Technorati (www.technorati.com) had crossed 90 million.[2] So this is not a niche trend; it is a major force changing the way humans share news and opinions.

Taken at face value, the ascendancy of consumer control appears to pose an enormous threat to marketers. However, if advertisers embrace the trend, it's actually an opportunity. Consumers won't choose to be involved with your brand if they have no interest in it. So, more often than not, consumers who seek out or participate in digital activities around a brand are well-disposed towards that brand. However, brand involvement doesn't happen by random luck. DigiMarketers require strategies that entice, encourage, and enable consumer contributions, including creating materials that people can easily personalize. Smart 21st century companies will leverage the energy and passion of their best consumers.

DigiMarketing Tenet 5: Consumers will initiate and direct more of the participant–marketer interchange. A large portion of content will come from consumers themselves. Marketers will play a role in this by encouraging and rewarding consumer content creation in a manner that is relevant to their brand(s).

From Push Marketing to Opt-In and Share Marketing

Consumers generally aren't interested in receiving information they haven't requested. They are also uninterested in a one-way relationship in which they have no choices. In digital channels, consumers demand to opt-in − to agree beforehand that they give you permission to contact them. This is a further manifestation of consumer control and it has a profound impact on the way in which marketers must now relate to consumers. Advertisers must shift their efforts from push marketing to approaches that service participants so they continue to opt-in.

Given the explosion of channels, there's more messaging than ever. The daily deluge of emails and SMSes is probably familiar to you, as is the stress of keeping up with your inbox. If you're nodding your head as you read this, then you are especially obligated to address this issue as you conduct your own DigiMarketing! Messaging should be done with some key principles in mind. The principles start with a requirement to always be permission-based. It really is the golden rule of digital marketing. Without consumer permission, you will be an irritant, and you will get branded as a spammer.

Spam

Spam is unwanted, unsolicited messages, usually sent by email, SMS, or other messaging platforms. Spammers send out billions of messages, using state-of-the-art tricks to avoid filtering software. We'll look at spam (and how not to send it) in more detail in chapter 5.

The opt-in process should gain more than just permission. The DigiMarketer should also seek consumer feedback on areas of interest and frequency of contact. Even your most loyal brand advocates might prefer to hear from you weekly instead of daily. Good opt-in data will enable you to communicate with each consumer in the manner most relevant to that individual. For example, a bank that mails all its customers repeatedly, suggesting that they open another account, is a spammer and an annoyance. However, if that same bank sends out an alert to an opted-in customer notifying her that she has an overdraft, and highlighting accounts with overdraft protection, they are seen as helpful. Changing your orientation to serve the needs of individual customers can really pay off.

In the future, as global positioning technology becomes more standard, messaging will be enhanced by more location-specific applications. Imagine, for example, that you're walking down the street near the local drug store and an SMS from your pharmacist reminds you that your prescription is about to expire. This is another example of how messaging can build the relationship with consumers by servicing them. This is the direction DigiMarketers must take.

Opted-in messaging is only part of the equation. Another part is harnessing the power of consumers messaging each other. Arguably, this will be as important as the marketers' direct messaging. Viral pass-on from one person to another is a very important part of brand building. First, there is a natural targeting process that occurs when people decide to forward material to each other. People generally forward material to someone they consider like-minded or whom they know will have a need or interest in that material. For example, you might share business content with colleagues, but probably not with family members. Second, when a person passes something on, there is an implied endorsement from the sender that this is worth the recipient's time and attention, even if it's just to amuse. DigiMarketing must include strategies to seed brands into people's interactions to leverage these benefits.

Let's also note here that viral pass-on is just one aspect of the evolving social dynamics of the digital world. Another important development is the growth of social networking sites, which act as virtual exchanges through which people connect. DigiMarketing plans need to include strategies for social networking sites as well. This might include embedding your brand into an existing networking site. Or it might result in your creating a social networking site for your brand, as Unilever's Sunsilk brand did in India with the "Gang of Girls" (www.sunsilkgangofgirls.com), developing a platform for young women to connect and network. As digital evolves, marketers are likely to see their role as creating platforms for interaction, with consumers providing most of the contact and content, all happening in a branded space.

DigiMarketing Tenet 6: Messaging with participants must be on an opt-in basis only, and tailored to each participant's indicated preferences. Companies will increasingly seek the exponential payback that comes from having consumers share information through social networking sites and virally with each other.

From Traditional Media Planning to New Media Planning

The media plan is a central fixture of marketing that is not likely to disappear soon. However, its purpose and content will need to change dramatically as marketers shift their budgets from traditional to digital media. As we saw in the last chapter, digital media has a direct response and activation function; it's not just about image and awareness. There are also new dimensions of time and location that need to be taken into consideration. To illustrate this, let's take the example of outdoor digital signage.

In a traditional media plan, billboards would be included to create awareness and possibly generate some response (probably through the inclusion of a phone number). However, once billboards become digital, marketers might prefer to display a video, not a static image. Depending upon the location of that digital signage, say in a central business district, the media plan would need to anticipate what video content is most appropriate to serve to that screen. That could depend upon the advertiser and the time of day; beer advertising, for example, would probably be more effective in the evening when people are leaving the office. A coffee brand, on the other hand, would probably have more interest in using that digital billboard in the morning or at lunch time. Consequently, the media plan would need to include the time of messaging, not just the location.

There are other dimensions to it too. The beer advertiser might be running a promotion or special events in and around the business district. So the inclusion of those interactive billboards in the plan might be to support an activation drive to the events. Or, the video in the billboards might encourage people to text back or possibly connect via a QR code to the brand's website to sign up for a special draw. When a specific consumer texts back, instant data-mining might indicate he is a high-value consumer and should be offered an incentive on the spot to encourage him to attend the beer advertiser's event that evening. Location tracking of the mobile phone used to send the SMS might indicate he is near to the event, so he could be sent a local area map showing how to get there, along with an offer for when he arrives.

There are a few implications of this brief example, which could go further. First, traditional media planning needs to become multi-dimensional. The new media plan now needs to integrate direct response planning and activation planning, not just image building. Also, the plan needs to reflect the connection of media and devices – in this example, the electronic billboard and the mobile phone. Real-time data enters as a key component too. Physical locations and dayparts might be involved in ways they have never been before.

At the same time, the new media plans must anticipate the content liberation we already discussed. Since content is more liquid and viral these days, content distribution strategies are required to seed material into the market, for consumers to pass virally to each other rather than simply relying on paid media channels. The old separation of media and creative doesn't make sense in a digital era. The two are inseparably intertwined in digital channels.

The shift to consumer initiation through search is a major, growing trend we've highlighted already. New media plans should include significant search components. Consumer hand-raising through search provides marketers with a better knowledge of consumers' interest and intent. So, part of the new dynamics of planning need to focus on how to leverage consumer intent into an ongoing dialogue.

There's a lot to learn about the digital media world. So if you want to be an effective DigiMarketer, you will have to invest the time to keep up. Otherwise, you will feel overwhelmed by the new terms and concepts. There are companies in the digital ecosystem to get to know – and potentially work with. There are new discussions to have: will you accept advertising on your site? Will you find partners for affiliate programs? Will you consider working with non-competing companies for new types of sponsorships? Marketers will need to be familiar with new media networks, how ad serving works, and a variety of new metrics and compensation models. Nobody ever said new media would be easy.

DigiMarketing Tenet 7: Marketers will need to understand a wide variety of new media options, many of which have pay-for-performance metrics. Search will play a key role in companies' DigiMarketing plans too.

From Managed PR to Digital Influence[3]

Digital is revolutionizing all aspects of marketing. This includes image management. Simply put, the days of image control are over. As traditional media gives way to new media, companies must shift from managed PR to digital influence.

Digital channels have helped spawn a profound shift in what people consider to be trustworthy information. Historically, companies have built trust for their brands through voices of authority – famous endorsers or experts that lend credibility to brand messages. However, consumers aren't readily following those authorities today; instead, they look to a broad base of peers to get what they feel are unbiased opinions. Look at all the websites where you can read consumer reviews of books or restaurants, or the sites dedicated to consumer comments about gadgets or cars.

This democratization of information means that consumers' opinions are no longer shaped by a limited number of traditional news and media outlets. Diverse groups of people, scattered across the globe, easily communicate and share opinions on topics of mutual interest. Their opinions move quickly through social networking and viral pass-on. We noted these already as citizen media.

Consequently, the image management process has to change dramatically, with marketers' loss of control again a major theme. What's required is a mindshift away from attempting to choreograph or control the discussion. Instead, marketers need to be prepared to participate in a fluid dialogue with a host of constituents. Marketers will still need to identify influencers, court media figures, and determine ways to get positive news out to the public. However, this will happen through digital channels. And, most critically, it will become fast-changing and dynamic. DigiMarketers will need to be ready to react in real-time to questions and responses from the general public. Otherwise, their opportunity to influence the situation will be lost.

As with new media planning, there are many new things that DigiMarketers need to learn. These include becoming familiar with digital monitoring tools, including services that provide real-time mapping of the digital conversation and the epicenters of digital influence. What's also required is a new approach to planning digital influence, which includes determining which blogs to monitor, how to best disseminate new material digitally, and being prepared to respond to a blog storm. For more on digital influence planning, please refer to chapter 13, or go to www.DigiMarketingNow. com/digitalinfluence to see a short video on the subject.

DigiMarketing Tenet 8: It is impossible to manage news in a digital world where consumers are faster than companies. Instead, DigiMarketers will have to adapt their approach to be a meaningful part of the public conversation, using all the digital tools available to them to influence – not dictate – the debate.

From Integrated Marketing to Unified Marketing

Integrated marketing communications (IMC) has been a popular marketing term for some time now. Most marketers and their agency partners would agree that it makes sense to have all the elements of a marketing campaign work together. However, integrated marketing often happens only at a superficial level. Some companies have succeeded in taking integration to deeper levels. However, even that is inadequate. Integration is still essentially one-way marketing thinking. In DigiMarketing, companies must shift gears beyond integration and seek unification of their marketing.

The difference is that while integration focuses on the consistency of the advertisers' message, unification shifts the focus to the continuity of the consumer's experience. The consumer's main interest is not integration of the brand's image. What the consumer cares about is whether his or her personal information, preferences, and needs are recognized by marketers, particularly if he or she is a loyal and long-standing customer. Unfortunately, this is where many companies are woefully inadequate. They are not focused or disciplined enough in learning about individual consumers through their interactions with them. As a result, the consumer experience is underwhelming – people aren't recognized at all as individuals, or if they are, it's patchy at best.

The shift to digital channels will enable marketers to do much better for the simple reason that addressable media yields individual-level data. If used appropriately, this data can help create a more continuous and customized participant journey with the brand. When marketing is unified, customer information is collected continuously, and the aggregated customer knowledge is redistributed immediately, informing all the digital touch points. Addressable channels enable customer preferences to be automatically present in every consumer interaction. Consequently, marketers should be able to get much closer to each individual's needs, serving more tailored offers and messages to each individual.

Unified marketing will require detailed planning and the identification of key data that will provide the thread to link customer interactions. We will address this aspect of your DigiMarketing planning in chapter 13 and touch upon how to better connect physical touchpoints with digital touchpoints.

DigiMarketing Tenet 9: The current approaches to integration of marketing communications are generally insufficient. Marketers will need to use more sophisticated approaches to connect digital and physical touchpoints. Plus, they will shift their focus from the integration of brand image to the unification of each customer's experience. The use of individual customer data will enable a continuous customer dialogue.

Participant Journey[4]

A participant journey – a planning technique developed by Ogilvy & Mather – describes the path that a person follows in considering, selecting, and then periodically reselecting a product or service. In traditional marketing, that journey was usually impacted by only a few elements, such as brand advertising and in-store materials. However, the explosion of channels means there are now many ways by which to connect with consumers along their path to purchase, and maintain brand relationships.

From Data Blind to Data-Driven

The next **DigiMarketing tenet** follows on from the previous points. Data, and the knowledge that can be derived from it, is the lifeblood that enables marketers to build customer relationships. Data enables companies to take a leap from the guesswork of traditional media to the precision of digital media. If your goal is to make the shift to DigiMarketing, you will need to be fully conversant with the collection, management, and application of data. Moreover, you will need to architect your marketing around data.

The key challenge for companies making the shift to data-driven marketing is to identify the most valuable information and how they can get it. Marketers must structure their digital marketing materials – websites, games, mobile marketing campaigns, and so on – in a way that generates and captures the most valuable information. The invisible data trail that the consumer leaves as he or she uses digital media holds the key to each consumer's preferences and interests. The big opportunity is to use the new media to learn what each consumer genuinely wants by analyzing what each actually does. The ultimate goal is to have a learning loop with consumers, so that each time you have customer contact, you can be better informed for the next customer contact.

Of course, we can also learn what consumers want by asking them directly. This doesn't mean hitting them over the head for information, as many online registration forms currently do. A better strategy is to ask for information at different points in the relationship-building process and find ways to reward consumers for sharing that information. Later, we will cover some of the most effective techniques for direct and indirect data gathering.

DigiMarketing data extends beyond demographics to psychographics and behavior. This is an important shift. Demographics, which are the basis for mass media buying, are very familiar to marketers. However, they're not sufficient to deal with today's more complex world. Marketers will use behavioral and contextual data to guide their targeting and engagement strategies. They will also assess communication channels based upon this type of data.

Companies can access and capture enormous volumes of customer data through tracking and monitoring tools. Many large companies already have extensive databases. These present both opportunities and challenges. Unsuspecting companies can quickly find themselves buried in mounds of data. And unless they prioritize that data, most of it will be under-utilized. Because data is both critical and available in unprecedented quantities today, you will need a clear plan to turn that data into information that you can use. This plan will need to address a variety of issues, including the methods by which the data will be captured, and how it will be analyzed.

DigiMarketing Tenet 10: Data will be recognized as the lifeblood of marketing. Data is the key to using addressable channels effectively. A good data plan will be the centerpiece of DigiMarketing. Marketers will use this data for more detailed psychographic and behavioral profiling of consumers.

From Post-Campaign Measurement to Real-Time Measurement

The eleventh tenet is also linked to data and reflects the need for a more dynamic brand management process. Marketers must move from old methods of measurement and analysis to sophisticated real-time techniques if they are to keep pace with the market.

Marketers generally use the best information available to them. However, in traditional marketing, most of that information is historical. Future media viewership is forecast from previous viewership; post-campaign studies look at the impact of a campaign over the previous period; and competitive reports include updates about what competitors have already done. Even if the data is fairly recent, it's still like driving forward while looking in the rear view mirror. Because traditional media gave us a long time-lag between exposure and consumer response, in the past we could get away with looking to the past. Digital media is not so forgiving. The gap between exposure and response narrows dramatically, so the necessity for real-time data becomes more acute.

Some historical data will always be useful to give perspective. However, the speed of market developments and the ability of your competition to make quick changes mean that it is critical to reduce the latency in your marketing. What most businesses really require is current information in a format that enables them to make decisions as close to real-time as possible. Companies that sell through the internet have this type of real-time data. They can see almost immediately the impact that a new online campaign launched yesterday is having on sales. Even if you are not conducting e-commerce, it's possible through digital channels to conduct real-time tracking of your digital advertising impact. Additionally, you can determine which channels and which creative executions are most effective at generating demand for your products in the form of qualified leads.

Marketing is moving towards an inevitable future in which real-time optimization becomes standard. This *performance marketing* approach uses technology to allocate media and marketing according to current participation levels and response rates. Traditional measures aren't likely to disappear altogether. However, as noted above about demographics, this rear-view data will be seen as rudimentary only: marketers' main focus will shift to what is happening *right now*.

DigiMarketing Tenet 11: The "rear-view" approach to marketing, which bases decisions primarily on historical information, is insufficient. Marketers will deploy real-time analysis of data to make quick, constant, and fact-based modifications to their DigiMarketing activities.

From Partial ROI to Optimization

The final shift reflects what marketers should strive to get out of DigiMarketing as a more measurable and accountable form of marketing – the ability to fully track and optimize their efforts.

Digital marketing is the future because of the inevitable changes in media and consumer habits. However, marketers should hasten their shift to DigiMarketing as it provides them with a more efficient business model. There's an old quip in the advertising business, attributed to John Wannamaker, that "I know half of my advertising is wasted; I just don't know which half." This has long been the sentiment among marketers. However, DigiMarketing – as the future evolution of more accountable marketing – can, and will, change this.

Marketers are under immense pressure today to ensure they squeeze the maximum value out of their efforts. Consequently, there's more focus than ever on methods that provide a measurable return on investment. Digital marketing through addressable channels is indeed measurable. But it's not simply the measurement that matters. In addition, the benefit of DigiMarketing is the ability it offers marketers to constantly optimize their programs, further reducing the latency and inefficiencies in their marketing. These optimizations can be made in a number of different areas, including creative work, messaging, use of search engines, website structure, channel selection, and the campaign performance. We look at optimization in chapter 12.

Marketers should be relentless in identifying and making these optimizations. After all, in the highly competitive marketplace in which companies now compete, every advantage counts.

DigiMarketing Tenet 12: Via addressable channels, everything in the marketing mix will be measured and optimized to ensure continuous improvement. DigiMarketing is the future evolution of more accountable marketing.

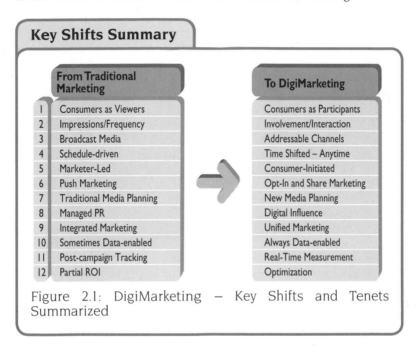

Key Shifts Summary

	From Traditional Marketing	To DigiMarketing
1	Consumers as Viewers	Consumers as Participants
2	Impressions/Frequency	Involvement/Interaction
3	Broadcast Media	Addressable Channels
4	Schedule-driven	Time Shifted – Anytime
5	Marketer-Led	Consumer-Initiated
6	Push Marketing	Opt-In and Share Marketing
7	Traditional Media Planning	New Media Planning
8	Managed PR	Digital Influence
9	Integrated Marketing	Unified Marketing
10	Sometimes Data-enabled	Always Data-enabled
11	Post-campaign Tracking	Real-Time Measurement
12	Partial ROI	Optimization

Figure 2.1: DigiMarketing – Key Shifts and Tenets Summarized

DigiMarketing in an Era of Experimentation

Will all companies heed the call to evolve their marketing to improved approaches? Probably not. After all, new thinking requires flexibility, and some find it hard to change. Plenty of marketers would rather turn back time to when traditional media was all that was needed to convince consumers about their products. But no-one can stop the march of progress. Marketers must be ready to embrace new media with winning plans if they hope to come out on top.

For more than a decade, leading companies have been experimenting with ways to harness digital media to grow their businesses. In the 1990s, the focus was on building an internet presence through brand websites and banners. Some marketers have stayed with that approach. However, others have sought new ways to harness the potential of digital channels to involve consumers in their products and brands. Consequently, there's now an array of approaches to e-commerce, branding, and relationship marketing through digital channels.

Some companies are creating their own branded channels. Others are embedding themselves into virtual worlds and online games. In the past couple of years, countless companies have decided to start blogs. No doubt, as new trends develop and new channels emerge, marketers will experiment further. Some marketers will seek to stay at the bleeding edge of marketing, while others will simply wish to maintain the contemporary relevancy of their brands. However, in this rapidly changing environment, marketers will need to be in what people are calling *perpetual beta* – a constant state of development and experimentation.

This represents an exciting new era in marketing. With many of the old rules being rewritten, companies have an opportunity to reinvent and add new dimensions to their marketing. However, this age of experimentation may also seem daunting for marketers, especially given the increased pressure to show results. Yet experimentation needs to be viewed as a natural – in fact, critical – part of DigiMarketing. Dynamic brand management will require companies to take a test-and-learn approach to emerging options. The process of engaging consumers using addressable channels, then using the data from their responses to improve, is essentially the evolution of direct marketing. Marketers will use the disciplines and knowledge developed over years in one-to-one marketing as the basis for DigiMarketing.

To be successful in DigiMarketing, you need to be familiar with digital channels. This means more than a passing interest in new media. Rather, it requires you to immerse yourself so you know the key drivers and nuances associated with using these channels. What follows is a detailed review of the main digital channels available today.

END NOTES
1 Estimates from Ogilvy & Mather. Represents viewership through all channels, inclusive of free Television exposure.
2 www.technorati.com/about/
3 Digital influence is a term coined by Ogilvy PR, a unit of Ogilvy & Mather Worldwide.
4 Participant journeys are sometimes called customer journeys.

Digital Channels

This next section provides an overview of the main digital channels available today. For ease of use, each chapter will cover the following:

KEY TRENDS YOU MUST KNOW

The chapters start with an overview of the main issues that have been driving the growth and increased consumer use of the respective channels. The intention is to give you a basic understanding of why that channel has become so important today, plus a brief scene setter for the remainder of the chapter.

DIGIMARKETING BEST PRACTICES

To help fast-forward your knowledge, each chapter includes a short case study or client examples to illustrate how leading marketers are already using new media channels for their DigiMarketing. We've also included notes on best practices and marketing implications that will serve as helpful guides for your DigiMarketing.

FUTURE TRENDS – WHERE IT'S HEADING

Since the digital world is evolving quickly, we have also noted how the current trends in each channel are likely to play out over the near term. Our focus is on the next few years – the key period in which you will need to assess which routes are most appropriate for your DigiMarketing.

Useful Links via www.DigiMarketingNow.com

Lastly, throughout the various chapters we have noted links to companies or examples. You can go to www.DigiMarketingNow.com/examples to use live links to view these examples or references. We encourage you to go online to see and experience what is happening in digital channels. Your DigiMarketing skills must start with a willingness to experiment and try things so your familiarity and comfort level with these channels increases.

Chapter 3

The Web

The web is no longer a side-show, no longer an add-on to other marketing channels. It already dominates many customers' interactions with marketers. This chapter charts the development of the web over the last 10 years, speculates on how it will continue to evolve, and delineates the marketing opportunities that the web continues to offer.

From a geekish start, the web developed into a colossal interlinked library of the world's documents, mixed with some basic e-commerce facilities: a starting point often referred to as Web 1.0.

More recently, Web 1.0 has evolved into a social space. No longer merely an information repository, the web is becoming a fluid stream of activity and events, involving people and their interconnections. This so-called Web 2.0 is developing into a tremendous resource for the DigiMarketer. Although the next generation, Web 3.0, is as yet only apparent in outline, it promises even more.

KEY TRENDS YOU MUST KNOW

Evolution: Three Generations of the Web

Fastest Penetration of Any Medium...Ever

The web has had the fastest adoption rate of any information medium in history. The telephone took 35 years to reach 25% of the US population; the television took 26 years; radio 22 years; and the mobile 13 years. The internet? Only seven years (and the US is far from the fastest internet adopter, but its developments are well documented).[1]

As we noted in chapter 1, all internet stats are constantly being updated and different sources provide different numbers. It does seem however that over 1.2 billion people were online globally by 2007, and at least a third of them were in Asia.[2] Not only is Asia the internet's biggest regional market, it also boasts the highest rates of broadband access, with some 114 million broadband hook ups[3] – almost 40% more broadband connections than in North and South America combined.

But it's worth remembering just how much further there is to go. By early 2007, less than 18% of the world was online. That penetration ranges: almost 70% in North America, just over 50% in Oceania/Australia, less than 40% in Europe, less than 20% in Latin America/Caribbean, just over 10% in Asia and the Middle East, and less than 4% in Africa. With only 12% penetration, and already over a third of the world's internet users, Asia is the region to watch.[4]

Web 1.0

The web is not what it was and definitely not what it will be! Figure 3.1 summarizes the stages of web development.

Web 1.0 was primarily a data repository, with a sprinkling of e-commerce – a library with a shop. Web 1.0 has been called "centralized them."[5] Websites were designed and completely

Digital Channels

controlled by the website owner. You visited *my* site, and looked at it. The website owner broadcast information. The website *told* the user. Marketers placed advertisements, wrote copy, posted goods for sale. The web was pretty much a vast electronic catalogue of information, goods and services, designed mainly by companies and some technically inclined individuals, for visitors to look at.

You searched for what you were looking for – or browsed around more or less aimlessly until you found it. Then you read it, looked at it, and/or bought it. Interaction was minimal; users' actions were pretty well limited to clicking on links and entering credit card and delivery data. When there was interaction, it was mainly user-to-website. User–user relationships were confined to mainly textual bulletin board postings.

But make no mistake; the break with traditional media was decisive even in Web 1.0. The web was less constrained by physical characteristics than any traditional medium. The web, built on software not hardware[6], is far more malleable than the print, billboard, radio and television that it is rapidly supplanting.[7]

Over the last 10 years, not only has the web become more and more important as a source of information and sales, it has also evolved. As Figure 3.1 shows, the web today is a very different animal from that of 10 years ago. It is this ability to evolve into almost whatever we dream of that really distinguishes digital media.

Web 2.0

Web 2.0, coined by O'Reilly Media in 2004[8], has already become a popular buzz-phrase. Web 2.0 is the second generation of the web. Already by early 2007, Web 2.0 sites accounted for 12% of US online traffic.[9]

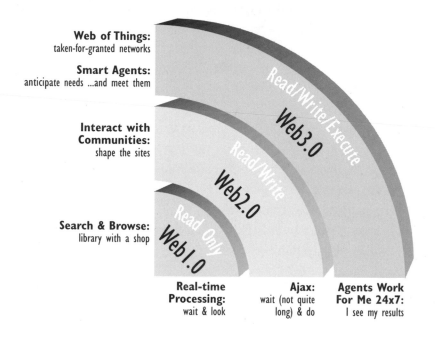

Web of Things:
taken-for-granted networks

Smart Agents:
anticipate needs ...and meet them

Interact with Communities:
shape the sites

Search & Browse:
library with a shop

Read/Write/Execute

Web3.0

Read/Write

Web2.0

Read Only

Web1.0

Real-time Processing:
wait & look

Ajax:
wait (not quite
long) & do

Agents Work For Me 24x7:
I see my results

Figure 3.1: Stages of Web Development

If Web 1.0 was a centralized *them* that told *us*; Web 2.0 is a *distributed us*[10] that asks what we want, and lets us modify things accordingly. The evolution is from centrally organized, top-down-created websites to democratic, bottom-up, user-contributed sites. The Web 2.0 experience is fundamentally decentralized – delivering what the user asks for, not what the centre thinks they want. To Web 1.0's centrally generated informational content and commerce, Web 2.0 adds community and consumer-created content.[11]

Web 2.0 is famously difficult to describe but easy to experience. It's like the elephant that the blind men touch, and in touching different parts completely disagree in their descriptions of the beast. As this is an evolution there is no single, clear-cut leap from 1.0 to 2.0.

But it does seem that the Web 2.0 phenomenon has four main aspects with important implications for the DigiMarketer:

- separation of presentation and data
- co-creation of content
- social networking
- the supporting technology: AJAX

Web 2.0: *Separation of Presentation and Data*

The basis of Web 2.0 is an increasing separation of presentation and data: of form and content. This allows information to be re-used, re-presented, so that meaning can be conveyed in different ways at almost no additional cost. These different ways may reflect the requirements of different devices or the needs of different users.

The meaning of a web page designed for a computer can be accurately and (almost) costlessly conveyed to the user's choice of device – mobile phone, game console, fridge, or whatever. What's more, the data can be presented in different ways to suit the whims of different users. Content becomes liquid: able to fit into any digital device, or shape itself to the needs of any particular user. Users can easily restructure data to meet their own criteria of usefulness. Presentation becomes a do-it-yourself project, allowing the user to tailor what they see to best meet their needs; 1:1 segmentation becomes a reality.

For marketers, this requires quite a change in perspective. With traditional media, the marketer is pretty much in control. The marketers' designers specify how things will look, and control exactly what the customer sees. In Web 2.0, marketers and their designers can control almost nothing. Users – not the marketers or designers – control what appears on their screens.

Each customer can display your website exactly as he or she wishes. If the customer wants, Bangkok can be at the center of the map. Another customer can put Toronto there. The same data can be tailored to every individual user…and of course it's the user who decides how to tailor *and* does the tailoring! As Web 2.0 sites spread, customization is pretty well costless to the marketer…and provided instructions, icons, signifiers and conventions are clear, the user can get it exactly as they want it.

Web 2.0: Co-creation of Content

Co-created content – namely, content which is developed jointly by the marketer and consumers – has been around since the earliest bulletin boards. But Web 2.0 takes this to a new level, making user-contributed-value fundamental to entire websites.

For example, the photography site Flickr (www.flickr.com) doesn't just allow users to store pictures. Users can decide who can see their pictures, and can tag – or allow others to tag – their pictures. Once tagged, these pictures become a searchable resource. As a centralized site, Flickr has zero content. The entire value of the site is the user-contributed, user-tagged photos. There is no central taxonomy. There is no Dewey decimal indexing system. The entire site is user-contributed, user-structured and user-catalogued. Some call this consumer-created content (ccc). It's not just a letters to the editor page, or a contributed story…it's the entire website's benefits. We will look at this phenomenon in more detail in chapter 8.

In a similar way, sites like Del.icio.us (http://del.icio.us) allow consumers to save and share bookmarks to web pages they find useful. Any user can then tag those bookmarks with words which that individual feels reflect the page's content and relate to the meaning of that bookmark to the individual user. These searchable tags become a shared web resource.

Letting users create content – posting stories, images, video, comments – and tag each other's content can help build community and long-term brand loyalty. It can also create dynamic, vibrant sites, reflecting customer needs. The DigiMarketer needs to remember that co-creating content takes consumer time away from traditional one-way transmission sites. If your DigiMarketing doesn't allow people to create content, they may find it more satisfying to go to a competitor's site that does.

An important part of this user-contributed value is the increasing use of mash-ups. Many Web 2.0 sites integrate the capabilities of multiple websites and services to meet the needs of specialized groups. They allow users to remix content, assembling something especially well-tuned to their community of interests. These mash-ups take the functionality of one site and combine it with that of another. For example, www.chicagocrime.org overlays crime figures on Google Maps to create a satellite view of your neighborhood, your house, your street, showing the incidence of different crimes. The user can actually see how safe their area is – a tremendously immediate, real, and user-tailored experience.

Web 2.0: Social Networking

A strong part of Web 2.0 is social. According to the *Pew Internet & American Life Project*[12], by the end of 2006 more than half of all online American teens were using social networking sites. These social networking sites are built around – really built *by* – the needs and interests of like-minded individuals. For many teens, hanging out at the mall has been replaced by hanging out on MySpace (www.myspace.com). College students are more likely at Facebook (www.facebook.com), and professionals at LinkedIn (www.LinkedIn.com). For the first time, the web has become an immediately malleable experience: truly an experience created by each user for that user – and of course their social network of users like them. A key concept to note here for when you do your own DigiMarketing is that designers must let go!

Web 2.0: Winner Takes All

As the point of these sites is to show off one's stuff, and to meet others, network effects are very strong. *Network effects* mean that a major part of the benefit of a product or service is created by the number of other people who have that product or service. Each person who has a telephone makes the telephone more useful to all. The user base drives the benefit of the product. In high network effect markets we tend to see a small number of big winners. eBay (www.eBay.com), for example, dominates in most – but not all – countries as an online auction site: buyers want to go where there are the most sellers, sellers want to go where there are the most buyers. So the biggest site gets bigger!

For social networking sites, the place where most people like you go is *the* place to go. Winning sites explode exponentially, until another site becomes in some way superior and surges ahead. Friendster (www.friendster.com) started in 2003 and quickly got to 20 million visitors. But, within a couple of years, as MySpace and other sites provided visitors with better music and video capabilities, Friendster slipped below a million users. YouTube (www.youtube.com) is reputed to have gone from zero to market leader in video search in just six weeks, passing Yahoo! in three weeks and Google by week six.[13]

It is extremely hard to predict which social networking sites will win out where. Orkut (www.orkut.com), a social networking and discussion site introduced by Google in 2004, is wildly popular in Brazil, and almost unknown in the US where it is based.

What is predictable is that social networking sites will become more niche oriented. As networking sites proliferate, the ones which survive will be those that have become most attuned to a very specific niche. Participatory sites take the long-tail (see Box Insert, Long-tail Wags the Dog) to a whole new dimension. Communities of interest form, create their own content, and build around the most bizarre niches. Web 2.0 is putting sophisticated design capabilities in the hands of impassioned amateurs – a sure-fire recipe for explosive success.

Long-tail Wags the Dog!

The long-tail – a term popularized by Chris Anderson[14] – refers to the well-known effect that if we graph product sales against type of product sold, we typically get a curve like the one below.

Sales

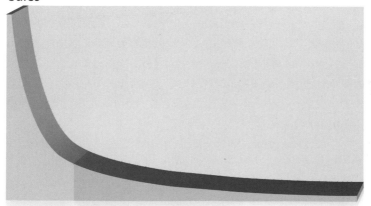

Products

Figure 3.2: The Long Tail

A small number of items sell very, very well, and a very, very large number of items sell only a little. This is often referred to as the Pareto Principle, or the 80:20 rule – 20% of the items make up 80% of the sales.

But that's because in the physical world cost to the retailer is driven by the space taken up by product selection. If a bookstore stocked every book which any customer had asked about that year, its inventory would be massive and rental costs prohibitive. What's more, most customers would find it hideously inconvenient to have to dig through all that inventory to find what they wanted. As a result, physical businesses tend to stay with the fat "head" of the chart above, and don't waste inventory (and customer effort) in catering to the long tail! The tail is truncated: the bookstore doesn't stock that esoteric title, so none are sold, further accentuating the fat head.

On the web, economics are different. Costs are almost unaffected by the number of items stocked. Listing another book doesn't entail much additional cost at all – until that book is ordered. Of course, the physical book has to be stored somewhere, but that will be in a low-rental, remote warehouse space, not in prime retail space. In fact, as books can now be printed economically on demand, in print runs of one, the physical book need not exist until it's ordered, completely removing inventory costs.

What's more, on the web search is easy. Your fingers – or other people's fingers – really do do the walking.

As Chris Anderson put it: "The average Barnes & Noble carries 130,000 titles. Yet more than half of Amazon's book sales come from outside its top 130,000 titles. Consider the implication: if the Amazon statistics are any guide, the market for books that are not even sold in the average bookstore is larger than the market for those that are..."[15]

Or as an Amazon employee reportedly said: "We sold more books today that didn't sell at all yesterday than we sold today of all the books that did sell yesterday."[16]

Web 2.0: The Supporting Technology: AJAX

Part of the technical secret of the Web 2.0 experience is what's become known as Ajax — asynchronous JavaScript and XML. There is no need for you to understand this jargon, although you might want to remember the acronym to throw at your web designers.

Ajax allows us to evolve beyond the click-and-wait experience of Web 1.0. Previously, the top-down web server sent you a page; you clicked and waited for the next page. No matter how fast your web connection, this always felt remote. An Ajax application introduces an intermediary — an Ajax engine — between the user and the server. The page that has already been served to your computer can respond to your requests for more information without calling home.

We put this driver last as we believe that technology should support, not lead. Taken together, these drivers — separation of presentation and data; co-creation of content; social networking; and the supporting technology — create a dynamic, evolving system whose value comes from the users.

Web 3.0

Although the outlines of Web 2.0 are already clear, Web 3.0 is still shrouded in the fog of the future. What does seem clear is that 3.0 will be even more user-centric than 2.0, with smart agents playing a key role so that the web will "work" for people, even when they're not online. We will cover Web 3.0 shortly, when we address future trends.

Implications of a Webbed World

The growing prominence of the web has challenged many physical world realities. We want to draw your attention to four major impacts for marketers and marketing:

- *Web* Impact 1: Leveling the playing field
- *Web* Impact 2: Disintermediation/Reintermediation
- *Web* Impact 3: The long-tail: infinite niches
- *Web* Impact 4: Marketing mix flexibility

Web Impact 1: Leveling the Playing Field

In his best-seller of the same name, Thomas L. Friedman said, "The world is flat." It's a catchy title, but he wasn't really contradicting Columbus: the world is still a sphere. What Friedman meant was "the playing field is flat." Some would say the playing field actually slopes now in favor of the local, market-oriented, entrepreneurial, smaller guy. Relationships still drive success, but those relationships, like the web, are geographically free, enabling the best value providers – no matter where they are located – to win.[17]

Speed of web connection has become more relevant than geographic centrality. Digital business is footloose, no longer tied to physical proximity. Teams from around the world can co-operate 24x365, passing work in progress seamlessly around the globe. The global digital supply chain can now incorporate the most geographically remote internet-connected workers. The web has created a worldwide tool for collaboration, giving small, specialized companies access to global markets.

Web Impact 2: Disintermediation/Reintermediation

"Crowned at Last" trumpeted *The Economist* in May 2005: "The claim that 'the customer is king' has always rung hollow. But now the digital marketplace has made it come true, says Paul Markillie."[18]

While the customer might not yet be king, the web has certainly put the capacity for direct action into customers' hands to an unprecedented extent. For example, consumers today can choose between enjoying the "theatre" of live shopping or the transactional efficiency of web shopping, with 24-hour unlimited access to products and information. E-commerce has even developed its own "theatre" of retail on the web. Increasing use of mobile devices for e-commerce purposes will soon mean that consumers are freed not only from the restraints of time but also of location.

Initially, it was suggested that the web would disintermediate markets: cutting out middlemen by providing customers with the information they needed to deal direct. The reality has been not quite so simple. At first, many customers chose to use the web as an information resource only. They researched their intended purchases online and used that learning to negotiate better deals with established intermediaries. Almost 10 years ago, JD Power was reporting that 25% of car buyers used the web to research their purchases. By 2000 that figure was more than 50%.[19] Yet still only 4% bought online.[20]

Even by 2005, although 25% of those using search engines to get information finally purchased, 92% of them did so offline.[21] Online purchases are growing rapidly (looking set to exceed $200 billion for 2007[22]), but still lag far behind online information gathering. Physical agents have indeed been removed from the system wherever the benefit they delivered failed to exceed the cost they extracted. For example, person-to-person (P2P) file sharing offers consumers the ability to share data files that they own. The first major casualty of P2P file sharing – perhaps the most reluctantly disintermediated intermediaries – were the record companies. File sharing of copyright materials has been declared illegal in many countries. However, despite taking legal action against file sharers – who were also of course their customers – the record companies and their notorious trade association The Recording Industry Association of America (RIAA) have been unable to stem the tide. It will be interesting to see how the movie distributors fare, as faster internet connections bring movies into the sights of P2P file sharers.

In other markets, however, disintermediation is proceeding rather more slowly than its proponents originally suggested. In fact, we sometimes see web-stimulated re-intermediation. New middlemen emerge, providing different services for a fee. It seems that consumers are still not happy with dealing completely on the web. They are willing to pay for the reassurance and advice of a human intermediary. In the US, we already see flat-fee car brokers. They will find the best price on the car you want to buy. The customer researches online, then the car broker finds the dealer with the best price for you. As we will discuss shortly, our prediction for Web 3.0 is that the car broker expertise will ultimately be automated in the form of a smart agent. Humanizing and gaining acceptance for such software will usher in the next wave of internet evolution.

Whatever the situation of intermediation/reintermediation in your market, what is certain is that consumer power is real and growing (if you still doubt this, take a look at the Box Insert iPod's Dirty Secret in chapter 8). DigiMarketers need to respect consumer power and work with it, not against it.

Web Impact 3: The Long-tail: Infinite Niches

We have already discussed the concept of the long-tail (see preceding Box Insert). For the DigiMarketer, the long-tail carries the prospect of infinite niches. Sales and profits can be driven from that long tail. The key is to get the niche product, and its associated communications, to the niche! There are three developments that assist in mining these infinite niches: collaborative filtering, blogs, and RSS. We mentioned them all in chapter 1; we'll reintroduce them here, and look at them in more detail in chapter 8.

Collaborative filtering: Remember, "Customers who bought this item also bought…" is all about customers helping each other. The actions of other customers are aggregated and fed back to inform our decision-making.

Blogs: Blogs or web-logs were originally online daily or near daily diaries. Now they are personal websites, the sophistication of which Web 2.0 is dramatically extending.

RSS: Real simple syndication is a set of web feed formats that help get frequently updated materials distributed over the web. Consumers choose to subscribe to (pull) feeds of headlines or summaries from sources which interest them.

The economics of the web allow DigiMarketers to offer more niche products and services than ever before. At the same time, web technologies allow us to reach niche consumers more accurately and less expensively than ever before. This will truly be the era of niche riches for savvy DigiMarketers.

Web Impact 4: Marketing Mix Flexibility

The web not only helps the DigiMarketer reach the niches of the long-tail, it also allows unprecedented flexibility in the marketing mix, a key part of personalization. Let's look at dynamic pricing as an example of marketing flexibility and potential personalization.

Dynamic pricing is setting different prices for different customers that reflect customers' varying price sensitivities (or even different prices for the same customer on different occasions reflecting changes in the customer's price sensitivity over time). If you're price insensitive, you will pay more. Dynamic pricing has always been possible via quantity discounts, cash discounts, advance order prices, and so on. The internet just makes it easier. Using cookies (see Box Insert, Cookies You Can't Eat) websites can be aware of customers' prior web experiences and adjust prices accordingly.

Cookies You Can't Eat

Cookies are small strings of data sent by a website to the user's web browser, generally without the user's knowledge. These cookies stay on the user's computer and can be read by the website (or allied sites) when the user returns. So cookies can be used to track browsing behavior within and (to some extent) across sites. Most browsers allow users to refuse cookies, but in many cases this will cause the website to deny the user access.

Dynamic pricing needs to be done with considerable care, as Amazon found out to its cost. Several years ago, Amazon appeared to experiment with dynamic pricing. However, in the global village, news travels fast. Consumers posting on www. dvdtalk.com quickly formed the impression that loyal, frequent Amazon buyers were paying more than new buyers.[23] There is nothing consumers hate more than finding that someone else got a better deal. And there was no greater impetus to delete Amazon cookies, thus eliminating an important part of the DigiMarketer's personalization program. Amazon sent mixed messages on this incident, apparently both confirming and denying it.

Dynamic pricing can be implemented in more user-friendly ways, including auctions (each customer bids and the highest bid wins, like most of the sales on eBay); reverse auctions (where the buyers set the price they will pay and suppliers bid for their orders, like Priceline, www.priceline.com); Dutch auctions (where the supplier quotes a high price and reduces it on a regular basis until all items are sold). Many B2B trading exchanges use reverse auctions, sometimes combined with barter.

DIGIMARKETING BEST PRACTICES

Give Tools to People With Passion: The Do-It-Ourselves Web

As we have noted, Web 2.0 allows data to be repurposed at almost no cost to the DigiMarketer. As Web 2.0 develops, consumers will come to expect such tailoring (personalization) as a basic requirement. What's more, they will expect personalization to have a strong customer-driven component. As we have already seen, customers will expect to be participants. Participants are customers, collaborators and producers all at once, with a definite preference for do-it-themselves. Successful DigiMarketers will be those who are not afraid to pass control to participants, allowing them to get information in their own way.

DigiMarketers need to think about their websites as part of a total "pick-n-mix" for participants. Sites need to be built with an eye for allowing interesting mash-ups to be created by enthusiasts. It will never hurt to seed some mash-up ideas, and provide the tools to create community and context in which participants can come together.

The net result of all this consumer enabling – giving consumers producers' tools, what some call creating *prosumers* – is that more than ever before consumers can actively control and shape what the web offers for them. This creates a highly relevant, high-benefit web, customized to the individual at little cost to the marketer – and (as smart agents develop) little cost to the user also.

As we see below, smart tools are already emerging that enable non-programmers to find, read, filter, use, mix, and remix the web to get exactly the information and presentation that they want. In a painting-by-numbers fashion, these tools are bringing sophisticated website development to the masses.

Utilize Widgets (also known as Badges and Gadgets)

To help stimulate users to interact with sites and pass along key components, more and more websites are being built of user-distributable individual software modules. These are called *widgets*, or sometimes *badges* or *gadgets*.

Widgets are small pieces of dynamic content – portable web parts – that can easily be cut and pasted into any web page, blog, or social networking site page to allow that page to display the widget's content. The widget itself is usually 150 x 300 pixels and is written in Flash or Javascript – allowing the widget to work on most PCs and most mobile platforms.

Newsweek has gone so far as to name 2007 "Year of the Widget,"[24] and a single widget syndicator claims to have already served 2.5 billion of them.[25] When built well, these portable elements spread virally and provide a route for marketers to get off their own page and onto tens of millions of users' pages. This shift from thinking about "getting traffic to my website" to thinking about "getting my content onto millions of participants' sites" is a key DigiMarketing insight for the future.

Widget Wisdom

Widgets offer some interesting branding possibilities. Target Corporation (the American retailing company) has a Christmas count-down widget; the Wrigley Company (chewing gum) provides a Winamp media player that looks like a pack of gum; UPS has a package-tracking widget. Nestlé Purina Petcare Company has a weather widget, so pet owners can check before they exercise the dog! Don't laugh: it got 15,000 downloads in its first two months, and of course that Purina logo probably still sits on the pet enthusiasts' desktops.

The most effective widgets – whether purpose-developed for the marketer or put together from free tools (like those at Google, desktop.google.com/plugins), or purchased from an independent widget syndicator (like Clearspring, www.clearspring.com) – have the same key characteristics:

- Genuine end-user value. Many marketers look at widgets as no more than digital flyers. But the widget will only get spread, and get attention, if it delivers a real customer benefit.
- Interactivity, both with the user (who can tweak and personalize them) and with the web, from which they extract the nuggets of value to the user.
- Try before you download: users want to know that it's good before they let it into their lives.
- A social, viral, dimension to get it shared around the web.
- Repeated updating, refining and developing. Good widgets continue to add functionality.

Provide Mash-Ups for All

As we saw before, mash-ups allow users to remix content, usually from several web sources. What's exciting for DigiMarketers is that several websites already provide applications (often called web apps) that allow anyone to create mash-ups in a few minutes.

For example, Yahoo Pipes (www.pipes.yahoo.com/pipes) is a web app that allows users to drag and drop to connect modules that search and extract information from almost any well-structured data feed. Feed items can be analyzed for content, combined and re-output as specialized information. What's more, a community is forming around the service: users can publish their pipes and remix other people's pipes.

The success of mash-up tools rests on ease-of-use and breadth of application. Users will gravitate to the easiest to use tools that can deal with the widest array of web raw materials. Mash-up tools need to be able to turn just about anything on the web into a customized service. As users get more accustomed to shaping the web, rather than having the web shape them, mash-up tools will be more and more sought after. DigiMarketers will need to think about the remixability of their sites and services.

Consider New Web Metrics

Web 2.0, widgets, mash-ups and social sites are driving a fundamental change in the basic metrics of the web. Traditional websites have been judged by their traffic to landing pages (that is, a web page specially designed to showcase the site's content as the destination page from an ad or a specific search). This was usually measured by pageviews (the number of times the constituent elements of a page were sent – served – to a browser). However, Web 2.0, widgets and mash-ups change all that.

A user might interact with a Web 2.0 page using Ajax for hours, and the page only gets served once. Remember, one attraction of Web 2.0 is the fluid interaction provided by having page elements already on the user's computer.

Widgets allow sites to be experienced without being visited! For example, the YouTube widget – probably the most popular on the web, appearing on almost every page of social networking sites – does not drive traffic to YouTube. Each YouTube video has a one-click "share" button at the end. Code is provided on the YouTube site which the user can cut and paste into their own site (or blog, or whatever). This is far different from the original web model of encouraging users to email a link to their friends.

The email approach built pageviews: friends visited the host site and site traffic looked good. For YouTube, sharing is a widget that actually moves to the user's site, and from there can be grabbed by other users, and so on and so on. The result is tens of millions of YouTube installations, all promoting the YouTube brand…and promoting that aspect of the brand (the particular video that the widget plays) that is likely to be the most appealing to that type of user. So the entire internet becomes the distribution system.

The idea of a website as something that is visited is starting to decay. The website is becoming a source for something that is used. So the DigiMarketers' metrics move from pageviews to reach. YouTube videos – along with any branding information within it – can be viewed without the YouTube site being visited. The widget cuts marketing impact free from the site visit.

Consider Microsites for Focused Topics

DigiMarketers can add interest and narrower targeting to their websites by creating microsites, also known as *minisites* or *weblets*. Microsites typically contain only a small number of pages (perhaps only one page), with a URL (address) separate from the main site, focusing on a specific occasion, event, product, or service.

Microsites can give the user and the search engine a rifle-shot focus on specifics which might get lost in the main site. In particular, microsites can effectively include interaction with quizzes, downloads, games, and so on that are all purpose designed.

Make Information Free

On August 2, 2006, AOL announced that it would begin giving away services for which it had in the past charged.[26] Probably the largest hold-out for subscription revenue-based services, AOL finally moved to free, advertising-financed content. Almost immediately AOL's advertising revenues surged. The norm on the web is that information is free and advertising-supported, which at least ensures a steady stream of advertising inventory for marketers.

Successful subscription models are few and far between, the most celebrated being *The Wall Street Journal*, whose online edition (www.wsj.com) now has almost one million paying subscribers – more than the paying subscribers to all but three US newspapers (only USA *Today*, *The Wall Street Journal*, print edition, and the *New York Times* have larger subscriber bases[27]).

Unless you have an exceptionally strong brand name and high-quality differentiated content, subscription models are unlikely to be successful.

Update Your Understanding of Participants

Because digital is changing quickly, you will need to constantly update your understanding of who is on the "other end." This will be particularly important when you do your DigiMarketing Planning and need to determine your Participant Print (see chapter 11).

As we have noted, the evolution of the web has introduced a qualitative change in the nature of the web and how it is used. Those who have grown up in a digital world – let's call them *digital citizens* – embrace all things digital with a casual nonchalance that those whose ideas were formed in a physical pre-digital world – call them the *digital immigrants* – can scarcely imagine. Digital citizenship does not necessarily map into customers' chronological ages (although the young are much more likely to be digital citizens). The main thing is to keep the profile of your participants up-to-date.

FUTURE TRENDS – WHERE IT'S HEADING

As we have already noted, the rough shape of Web 3.0 is already discernible. A number of these emerging features of Web 3.0 are likely to drive the future of the internet. We have grouped these into six underlying trends:

Web Trend 1: Unstructuring the web experience
Web Trend 2: The long-tail on steroids
Web Trend 3: Software as a service (SaaS)
Web Trend 4: Web takes over other communications
Web Trend 5: The real global village
Web Trend 6: Web-wide single sign-on

Web Trend 1: Unstructuring the Web Experience

This will be a continuation of the Web 2.0 phenomenon discussed above. Most of today's web is still a structured experience of websites, blogs, homepages, search engines, and so on, where form and content are determined by web designers. As we have seen above, this designer-structured web world is already collapsing and a do-it-ourselves – or do-it-my-way – web is emerging. Website creators may suggest the types of experiences users can have by how they design the site. But it is users who are supplying content and fine-tuning look and feel.

All non-essential control will be passed to users. Users contribute content, participate socially, and shape the site itself. The premise is that motivated, involved users will do a surprising amount of the hard work necessary to make a site successful, right down to creating the very site content and even marketing it, by inviting their friends and family members to use it.

The web of the future will be much more about doing things than going to websites. Whereas the old web was about surfing – enjoyable, only partly controlled, traveling to locations that were all too often determined by chance and serendipity – the new web will be far more businesslike. It's inevitable as the web becomes the heart of business. As Ross Mayfield puts it, "the Web is increasingly less about places and other nouns, but [about] verbs."[28]

We access information in order to do things. Currently the information and the doing are separate activities. Although the information is typically accessed online, as we have seen, the doing is still often offline. Smart agents will change all that, making the web of the future a web of action.

As we look to the future, we can see at least three themes emerging: the semantic web; smart agents and the pervasive web – the web of things. We'll briefly examine each of these.

The Semantic Web

The semantic web is a web that computers *understand* not just display. Semantics is the science of meaning. If a computer understands the semantics of a document, it doesn't just interpret the series of characters that make up that document: it understands the document's meaning.[29] The semantic web has been a dream of some of the original developers of the internet, featuring most famously in an article co-authored by Tim Berners-Lee (one of the world wide web's key architects) in *Scientific American* in 2001.[30] The idea is that machine-readable information could be added to the web, allowing computers to comprehend rather than simply display words: to search for meaning rather than simply search by matching words and phrases.

Interestingly enough, the semantic web is now becoming a reality both from the bottom-up and from the top-down. The bottom-up semantic web is already here, created by consumers tagging pictures, videos, bookmarks, and so on, as discussed above. Tagging means that individuals are teaching the internet the meaning of the items stored there.

At the same time, software like Blue Organizer (an add-on to the Firefox web browser available at www.adaptiveblue.com) creates contextual menus on the web pages you visit. These menus are based on the software's understanding of the page and your past browsing. Blue Organizer is an early example of increasing software intelligence...the start of smart agents, which is our next topic.

Smart Agents

The semantic web is a key starting point for smart agents, also known as *bots*. Configuring those Web 2.0 sites takes my time. Personalizing my Facebook profile takes time that I can ill-afford to spend. Booking those trips for myself online saves the expense of the travel agent – and ensures that the trip really fits my needs (in as far as I can afford it) – but it takes my time and effort. I have to do it, in real time.

As the web proliferates, our human ability to use it will be severely taxed. The smart agents of Web 3.0 will be programs that go out and perform web tasks on your behalf. Your smart agent can be configured – or will configure itself – to know what you want: to know how you will wish your Facebook entry to appear. Your smart agent will learn from what you do, what you have downloaded, the entries in your calendar, and the emails you have sent.

Once your smart agent understands your preferences, it can work in the background while you do something else. Your smart agent will know what you want, perhaps even before you know you want it, and will deliver on your wants without your active intervention – without taking up your precious day. Internet use will move out of real time. The web will move into the fourth dimension: time. Users will be freed from the tyranny of time online to get things done.

Your smart agents will also interact with other smart agents. In chapter 1, we looked at how your smart agent might scope out a restaurant, close to where you are, that serves your favorite food, and direct you to it. The same smart agent can coordinate with your business partner's smart agent, compare calendars, find when you're both free, determine your joint favorite restaurant, make the reservations, and direct each of you there.

All this smart agent interaction will happen "in the cloud" (that is, without the active intervention of users, and without them even noticing that it is happening). Our agents will learn our preferences and apply them in screening the mass of web data to isolate what is worthwhile information for each one of us. How we will monitor and control these smart daemons is a design challenge that remains to be explored.

The Pervasive Web

Already the web reaches almost everywhere; we are almost at pervasive or ubiquitous computing. At the same time that the web takes over more functions, its very existence will become less obvious. The web will be taken for granted, much like electricity today – notable only when it fails. The independent existence of computers themselves will become vague. Already mobile devices (discussed in chapter 6) and gaming devices (chapter 7) are almost indistinguishable from computers. What's more, RFID (radio frequency identification) chips (chapter 9) offer the capability of placing intelligence in every can, jar, and package on the supermarket shelf! We can foresee a world, not so far in the future, where almost all appliances – and even objects – are intelligent and networked: an internet of things rather than websites.

If users choose, their scales will interface wirelessly with their fridge and microwave. The fridge will refuse to release food in excess of the user's diet requirements, and the microwave will refuse to cook it. Perhaps that cut-price health insurance policy will come with such impositions, and will remotely monitor compliance! Yet again the tension between privacy and personalization rears its ugly head.

As compared to the centrally generated content and e-commerce of Web 1.0, and the community and user-generated content of Web 2.0, Web 3.0 seems likely to add context, or personalization, with an understanding of each specific customer so thorough that the Web 3.0 experience will be reorganized around his or her personal interests.[31]

Web Trend 2: The Long-Tail on Steroids

As smart agents develop, increased levels of specialization will become more manageable. Communities, blogs and e-commerce will continue to become more and more specialized: value will flow to the edges. The mainstream will continue to become more and more competitive. The attractive markets will be at the edge: the niches that cater exactly to the tastes of a few...and can then be (almost costlessly) restructured to exactly meet the tastes of another few...and then another few, and so on.

The participants who visit these niche sites will also be the sites' producers and editors. Successful DigiMarketers of the future will provide basic information and tools on their websites. The real trick will be to attract and motivate enthusiastic amateurs, who will use the tools provided to reconstruct the DigiMarketers' data to precisely meet their niche's needs. This will inevitably mean making sure that those amateurs – or at least the niche as a whole – are able to capture some of the financial value associated with their efforts, just as YouTube already compensates posters of its most popular videos[32] and Google AdSense allows individuals to monetize their websites and blogs by allowing targeted ads to be shown.[33]

Web Trend 3: Software as a Service (SaaS)

Rich, desktop-like applications are already becoming available on the web. Some are traditional desktop applications like word processing, spreadsheets, and email, now offered via a web interface, rather than as a purchased product.

Other web applications are purpose-built to take advantage of the unique strengths of the internet. Some are based on analysis of collective actions (collaborative filtering, discussed above); others are based on aggregation of data accessed in close to real time (stock quotes, news, and so on); still others are based around publishing from individuals to friends, to family, or to the world (blogs, Flickr).

Software provided as a service, delivered on the web, rather than a product bought or downloaded, is poised to explode. In 2006, the market for software as a service (SaaS) reached $6.3 billion and is forecast to get to $19.3 billion by 2011.[34] There are several revenue models at the moment, including subscriptions and pay-per-use. But many see the future as free SaaS access supported by advertising. This will provide yet another important digital communication channel for the DigiMarketer.

Web Trend 4: Web Takes Over Other Communications

Voice over IP – or voice over internet protocol, or VOIP – is quickly becoming a major force in the telecommunications business. The most familiar providers are probably Skype (www.skype.com) and Vonage (www.vonage.com), but there are a host of others. In all cases, voice is digitized and becomes just another data stream across the internet. Telcos have traditionally priced phone calls by distance. But as we have already seen, the web is geography free: transmission costs have almost no relationship to distance. As a result, VOIP has made its greatest inroads in two areas: first, in international calling where its fixed tariffs dramatically undercut the distance-based telco charges, and second, in computer-originated and terminated calls (computer-to-computer calls) where the VOIP providers have no need to pay fees to existing telcos, and so can provide free or near-free service.

VOIP brings with it all the advantages of a digital channel. Your telephone number is globally portable – one number can link to a computer, or a mobile phone with an internet connection, or a VOIP phone (a VOIP phone is capable of digitizing a voice call, and transmitting it over the internet, without the user needing a computer). Video is simple to add to any call (provided your internet connection is fast enough). Some consider VOIP to be the potential killer of large telcos. Some researchers expect VOIP to be worth over $23 billion in North America alone by 2009[35], with 34% of US phones predicted to be VOIP phones by 2010.[36]

Expansion to Everything Over Internet Protocol is imminent. By 2007, Google had already acquired Marratech (www.marratech.com), an e-meeting company allowing users to communicate via text chat, VOIP and video, and share applications in virtual meetings.

Web Trend 5: The Real Global Village

The web makes Marshall McLuhan's prescient notion of a global village a reality. We now live in a village where happenings at even the remotest hut are almost instantaneously public knowledge. As we have noted several times already, the web has destroyed geography, with virtual groups collaborating around the globe. Yet many marketers (and politicians) still cling to geographic separation.

Marketers frequently use geography as a segmentation variable, charging different prices, using different positionings, different product specs, and different product assortments in different geographic markets. In the pre-web world, this worked quite well. Aside from some grey market flows (where middlemen bought in low-priced markets and sold in high-priced markets), geography separated things pretty well. Conventional media tended to fit the geographic model; language differences, differences in standards (such as voltages and video protocols, NTSC versus PAL), and shipping costs all helped.

But the web changed all that. Digital media are global. As automated translation sites continue to improve, even language is scarcely a barrier. Digital standards (such as mp3 audio, mp4 video) are already global. Transmission costs are distance independent. All in all, geographical segmentation starts to decay. The attempt to zone DVDs, to allow release dates and prices to be set regionally, was perhaps the last hurrah of geographic segmentation. The manufacturers of DVD players soon produced zone-free players, making zone codes redundant.

The global village of the web also means that it is all but impossible to guarantee that web content will not be offensive to some regional or cultural group. Given the increasing difficulty of web-censorship — it has been said that the web routes around censorship as it does power outages — we may well see smart agents that filter content based on users' beliefs and sensibilities.

Web Trend 6: Web-Wide Single Sign-On

Since the start of the web there have been calls for a single sign-on (SSO) — one login to permit access to all controlled sites. In practice, this is by no means simple. Although some mega-sites (for example, Yahoo!) offer a single log-in across all sites, as of early 2007 it is still not possible to move information or resources from one Yahoo site to another. Each remains a separate fiefdom.

The initial authentication system for the web – often called Identity 1.0 (will everything come in numbered versions now?) and still used on most sites – relies on user authentication based on a look-up in the site's directory. When you log in, the site's database is checked to ascertain that you are a registered user, and to confirm that your password matches with your username. Of course each site is completely separate, requiring separate, and repeated, logins.

Identity 2.0 initiatives like OpenID (www.myopenld. com) allow the user to apply the logon they have established at OpenID to other sites. When users visit a site that accepts OpenID, they enter their OpenID login and the site refers back to OpenID. Users then decide whether to allow that site to access their OpenID credentials. Sxipper (www.sxipper. com) is a Firefox add-on that uses the OpenID authentication mechanism to allow users to maintain multiple identities and automate logins on different sites.

SUMMARY: THE WEB

The web will continue to play a vital role in the digital world. However, there will be substantial changes to its form and function:

- It will be more guided by participants than advertisers.
- Marketers may create the forums (sites), but participants will populate them.
- Over time, web agents will do more of the work of the web, relieving users of many tasks they must now do themselves.

- As this happens, the web will reach even deeper into people's lives, filling every niche of interest and need.

Next we will look at another topic related to the web: the advertising and media placement options available today.

END NOTES
1   US Centre for Policy Analysis; *Reeling in the Years*, 1998.
2   www.internetworldstats.com/stats.htm
3   *World Broadband Statistics*, Q1 2007, Point Topic Ltd
4   www.internetworldstats.com/stats.htm
5   www.outofrhythm.com/
6   Although of course hardware in the form of a computer or mobile device is required to use the web, the web itself is built and evolves on software.
7   See the discussion on asn.planetwork.net/AugmentedSocialNetwork.pdf for example.
8   www.oreillynet.com/pub/a/oreilly/tim/news/2005/09/30/what-is-web 20.html
9   www.hitwise.com/press-center/hitwiseHS2004/web20.php
10 www.outofrhythm.com/
11 See, for example, sramanamitra.com/blog/572
12 *Pew Internet & American Life Project*, January 2007.
13 www.readwriteweb.com/archives/web_20_expo_data.php#more
14 *Wired* 12.10, "The Long Tail", www.wired.com/wired/archive/12.10/tail pr.html
15 *ibid*.
16 longtail.typepad.com/the_long_tail/2005/01/definitions_fin.html
17 See www.uclaforecast.com/reviews/Leamer_FlatWorld_060221.pdf "A Flat World, A Level Playing Field, a Small World After All, or None of the Above? Review of Thomas L Friedman, *The World is Flat*". Edward E Leamer, April 16, 2006.
18 "Crowned at Last", *The Economist*, March 31, 2005.
19 "Revving up Auto Branding", *McKinsey Quarterly*.
20 "Online Car Sales Will Stall", www.ecommercetimes.com/story/3454.html
21 www.buythisdesign.com/blog/archives/5-Local-Search-the-phone-book-advertisement-Killer-app!.html
22 www.webpronews.com/topnews/2007/07/30/non-travel-e-commerce-flies-high
23 www.washingtonpost.com/ac2/wp-dyn/A15159-2000Sep25?language=printer
24 www.msnbc.msn.com/id/3637973/site/newsweek/
25 "Widgetsphere: New Playground For Marketers", www.readwriteweb.com/ archives/widgetsphere_expo07.php
26 money.cnn.com/2006/08/02/news/companies/timewarner_earnings/index.htm
27 www.opinionjournal.com/editorial/feature.html?id=110010038
28 ross.typepad.com/blog/2005/08/web_of_verbs.html
29 www-128.ibm.com/developerworks/web/library/wa-semweb/
30 Tim Berners-Lee, James Hendler and Ora Lassila, "The Semantic Web", *Scientific American*, May 2001.
31 See, for example, sramanamitra.com/blog/572
32 www.cnn.com/2007/BUSINESS/05/04/you.tube/index.html
33 web.2point0.be/2007/02/12/interview-with-bart-decrem-ex-ceo-flock/
34 biz.yahoo.com/bw/070306/20070306005384.html?.v=1
35 blogs.zdnet.com/ITFacts/?p=9925
36 blogs.zdnet.com/ITFacts/?p=12418

Chapter 4

Internet Media: Display, Search, Affiliates, and Sponsorships

As consumers' web usage increases, and as marketers use more web touchpoints, online advertising spend will rise. Forecasts are that online advertising will exceed $80 billion by 2011, an annual growth rate of 21% from 2006 to 2011.[1]

The internet now offers not just display ads – the banners and buttons so common when the web started – but also rapidly growing search engine optimization and search engine advertising options. Undoubtedly, the next few years will see the emergence of many more web advertising vehicles. Plus, niche online content will allow finer segmentation and provides a viable communication route for smaller advertisers that can't afford mass channels. This chapter reviews the most common advertising formats available on the web, outlines future trends and options, and highlights some best practice marketing activities.

KEY TRENDS YOU MUST KNOW

From Portals to Search

In the early days of the web, most web surfers used portal sites to enter the internet world. These portals linked directly to the most used websites. As websites proliferated, so directories and search engines developed. Initially there was a sharp distinction between directories and search engines. Directories like Yahoo! (launched in 1994) listed selected (quality) sites, sorted into categories by real people. Search engines, like AltaVista, crawled the entire web, indexing every page. Gradually directories came to also include search engines and the distinction blurred.[2]

Although portal sites continue to have great reach, most users go through the portal to other sites. As a result, portal traffic is both fleeting and untargeted (although, as we will see, targeting is improving). Search is reportedly *the* most commonly used application on the web[3], having become the major on-ramp to the web; 90% of web users have used search to find out about a product or service.[4]

Of course, access to search sites – like access to portals – is short duration. Search is a path elsewhere. But as we noted in chapter 2, search is the database of intentions.[5] Search users are actively looking for something. As a result they can be easily targeted by what that something is, and are (presumably) receptive to relevant information and offers.

At first, many marketers seemed to think about the web with a real estate metaphor. Website addresses (URLs) became valuable "web properties." The widespread use of search has changed that. Now we are more likely to find content by search than by its address. So blogger Robert Scoble went from scoble.weblogs.com to scobelizer.wordpress.com to www.scobelizer.com with scarcely a flutter in his technorati ratings.

Why? Because those who wanted to find him used search, not a website address.[6]

Google is the increasingly dominant search engine in most, but definitely not all, countries.[7] Google's advertising revenues now represent almost 20% of global online ad spend[8]; they take up almost 50% of US searches, and are targeting a 70% to 80% share.[9] However, local search and new search technologies have the potential to change all this.

Web-based Advertising Options Diversify

The evolution of the web, which we outlined in the previous chapter, is having a large knock-on effect in terms of the options available to advertisers. Back when people went primarily to portals, banner advertising predominated. However, now that consumers want to visit diverse, niche appeal sites, and use search to find them, there are important new options for marketers to consider. We can group these options into four broad types of internet media that digital marketers should consider:

1. Display ads
2. Search – SEO and SEM
3. Affiliate programs
4. Sponsorships and negotiated space

1. Display Ads

In the early days of the web, way back in 1996, display ads – mainly using banners and buttons – were the form of DigiMarketing. This is still what most people think of as online advertising, and display ads are certainly still important. By late 2006, *eMarketer* put online display ad spending at about $3.3 billion, and forecast growth to $4.5 billion by 2010. Although (as we will see) search is hot, internet users spend only 5% of their time actually searching: the rest of their time is spent with the results of search, and represents opportunities for display ad communication.[10]

Although initially display ads were fairly untargeted, the advent of cookies (see Box Insert, chapter 3), the growth of online advertising networks, and major data-mining computing capacity has changed all that. Display advertising is likely to remain a fixture of the internet, providing particularly interesting opportunities on niche sites.

Display Formats

As the internet has evolved from start-up to mainstay, internet display ad formats have also become well standardized with banners, buttons, and vertical banners (skyscrapers). The Internet Advertising Board's site (www.iab.com) illustrates typical display ad dimensions that most site publishers follow. Standardization of sizes is certainly helpful, but display advertising continues to evolve, particularly in regard to what happens in those display boxes.

Display ads are increasingly using rich media including motion, Flash animation, streaming video and audio, and interactive opportunities – with mini-forms to fill out to obtain more relevant details, and even games. Banners and buttons are now often expandable. If a user interacts with them by clicking or even mouse-over, they enlarge to reveal additional information. When this additional information is video, these are sometimes called video strips. As the banner expands, it usually slides site content down the screen rather than concealing it (so-called push-down banners). Other times the additional information remains within the original confines of the banner (often called polite banners). Disney's *Pirates of the Caribbean: At World's End* movie used a banner holding streaming back-to-back videos, showcasing up to 20 clips from the movie.[11]

Other forms of display (sometimes called out-of-banner ads) include a variety of pop-ups that appear as new windows (usually small) containing advertisements. Technically these are often not really windows but transparent layers. Variations on the pop-up theme include pop-overs that appear on top of the user's active window, and often stay on the screen even as the user scrolls down (also known as hover ads, or floating ads); after a few seconds they may revert to regular banner ads. And pop-unders open beneath the active window. Pop-unders are less intrusive and, as they cannot be seen until the main window is closed, may not be recognized as advertising and gain additional attention. Many users see pop-ups as very intrusive and web browsers can now usually be set to defeat them.

There are also a variety of interstitial display ad possibilities. Interstitials appear between web pages (that is, before the browser displays a new page). Some call them commercial breaks, or intermediate pages, or page takeovers. Snap-backs appear when the page is first loaded, with the ad expanding on the page, and then after a moment automatically snapping back to a standard size, until the user interacts or mouses over, when the larger message opens again. Full-page overlays cover the page with a semi-transparent ad-carrying layer. Wallpaper ads replace the site's background with an ad.

Then we have mobile ad formats to consider. As an example, the Nate MOA services from SK Telecom in Korea allows advertisers to buy seven-second video clips as a standard unit that runs when subscribers turn on their mobile phones.

As you can see, there are now myriad formats with which a DigiMarketer must become familiar. While this looks like a complication, it's really providing a greater array of choices. It's important to know the full range of display options available in your market when you start your digital media planning process.

Ad Serving

Ad serving is the process by which display ads get placed on websites. While this might sound like a technical issue, it's an important topic for digital marketers to understand, so they know how the process works and who plays what role.

Many of the people who create and own websites – the publishers – don't want to deal with all the issues related to managing advertising on their websites. Many would rather focus on creating great sites, not dealing with all the potential advertisers. Therefore, ad serving companies take on this role and provide software to websites and advertisers. The ad serving companies manage the flow of all ads onto each site. Of all the display ads that advertisers have paid to run on a site, the ad server software chooses which one to serve. Advertisers may restrict the times at which their ad is served, and/or they may restrict ads depending upon the location of the viewer (for example, only show a given banner to Asian IP addresses – often called geo-targeting or IP-targeting). Other advertisers may restrict the number of times an ad is shown to each user (frequency capping), or may restrict the order in which ads are displayed to users (surround sessions).

From an advertiser's viewpoint, the ad server tries to serve the ad most likely to result in the advertiser's desired effect. For example, if the ad is aimed at purchase, the ad serving software attempts to estimate which ad is most likely to result in a sale for that type of user. This entails estimating which type of ad the user is most likely to click on (the click through rate, or ctr) and how many of those clicks will actually result in a sale (the conversion rate).

Choice of ad to display may include user-profiling based, for example, on past browsing behavior; a user who visited a site about stereos and then visits a general purpose portal will be served ads for stereos (this is called behavioral targeting). Ad serving may also be affected by the characteristics of the website and the page itself. A particular ad color may do well on a particular type of page. Or the topics on the page may affect the ads shown. This is called contextual targeting, Google AdSense (see below) was the first major user of contextual targeting, which is already playing a major role in advertising on the internet.

An advertising network (for example DoubleClick – now owned by Google) buys ad space on many websites and resells this aggregated ad inventory to advertisers. The network stores the ads to be served on a central ad server and serves them to the appropriate website visitor. If the sites on which you advertise are part of an advertising network you can deal with a single source and have results aggregated across all the sites. The advertising network will also be able to track users across the web, allowing users' actions at websites visited earlier to inform ad targeting (that is, allowing behavioral targeting).

Sites that are not part of an advertising network simply serve the ads themselves. These sites are often more targeted and niche oriented. But the advertiser has to deal with each individual site separately, and needs to develop some means of aggregating response data – clicks, sales, or whatever – across sites. This response aggregation is important as effective DigiMarketing will require real-time optimization using aggregated data.

Although display dominated the early years of the internet, as search engines have grown, so has the importance of search engine marketing. By 2010, paid search is expected to be 70% of total online ad spend.[12] However, some reports see display rebounding as per-click costs of keywords rise. Intriguingly, in 2007 Google made more history by signing to sell display ads on a third-party site (on www.glam.com)[13] and purchased the leading display advertising network (DoubleClick), suggesting further integration of display and search.

2. *Search* – SEO *and* SEM

While display advertising is fundamentally marketer initiated (although increasingly based on consumer behavior triggers), search is consumer initiated. Of course smart DigiMarketers incorporate both sides into their campaigns.

As of mid-2007, search is the fastest growing part of internet marketing. Marketers have realized that searchers are already actively in the market for something. They have indicated their interest via a search enquiry; they have qualified themselves at least as customers for answers. Search is the ultimate opt-in: a request from consumers for information.

Search engine marketing covers two interrelated activities: search engine optimization (sometimes called organic search optimization) or SEO, and paid placement (sometimes called search engine marketing or SEM).

Typically searches generate hundreds of thousands, if not millions, of results. Users rarely get beyond the very first of all these search engine results pages (SERPs). Therefore, companies now deploy search engine optimization (SEO) strategies to try to ensure that they will be on that very first results page for searches using key phrases relevant to their site. The main idea behind SEO, which focuses on the free or organic search results, is to make the construction of a website more "friendly" to being found by the search engines. We will discuss the details of this further in just a moment. In the major general purpose search engines – Google, Yahoo! Live Search, Microsoft – organic (unpaid) results appear on the left of the page.

Paid placement focuses on the paid results which (in the major search engines) appear on the right, or occasionally at the very top of the page. Paid placement evolved from the early days of the internet when Yahoo! (then strictly a directory, remember) both screened – with human editors – every site it listed and charged for the privilege of inclusion. GoTo (later renamed Overture, and now a division of Yahoo!) took this a step further by simply selling positions in the search listings. Marketers could bid on search phrases, with the highest bidding site ensuring first-placed listing in searches using that phrase. What's more, the marketer only paid when the ad was clicked, not when it was displayed. This was a radical change from traditional media where payment was based on exposure (cost-per-thousand, cpm). GoTo exploited the greater tracking power of digital media, by allowing action-based pricing (pay-per-click, ppc).

By 2007, pay-per-click programs were the major revenue drivers for all the main search engines. Google AdWords (http://adwords.google.com) was by far the largest, with Yahoo! Search Marketing (http://searchmarketingyahoo.com) and Microsoft AdCenter (http://adcenter.microsoft.com) also major players. Reportedly, 99% of Google's 2005 revenues came from keyword advertising – meaning Google made more from ads than any television network or newspaper chain.[14]

Google AdWords successfully tweaked the GoTo model in three very important ways:

Clear Separation of Ads

Clear separation of ads from unbiased (organic) search results. AdWords ads usually appear on the right-hand side of the page, whereas the organic results appear on the left. Occasionally paid results will show at the top on the left, but they have a distinctive background. This clear separation of ads and search results seems to have maintained the perceived integrity of search listings.

Ordering Based on Revenue

The order in which ads appear is based on their revenue to Google. AdWords ranks the ads not based on the amount bid per click but on the total revenue earned for Google by the ad; that is, cost-per-click multiplied by the number of clicks that ad generates. An ad can get the coveted top place if its click through rate is high, even though it might not have the highest bid per click. As a result, an effective offer, and/or effective copy, can support lower per click bids. This means that the ads served highest on the page are likely to be relevant and persuasive. Boring ads pay more!

Ads Appear On Non-Search, Non-Google Sites

The AdSense program allows any site (which meets Google's screening criteria) to receive contextual ads. These appear in a part of the site designated by the site's owner, looking very like the AdWords ads on the Google search engine. Again the advertiser only pays when the ad is clicked – and the payment is split between Google and the site on which the ad appeared. Google attempts to serve ads which fit the site's content. Both site and advertiser can set ads/sites which they will not accept. If the AdSense algorithm works well, the contextual ads are highly relevant to the site's content. In the US, the AdSense program now extends to audio ads on the radio. Many advertisers found that AdSense program ads generated lower quality clicks (that is, conversion rates were lower) because viewers were not actively engaged in search and so were less open to offers. So, Google recently introduced smart pricing (the Yahoo! version is called quality-based pricing), whereby clicks from sites that yield lower conversion rates actually cost less.

The AdSense model is now followed in essence by Yahoo! (as Yahoo! Publisher Network), and by Microsoft adCenter.

Search Engine Optimization

Search engine optimization (SEO) is all about getting a good place in search results. SEO is complex and rapidly evolving. It is impossible to present SEO here in definitive detail. You will almost certainly want to use an expert consultant in the field. But the DigiMarketer should appreciate the broad outlines of SEO, and first heed two warnings:

1. No-one outside of the search engines knows exactly how the engines rank web pages. And the ways they do it (the algorithms they use) are continually evolving to defeat search engine optimizers who try to game the system by getting unworthy sites into the high ranks.

2. Trust no-one who promises to guarantee a continued first-place result. Sites that employ tricks – like providing the search engines with pages different from those seen by regular visitors – or are even suspected of playing tricks – risk getting blacklisted by the search engines and being completely eliminated from all listings. If your site gets into that search engine black-hole it can be extremely difficult to get out. The search engines want to make sure that users (their customers) quickly find the things for which they are looking. The search engines want to list the most relevant pages for a search phrase first. If your pages are not very relevant to the search phrase, you are unlikely to ever get a high rank for that phrase, and if you do get a high position, you won't be able to sustain it.

Then: *think like a search engine*! Search engines look at individual pages, not websites. Each page on your site can be constructed to rank highly for different key phrases.

Think key phrases not keywords: most users search for phrases not words. Start by listing all the key phrases for which you want to be found. Then allocate each phrase to the page(s) to which it already fits best. If there are some phrases that don't seem to belong to any particular page, ask yourself if that phrase is really relevant to your site. If it is, then build the page appropriate for the phrase. As you can see, you should be thinking about the search implications when you build your website: don't treat search as an afterthought.

Search engines can't yet make much sense of pictures. So every picture should have a descriptive verbal tag (called an alt tag) in the page code (the HTML). Most people think that search engines can't make much sense of Flash animations either. So whatever content is in Flash should be in text somewhere also. Search engines can't fill in dialogue boxes, logins, or passwords. So again any content that you want the search engine to see should also be in a readily accessible part of the site.

Search engines probably give more weight to content that is frequently updated (this makes sure that they can spot news). So you might make sure that at least part of the site is updated daily. Google uses a concept of query deserves freshness (QDF)[15] whereby the search engine attempts to decide whether a given search phrase is looking for freshly breaking stories, or long-established authorities (they do this by looking at how much that search phrase is used in up-to-the-minute sites like blogs). If pages on your site are using some trendy key phrases, it is probably a good idea to update content on those pages frequently.

On-Page and Off-Page Criteria: Search engines use many criteria in ranking sites for key phrases. Google reportedly has over 200 signals that it uses to rank sites.

These are believed to fall into two main sets: on-page criteria and off-page criteria.

On-page criteria focus on how many times the search phrase occurs on the page and how important it appears to be. Appearing in the domain name, in the page title, in the main heading, being repeated in text (or in alt tags), and in the HTML meta tags are indications of importance – in roughly declining order of merit.

The search engine also attempts to measure how naturally the phrase occurs, so simply listing the same phrase mindlessly is unlikely to help – and will probably get you penalized. Pages that are clearly focused on a key phrase will be more highly ranked for that phrase. Because on-page criteria are controlled by the web designer, and so are easy to game, off-page criteria are probably more important.

Off-page criteria look at how other web pages relate to your page. The basic metric is "how many other pages link to this page, and how important are those linking pages?" The links into your page are a reflection of how important the entire web considers your page to be. Links to the pages that link to you become an index of how important those pages are, and so on. This is the well-publicized concept of Google page rank.

The quantity, quality and context of incoming links to each page   and to your entire site – have a big impact on how high the page is ranked with respect to a particular key phrase. The type of site that links to you is also important.[16] Some think that the less commercial the site, the more important is a link from that site. So try to get links in from high trust sites that have a genuine fit to your content. The specific words used in the links are also important. The link's wording is assumed to reflect the content of your page. This is the basis of Google-bombing (see Box Insert in chapter 8).

As search engines evolve, SEO strategies must adapt. Google is now listing its vertical search options. These allow users to confine their search to websites, or other content, of a particular type. A user can choose to search blogs, books, catalogs, images, maps, patents, products, video, and so on. This opens up the possibility of developing content on your site that would rank well in a particular vertical.

As personalized search develops, search engine ranking will take on a different meaning. Off-page criteria will include information about the searcher. There will be no consistent first place in search results. The search results that I get will be personalized to what the search engine thinks will interest me. The search engine's opinion of my interests will be based on analysis of my past searches, my browsing history, other items on my computer, perhaps even my email, my calendar and the contents of my mobile phone. There will be a #1 on my search results, but it won't be the same as the #1 on your search results!

Click Fraud

Click fraud occurs when a person – or more usually an automated script, or computer program – clicks on an ad to generate per click charges, without a genuine interest in opening the link. This can be done as a dastardly scheme by a company that wants to drive up the cost of advertising for its competitors (or exhaust their budgets so competitive ads don't get shown), or by angry consumers that wish to exact payback from companies that have aggrieved them, or as a revenue earner by the sites showing the ads (remember the site gets a cut of the ad revenue).

Click fraud is illegal in several countries. However, as an operational definition of "without a genuine interest in opening the link" is not really possible, the precise delineation of click fraud is fraught with ambiguity. By the end of 2006, estimates of click fraud ranged from 14% for search engine ads (like AdWords) to 19% for content networks (like AdSense)[17] – with higher rates for more costly cost-per-click (cpc) ads. Understandably, Google disputes these click fraud estimates[18], claiming much lower rates of "undetected" click fraud, perhaps less than 2%.[19]

Typically the major cpc advertising brokers employ sophisticated click fraud detection algorithms, and claim not to charge for fraudulent clicks. Obviously fraud detection methods are not disclosed, but they certainly include checks for repeated clicks in short periods of time, and clicks from the same IP address.

Click fraud associated with click farms – real people in low-wage countries, paid to click on ads – is harder to identify, as is fraud from zombie computers. Zombies are caused by computer viruses (for example, Trojans) that like the wooden horse of Troy are allowed onto a user's computer only to later use that computer to (among other things) generate ad clicks. Some believe that click fraud will eventually force pay-per-click to change to pay-per-action (ppa). Then, advertisers will pay only when a click results in a specified action (for example, a sale or registration or whatever). In recent years both Yahoo! and Google have settled class action lawsuits alleging they did not do enough to prevent click fraud.[20] In the future we may see some sort of an independent click fraud auditor.

3. Affiliate Programs

Affiliate marketing is a growing digital media trend. Like paid placement, affiliate programs are performance based.

Instead of paying for display ads, or for search phrase-related ads, affiliates "advertise" your products and services for free, receiving compensation only when the ads lead a prospect to undertake the required action – which may be visiting a site, or signing up for a newsletter, but in the vast majority of cases is making an actual purchase.[21] Affiliates often advertise your products and services in their editorial content.

One of the earliest affiliate programs was started by CDNow (www.cdnow.com, currently operated by Amazon) which encouraged music-oriented websites to link to the CDNow site. Purchases by visitors who followed such links resulted in commissions to the referring site. Amazon (www. amazon.com) of course launched a similar book-oriented affiliate program.

Affiliate marketing is an often overlooked option for the DigiMarketer. Affiliate marketing can be an effective way to harness the energy of smaller, niche-oriented sites that don't get the kind of traffic or advertiser interest of the big sites or portals. These smaller sites are often very targeted, yielding a highly focused audience. If the site's audience fits your target market, then you might actually get a more qualified lead than you would through search results.

It's also worth noting that affiliate relationships can work both ways. While you gain traffic to your site from the affiliate, you might also generate traffic to theirs. In addition to potentially giving you some revenue, affiliate marketing can also lead to interesting co-marketing activities with synergistic brands.

4. *Sponsorship and Negotiated Space*

This is perhaps the most interesting area of all, given the opportunities to negotiate something completely new with media owners. Certainly, many sites, games, and mobile destinations have standard sponsorship packages, some of which are worth consideration. However, channel owners and marketers are all looking for fresh, innovative ways to build their respective businesses. The digital marketing space is still being defined, so there are ample opportunities to negotiate something new. For example, you could sponsor a new, brand-relevant section of a portal or of a game. An airline might sponsor a portal's travel section. Or a branded department store might negotiate to put an outlet in a new mall in *Second Life* (discussed further in chapter 7).

Most marketers are familiar with traditional sponsorships in which companies put their branding on a media property, an event, or even an F1 car. This certainly provides brand exposure. But sponsorship can be limited in terms of a truly relevant connection between the advertiser and the sponsored property. However, in digital channels, sponsorship can be around content. This might mean, in the example just noted, that an airline supplies interesting travel information to the portal as part of the sponsorship. This alignment of advertiser and marketer around content creates more relevance to the sponsorship. Plus, since it's in a digital channel, consumers can easily click through from the sponsored material to the advertiser – something you can't do as well with traditional sponsorships.

As you consider sponsorships or negotiated space options, you should try to anticipate the longer term steps you might want to take if it's a success. This will enable you to secure valuable long-term rights. If you are going to sponsor that portal's travel section, you might want to lock-in option rights as the primary advertiser for any travel specials on the site. Or you might want to reserve rights to create affiliate links within the sponsored section to travel agents. In a negotiation, everything is worth a try. After all, the worst that can happen is that the channel owner says "no!"

DIGIMARKETING BEST PRACTICES

Ensure Your Advertising is User-friendly, Not Annoying

DigiMarketers must always remember that the user is in control. Poorly targeted, irrelevant, intrusive ads which are not consumer friendly will cause viewers to leave the site and/or block future ads. User friendliness dictates that all rich media ads should have clear mute, pause, stop, and close buttons, which should not be confusingly similar to Windows buttons, or other operating system warnings. Anything that intrudes on the site's content (floating ads, snap-backs, and so on) should appear for no more than a few seconds, unless the viewer shows interest by interacting with them in some way.

Deliver Intensely Relevant Display Ads

The DigiMarketing environment is extremely data rich. There is really no excuse for failing to target your advertising. There are optimizers capable of analyzing web pages, browsing histories, contexts and adapting advertising – even down to the creative – in real time so as to serve the most relevant ad. Ad optimizers can run 5,000 to 10,000 calculations to evaluate ad performance, all in real time. Optimized ads perform 15% to 30% better than standardized display ads. If a user who has consulted a web page involving alternative fuels or energy conservation subsequently visits an auto site (even in a new browsing session), he can be served ads about hybrid cars.[22] Or a user who browses a site, accesses the shipping cost page, but then doesn't buy, can be tagged as a hot prospect. If that person subsequently visits another site fed by the same advertising network, she could see a special targeted ad, with a better offer (perhaps free shipping). Clicking that ad would take her back to the original site with the free shipping code pre-inserted for her.

Such behaviorally targeted ads – designed and served to reflect shopper's actual actions – are rapidly becoming the norm for DigiMarketers' display advertising. For example, the data miners claim they can tell with 75% certainty which of the 300,000 monthly visitors to Yahoo! Autos will actually purchase a car within the next three months.[23]

As tightly targeted ads become the norm, even small businesses – who up to now have been unable to finance much advertising in conventional media – will be able to access the infinite niches we discussed in chapter 3.

Integrate Your Organic and Paid Search Efforts

Natural search (SEO) and paid search (SEM) are two sides of the same coin. Marketers sometimes think they should choose one or the other. However, the truth is they should be doing both. A holistic search marketing strategy, initiated early in the DigiMarketing planning process, is essential. Search marketing requires a lot of forethought.

The ideal situation for DigiMarketers is when a search phrase brings up at least one link to their site on the organic (left-hand side) results *and* a paid placement ad on the right-hand side. The customer is most likely to click the left-hand link (preferring organic results) thus the DigiMarketer will have no charge for the appearance of the paid placement ad (assuming it is on a cpc basis). Yet that paid placement had an awareness impact on the customer, provided a chance to focus on the exact search phrase the consumer used, and to highlight the site's content related to that search term. The paid placement reinforces the organic position, at no cost to the DigiMarketer.[24]

Get the Most Out of Paid Search Placement (SEM)

It's Not Essential to Be in the #1 Placed Ad

Research suggests that the top-placed ad will indeed get clicked on a lot more – maybe as much as 40% more for Google AdWords.[25] But the quality of those clicks may be lower than for lower placed ads. The top-placed ads get more clicks, but the traffic may be much less likely to convert. People who click on the top-most ad may be less committed and less interested in action than those who take the trouble to read and click on lower ranked ads.

Look at ROI

ROI from paid placement depends on the traffic from the ad and the conversion rate and the margin from that conversion and the cost of the ad. Those top-placed ads are paying more per click – often much, much more.

Look at the Long-tail Keywords

Instead of bidding for the expensive frequently searched phrases, buy more less-searched phrases. Google recently reported that 20% to 25% of searches were unique.[26] These more specific, long-tail, keywords will be cheaper, and provided the ad is tailored to the search words, may give better conversion rates.

Make Sure the Search Phrase is in the Ad Headline

Most paid placement programs let the DigiMarketer create as many ads as they wish. For text ads, production cost is almost zero. So make each of those long-tail phrases deliver an ad with that exact phrase in the ad headline. This delivers three benefits. First, the search phrase will be highlighted in the ad – so your headline gets a boost. Second, searchers will be attuned to their exact search phrase, so the ad gets a relevancy gain. Third, because of these two factors you get more clicks, so you can hold high places for your ads without necessarily out-bidding the competition. Remember: Google rewards return to Google! Ad rank depends on the cpc you bid and the click-through-rate.

Don't Bid Against Yourself

Careless DigiMarketers don't only bid against their own affiliates, they may finish up bidding against other parts of their own company. Keyword bidding needs to be centralized.

Look for Others to Share the Cost

Can your suppliers or distributors, or suppliers of complementary products or services, be persuaded to share the cost of your keywords? Both Intel and Microsoft work with customers to share paid placement costs for products that contain their components. Perhaps you can set up a system to monitor how the keyword traffic flows to your site, and out to allied sites. Rather than fighting over the keyword bids, to the benefit of the search engine, you could split the cost according to how you and your allied sites benefit from the traffic.

Co-ordinate Your Affiliate Programs so They Represent Your Brand the Way You Want

Affiliate programs can provide tremendous reach and can harness a wide range of niche sites to market your brand and capture referral business. But the DigiMarketer needs to be in full control of how affiliates are using the brand and to police their communications to make certain they are right on brand.

If affiliates use intrusive, disruptive, aggressive advertising it will be your brand that gets the blame. The smart DigiMarketer will also ensure that affiliates have proper privacy policies in place. Any cause for the consumer to lose confidence will rebound on you, not on the affiliate. It's also necessary to ensure that affiliates are not bidding against each other on key search terms.

Integrate Your Digital Media

There is evidence that exposure to display ads can impact phrases used in search. In a Yahoo! test using ads for the brokerage company Harris Direct (www.harrisdirect.com, now part of E-Trade), those exposed to display ads for the brokerage were 160% more likely to search in the category over the next three weeks – and far more likely to click on a text ad for Harris Direct when it appeared in paid search results.[27]

In 2005, Google added display ads to its AdSense network. Display ads are placed in the same way as AdSense places text ads, matching with pages' keywords. In 2007, Google acquired DoubleClick – the leader in web display advertising. DoubleClick has collected a massive amount of data on individuals' browsing and click-stream activities using cookies left on users' computers to allow their activity to be linked across websites. This could now be integrated with users' search histories and even emails. Google claims that only "nonpersonally identifiable data" will be merged to better target ads.[28] The acquisition will allow DoubleClick to better target its banners, based around the same AdSense algorithms. In 2007, Privacy International, a "cyber rights" group, ranked Google as having the worst privacy policies of 20 popular internet companies, claiming Google was "hostile" to privacy.[29] Irrespective of Google's specific issues, integrating your various digital media components makes good sense.

FUTURE TRENDS – WHERE IT'S HEADING

Looking to the future, digital media options are likely to evolve as quickly as all the other elements of the digital landscape.

While there are likely to be many changes, there are three areas that will constitute the major trends for the future:

Media Trend 1: Video predominates
Media Trend 2: Search diversifies further
Media Trend 3: Personalization becomes the norm

Media Trend 1: Video Predominates

Late 2006 saw Cisco CEO John Chambers declare that "if there is a killer app, it is video."[30] The largest and fastest growing websites are almost all heavily involved in streaming video. Estimates are that video already accounts for over 60% of internet traffic.[31] As an advertising medium, video is of course a format marketers can easily relate to and is likely to drive a major move of advertising from television to web.

Traditional broadcasters are already getting online. CBS, for example, is already distributing content over ten different online destinations, including AOL and Joost (Joost is an online television station, discussed in chapter 10) as part of the CBS Interactive Audience Network. CBS is reportedly already working on deals to distribute their video content over social network sites. But much of the surge in online video is consumer-created and will be discussed in detail in chapter 8.

Video Search

If advertisements shown during a video are to achieve the same acceptance as AdWords, they will need to be relevant to the video being viewed. The leading general purpose search engines have very limited video indexing abilities. In a recent US study, a substantial number of people complained that web video was chaotically organized and difficult to search.[32] As a result, specialized video search is attracting great interest.

These solutions try to assess video content on a moment by moment basis, allowing different ads to be targeted at different points in the video.

Blinkx[33] (www.blinkx.com, and see Box Insert below) claims to have indexed more than 18 million hours of audio and video content, using patented conceptual search, speech recognition and video analysis. Currently, Blinkx seems to have a larger index base of rich media than Google or Yahoo! and powers video search for several major engines, including parts of MSN, Lycos and Infospace.[34] Among other features, Blinkx can produce a list at the end of each video of every product and service mentioned in the video, allowing advertisers to place ads against already occurring uses of their products rather than having to pay for product placement.[35]

An alternate service from ScanScout (www.scanscout.com) offers contextual text ads keyed to specific scenes in a video. It will also avoid showing ads against scenes unsuitable for the brand. These text ads can open into videos when clicked.

Blinkx: Don't Miss It

www.blinkx.com is a vertical (specialized) search engine for video and audio content. Blinkx, now based in San Francisco, uses speech recognition technology originally developed in the UK to index audio content – including the audio track of videos. This is supplemented by indexing any text associated with the video. Blinkx already has agreements with over 200 content providers and has indexed over 18 million hours of audio and video content. Blinkx's technology powers the video search of parts of MSN, Live.com, Lycos, Infospace and parts of AOL. IPO-ing in the London Alternative Investment Market, in

May 2007, Blinkx produced the second highest trading day for an IPO in London for the last two years.

As with other successful vertical search systems, Blinkx presents an array of products/services, not just search. Users can search video, create personal playlists, or build a customized Video Wall for their blog or social networking page.

Blinkx Remote searches for full-length television episodes on the web, supplemented with background information from other sites (for example, Wikipedia and the Internet Movie Database, IMDb). Blinkx Remote will also alert users when new episodes are available.

Blinkx Video Wall is a widget[36] that lets sites (and blogs) create a display of video previews on their sites. Think conventional television's picture-in-a-picture feature – multiplied by 25: Blinkx Video Wall delivers 25 preview clips running simultaneously. Users can click a Wall it! button to show any Blinkx results as a wall of video previews. Mouse-overing any item in the wall enlarges it. The wall can hold favorite videos or the (constantly updated) results of a Blinkx video search.

Blinkx it is another widget that selects text from the user's website (or blog), searches for videos relevant to that text, and displays the video clips on the user's site. Results are updated as the site text changes. Blinkx it could easily deliver contextually relevant video to sites across the web (as AdSense does for text).

Pico is a toolbar that runs in a text editor or a web browser working in the background to find web sources similar to what is already being read.

In 2007 Google embarked on extensive experimentation with ad formats on its YouTube site (www.youtube.com, acquired in 2006). This included tests on duration[37], placement[38] and triggering, with some videos showing clickable text ads (which launch an ad video[39]) and others showing thumbnails of suggested (similar) videos, some of which may be paid advertising.[40] By mid-2007, Google had launched an advertising solution on YouTube, featuring a semi-transparent layer across the bottom part of videos, which appears after 15 seconds of play. The ads can animate for a few seconds, and can be clicked away or clicked on. If a user clicks in the ad, the video he or she was watching pauses and a video ad launches inside the player. Unlike AdWords, YouTube is using a cpm model at the time of writing, with a flat fee of $20 per 1,000 video impressions.[41] Initially ads are only appearing on videos from YouTube's professional content partners and odd members of its member partner program.[42] Within five days of YouTube launching ads at least two free blockers were available to allow users to view video without being bothered by advertising![43]

As search tools continue to develop, it seems certain that we will be able to place contextually relevant ads on or around video. Whether these ads can be displayed, like AdWords, in a format that is sufficiently appealing without being too intrusive remains to be seen.

It seems very unlikely that 30-second television-style commercials will emerge. At present, tolerated ad duration seems more like 5 to 15 seconds. In the UK, a 2007 YouGuv survey found 93% of respondents amenable to viewing pre-roll ads if no longer than 15 seconds in length.[44] Neither pre-roll nor post-roll video ads achieve quite the separation of ads and content delivered with text search. AdBrite's InVideo (www.adbrite.com) provides a custom player which can carry branding information (superimposed on every frame) and advertising. When the video is shared to other sites, the branding and the ads carry with it, and the original video publisher continues to receive ad revenue. It remains to be seen whether ads around video can be managed with the unobtrusiveness and relevance achieved by AdWords.

Media Trend 2: Search Diversifies Further

Regular search at general purpose search engines is called horizontal search. Searches are conducted across a broad range of materials. As the web becomes more detailed and micro-niched, we can expect a dramatic growth in vertical search engines (VSEs), also known as *specialized* or *alternative search*. Vertical search will focus only on sites involving a single topic (for example, medicine) or particular types of content (for example, blogs or videos). Video search (discussed above) is really a type of vertical search.

The attraction of vertical, specialized search will be the elimination of many irrelevant results arising from ambiguous words. So a vertical search for apple on a specialized electronic devices search engine will turn up references to computers, unsullied by pages about fruit!

Google launched Universal Search in mid-2007, integrating its vertical search results from news, video, images, local and book search engines with those from crawling web pages. It even allows video (including, conceptually, video ads) to be opened within the search results.

The best vertical search engines provide specialized user interfaces, related services, and even communities with bulletin boards and self-help areas. The real estate vertical search sites Trulia (www.trulia.com) and Willow (www.willow. com) provide mash-ups of real estate values per square foot and mapping data to produce "heat maps" of home cost per square foot. Users can zoom in on maps to see areas they can afford – or try to spot adjacent lower cost areas.[45] www.wize.

com collects together consumer reviews and comments and attempts to build product ratings (see also the Boxed Insert on www.blinkx.com). There is even a specialized music search and recommendation engine at www.seeqpod.com which provides "playable search" by allowing users to actually play the music they find. And there is an intriguing image-based search in beta from www.tiltomo.com.

Technorati (www.technorati.com) is probably the leading vertical search for blogs, while Sphere (www.sphere.com) provides a widget (see chapter 3) which, when clicked, will find blog posts and media articles similar to the one being read. We even have vocal search emerging: talking search engines. For US users, Google provides a free, phone-based, completely automated Directory Enquiries/Information service. Effectively, this gives Google the potential to launch a voice-activated interface to web search and search results.

Shopping Search

One rapidly emerging category of vertical search uses "shopping bots" to do comparison shopping; see for example www.pricegrabber.com, www.shopzilla.com and www.shopping.com (bought by eBay in 2005). Many shopping search sites allow paid placement by retailers at the top of the results lists, and involve some form of reputation scoring (see chapter 8) and user feedback. Shopping search sites are particularly attractive to marketers as searchers are close to buying, probably higher spending, and yield higher conversion rates.

Autonomy (www.autonomy.com), a UK search company (who spun off Blinkx), has search abilities based around implicit query technology. This runs constantly in the background, looking for data that could be relevant to what a user is doing. One of Autonomy's shopping-based applications is a transaction hijack capability that allows vendors to identify customers who are about to purchase at a competitor's website and present their offer of a similar product.[46]

Local Search

Local search, especially when coupled with mobile devices, will probably be one of the hottest future trends. Advertising opportunities in local search are likely to be particularly attractive to small businesses, who (by some estimates) already make up 70% of the AdWords base.[47]

Some aspects of local search are built right into the major search engines. For example, Google will interpret enquires within a national context, so searches for "government" will turn up sites relevant to the government of the country from which the search is conducted.[48] For some languages, they will even translate into English queries framed in that language, perform the search, and translate search results into the original language of the query, even translating pages the user chooses.

Although location-specific results can be obtained from general purpose search engines, specialized engines have the opportunity to build additional functionality. Yelp (www.yelp.com) and mojopages (www.mojopages.com) add user-submitted reviews of restaurants, cafes, bars and so on for major US cities, and offer the possibility of paid advertising adjacent to reviews

At present, local searches are fragmented over many sources. As we have seen, these include the general search engines, geographic or local vertical engines, proprietary internet directories, user review sites, community guides, newspapers sites, and so on. While many of these search sites are using data from the same aggregators (for example, InfoUSA, Acxiom, and Amacai), almost every service does its own cleaning and processing of the data.[49] In addition, most local search is very US-centric. Although it is possible to Google a restaurant with a street on your mobile device, unless you live in the US, the results are far from satisfactory. Craigslist (www.craigslist.com), although really a classified advertising site, is probably the most global of the local search sites. We can expect to see more social networking sites including local search.

Maps Search

The popular Google Maps (www.maps.google.com) are now experimenting with advertising. The location of your business can be listed with Google Maps and will appear in directory listings beside the map, with a location marker on the map itself. Others have taken advantage of the satellite imagery feature to advertise on rooftops!

AdWords now extends to maps, with a maplets feature that allows content – like building descriptions or advertising – to pop-up when users mouse over a push-pin on the map. The push-pin itself can be customized around logos. If a user clicks on a link from the pop-up, Google and the site on which the map appeared share the cpc revenue. Google Street View provides panoramic video views of actual streetscapes in major US cities. This has tremendous potential for local search and local advertising.

Mobile Search

The most logical place to use local search is on a mobile device. Typically, the consumer is out and on-the-move when they most need local search. For the marketer, these are motivated consumers with an immediate need for information, not to mention that there are far more mobile devices than PCs – probably about three times as many – and they're growing at twice the rate, with two-thirds of the world living within reach of a mobile network.[50] Mobile devices and their DigiMarketing potential are discussed in the next chapter.

Indeed, consumer-initiated search on mobile devices with relevant results, and relevant advertising, is one of the keys to the mobile marketing future. As a result, many players are moving into this space. In addition to mobile versions from the general search engines (www.google.com/mobile, m.yahoo.com, and beta.mobile.msn.com), we already have entries from the mobile phone companies (for example, Nokia already offers mobile search and maps), and so-called white-label search services available for carrier branding (for example, www.mediosystems.com and www.jumptap. com), and of course mobile specialists start-ups (for example, www.mogmo.com).

Some mobile search is SMS-based – all the majors provide this service, as do some specialized suppliers (for example, 4info.net). Some is voice-recognition based (for example, 1-800-Free411 and www.promptu.com). However, as connection speeds improve, most mobile search is using a simplified web interface. For the advertiser, limited screen real estate is a real handicap, especially if the user's need for information, and possibly maps, is to be respected. Although larger, flexible displays are on their way (see chapter 6), at present mobile browsers often compress the page (using services like Skweezer, www.skweezer.net, from Greenlight Wireless), which can actually remove advertising from the web page.

Yahoo! perhaps has an edge over Google in mobile search. At the time of writing, Yahoo! oneSearch is being rolled out. As with other specialized mobile search suppliers, oneSearch attempts to increase its result relevance not only by factoring in location, but also judging the intent of the searcher. Based on the contemporary behavior of other searchers, oneSearch attempts to better understand the query, and better order search results.

In particular, oneSearch assumes that as you are searching from a mobile device, you want local, topical answers rather than general interest links. A search for "pizza" returns phone numbers and addresses of local pizza restaurants rather than websites about pizza. Like, all the best vertical search engines, this is combined with ratings and reviews from other users. Searching on a city name brings up a link to city guide, which then links to flickr photos which have been tagged in that city and to today in the city, with weather and traffic reports. Yahoo!'s prototype ZoneTag automatically geotags uploaded photos with the cell tower's location.[51] Pay-per-click advertising is shown and, to conserve screen space, only the two highest bidders appear.

Users appear very accepting of advertising on their mobiles, provided the ads are unobtrusive and relevant. An Enpocket study of mobile users found that 78% of consumers said that "they would be happy to receive advertising that is tailored to their interests" and almost two-thirds of those would be willing to provide personal details to improve relevance.[52]

Google recently made a patent application for an interesting call-on-select function which would allow an ad to automatically trigger a phone call. This would indeed make ads more relevant and easier to use for the customer. Whether a link opened a new page or made a phone call would depend on the user's screen size, connection speed, input capabilities, and on the cpc price[53] – the start of smart agents. Reportedly, Google has started testing such ads on its site, and as many small businesses prefer a phone contact to a web page view, these ads may be premium priced.

Mobile search is particularly promising for small and medium local businesses looking for an effective, low-cost advertising medium, since it is as accessible to a local shop as to a super-chain.

Contextual Search

We are already seeing the first steps towards the semantic web discussed in chapter 3. In the near future we can expect a radical improvement in the web's ability to understand itself and to interpret text and video content. As of 2007, the major search engines are still index-based: crawling the web, attempting to ascertain the importance of pages, and using keywords to tag them. However, natural language search engines are starting to emerge, using artificial intelligence to attempt to understand the structure and nuances of natural language.[54]

Powerset (www.powerset.com) – although limited to a few sample search results at the time of writing – highlights some of the limitations of index-based engines. To search for "what did Steve Jobs say about the iPod" in a conventional search engine produces an overwhelming volume of hits, very few of which actually involve Steve Jobs saying anything, and even fewer involve him saying something about the iPod. If the searcher controls the order of words to ensure that Steve Jobs is doing the saying, and what is said about the iPod, no results are returned. Powerset, on the other hand, returns a much smaller set of totally relevant results.

Social Search

Some new entrants to the search field are putting humans (real people) back into the search system. Some let users suggest or vote on the best pages for a topic, sometimes with editors screening suggestions (for example, Squidoo, www.squidoo. com). Bessed, pronounced "Best" – www.bessed.com – lets users comment on the search results (combining blogging and search). ChaCha (www.chacha.com) even lets users chat online with a human search assistant. Mahalo (www.mahalo.com) aims to provide search pages for popular search terms that are pre-prepared by humans to avoid the "spam" pages that infest Google's results for commercially valuable searches.[55] Anything to try to get an edge.

3. Personalization Becomes the Norm

Yahoo! recently made a splash when a VP reportedly declared that "Search is no longer the dominant paradigm...The future of the web is about personalization."[56] While the company wasted no time in asserting that search was still a top priority, all the major search engines are already talking more and more about personalization.[57]

As we saw in chapter 3, rather than users searching the web and screening the results, as they do today, the future of the web will be in screened, relevant information coming to users. We are already starting to see this with RSS feeds where, remember, users choose the feeds that interest them and then receive headlines or summaries from these sources. Eventually this screening will happen at the behest of users' smart agents, with minimal intervention by users themselves. The Australian-based Particls (www.particls.com) relevancy service adds a proportioning alert filter to RSS. Particls learns from the users' browsing which items are likely to be of most interest to them. These important items are presented intrusively (users can even receive them as SMSes to their mobile). Items that are unimportant are not presented, only logged. Other items can be tickered across the screen, or popped-up, and so on, depending on the user's preferences. The collaborative filtering approaches of Digg, digg.com, and Spotplex, www.spotplex.com (see chapter 8), and the widget-driven steps (see chapter 3) of Netvibes (www.netvibes.com) are a smart agent direction.

122

As we noted in the Box Insert, personalized search really undercuts SEO (search engine optimization). Each individual will receive a different set of search results, tailored to his or her interests. The computer technician who searches for "apple" will see computers; the fruit grower who does the same search will see varieties of fruit; the 60s music buff will find the Beatles. So there will be no overall #1 on the search engine. Ranking will depend on the individual.[58]

The interesting question will be whether the currently dominant search sites will continue to drive personalized search. Some feel that the sites best able to deliver personalized search will be those with the most intimate knowledge of their users.[59] These may well turn out to be the social networking sites like Facebook (www.facebook.com) and MySpace (www.myspace.com) or their successors.

Google and Yahoo! are racing to aggregate details of their users from across their diverse properties (for example, search histories, del.icio.us bookmarks, Flickr photos, calendar entries, email topics, and so on). Although the ultimate goal of personalization is to benefit the customer by delivering exactly what that specific user wants – without the user having to articulate his or her exact needs – privacy concerns are undoubtedly uppermost in the user's mind. As we will see again and again in the world of digital media, personalization and privacy are often at odds.

SUMMARY: INTERNET MEDIA

Digital media and advertising options are expanding. Therefore, DigiMarketers have a number of new media opportunities to explore:

- There are a variety of new display formats that should be considered.

- In addition, affiliate programs and various negotiated space and sponsorship options are available.
- Search – consisting of both SEO and SEM – is increasingly central to DigiMarketing plans.
- Video will eventually predominate as the media and advertising standard for digital.
- More placements and media deals will be contextual in nature, leading to greater targeting and relevancy to individuals.

The next topics – email and viral marketing – are perhaps the most widely used techniques today on the web.

END NOTES
1   *The User Revolution: The New Advertising Ecosystem and the Rise of the Internet as a Mass Medium*, February 2007, Piper Jaffray.
2   This is not to say that the remaining directories are unimportant. Search engines are thought to pay attention to directory listings as one factor in substantiating site credibility and so driving better listings in the SERP; searchenginewatchcom/showPage. html?page=3625170. Nor is it to say that indexing by real people is unimportant. See www.nytimes.com/2007/06/24/business/yourmoney/24digi.html?ei=5090&en=7c0c119d 030c477c&ex=1340337600&pagewanted=print
3   searchenginewatch.com/showPage.html?page=3625170
4   Pew Internet & American Life Project, December 2005.
5   John Battelle, *The Search: How Google and Its Rivals Rewrote the Rules of Business and Transformed Our Culture*, Penguin Group, New York, 2005.
6   innovationcreators.com/wp/?p=310
7   A notable exception is South Korea, where Google has less than 2% of search, with the Korean site www.naver.com dominating the market with a 77% share, followed by another home-grown site www.daum.net with just over 10%. See www.precursorblog. com/node/454
8   *The User Revolution: The New Advertising Ecosystem and the Rise of the Internet as a Mass Medium*, February 2007, Piper Jaffray.
9   weblogs.hitwise.com/leeann-prescott/2007/04/local_search_marketing_panel_a.html
10 money.cnn.com/magazines/business2/business2_archive/2007/03/01/8401043/ index.htm
11 clickz.com/showPage.html?page=3626106
12 www.businessweek.com/technology/content/apr2007/tc20070414_675511 htm?campaign_id=rss_daily
13 www.redherring.com/Article.aspx?a=22487
14 www.wired.com/wired/archive/14.01/fraud.html. *Wired*, quoting a Goldman Sachs analyst, claimed 56% of 2005 Google revenues were from AdWords and 43% from AdSense.
15 www.nytimes.com/2007/06/03/business/yourmoney/03google.html?_r=1&oref=slogin& pagewanted=all
16 Some talk of search engine bowling as a technique to make a competing site (or one carrying unfavorable reviews of your product or service) look like it is trying to game the search engines and thereby get demoted to a very low rank, or even disregarded completely. See Box Insert chapter 10.
17 www.clickforensics.com/news/pressreleases/01-30-07.html
18 shumans.com/articles/000048.php

19 www.marketingpilgrim.com/2006/12/google-click-fraud-rate-two-percent.html
20 www.imediaconnection.com/content/10294.asp
21 en.wikipedia.org/wiki/Affiliate_marketing
22 money.cnn.com/magazines/business2/business2_archive/2007/03/01/8401043/index.htm
23 *ibid.*
24 The only snag will be that the lower ctr for the ads means that a higher bid will be needed to maintain prime positions, and if the ctr rates are very low the search engine may pull the ad.
25 www.clickz.com/showPage.html?page=3379931
26 www.readwriteweb.com/archives/udi_manber_search_is_a_hard_problem php#more
27 money.cnn.com/magazines/business2/business2_archive/2007/03/01/8401043/index.htm
28 news.com.com/Privacy+concerns+dog+Google-DoubleClick+deal/2100-1024_3-6177029.html
29 news.bbc.co.uk/2/hi/technology/6740075.stm
30 gigaom.com/2006/12/12/chambers-video-is-the-killer-app/
31 www.nytimes.com/2007/02/25/business/yourmoney/25slip.html?ex=1182830400&en=41d2df69738bc088&ei=5070
32 32% of web video searchers are frustrated by the amount of ads.
33 www.blinkx.com
34 en.wikipedia.org/wiki/Blinkx
35 www.marketingpilgrim.com/2007/06/blinkx-developing-video-for-adsense release-set-monday.html
36 As we saw in chapter 3, a widget is a small piece of code that can be cut and pasted into any website (or blog) to allow that site to display whatever it is that the widget delivers.
37 Non-profits could get listed free.
38 www.redherring.com/Article.aspx?a=22095&hed=YouTube+Lining+Up+Summer+Ads
39 newteevee.com/2007/05/11/youtubes-new-inline-ads-screenshots/
40 www.searchenginejournal.com/new-youtube-embedded-player-features-google-video-ads/5064/
41 www.readwriteweb.com/archives/google_launches_youtube_video_ads_is_video_adsense_far_behind.php#more
42 www.last100.com/2007/08/22/google-unveils-youtube-ads-theyre-not-that-bad/
43 See www.ghacks.net/2007/08/23/how-to-block-youtube-video-ads
44 Reported in IAB *Video Marketing Handbook*, www.iabuk.net/media/images/The%20IAB%20video%20marketing%20handbook_1736.pdf
45 Apparently it's not possible to switch the whole thing into cost per square meter…so it's not quite there yet.
46 www.autonomy.com/content/Verticals/ecommerce/index.en.html
47 searchengineland.com/070102-150920.php
48 www.readwriteweb.com/archives/udi_manber_search_is_a_hard_problem php#more
49 searchengineland.com/070604-093700.php
50 www.ft.com/cms/s/2/fbc969aa-e8f2-11da-b110-0000779e2340 html
51 research.yahoo.com/zonctag/
52 www.enpocket.com/news/press-releases/research-shows-that-targeting-and-relevance-are-key-to-making-mobile-advertising-work
53 www.clickz.com/showPage.html?page=3576931
54 For example, AskMeNow (www.askmenow.com) – already available in the US on mobile devices; Hakia (www.hakia.com) – from Europe; TextDigger (www.digger.com) – currently in private beta.
55 www.nytimes.com/2007/06/24/business/yourmoney/24digi.html?ei=5090&en=7c0c119d030c477c&ex=1340337600&pagewanted=print
56 technology.timesonline.co.uk/tol/news/tech_and_web/the_web/article1883175ece
57 www.ft.com/cms/s/c3e49548-088e-11dc-b11e-000b5df10621.html
58 searchengineland.com/070202-224617.php
59 www.readwriteweb.com/archives/yahoo_search_not_history.php#more

Chapter 5

Email and Viral Marketing

T his chapter covers the most fundamental and long-standing DigiMarketing technique: email – and its evil twin: spam. Most readers of this book will have experienced email marketing, both as recipients (probably on a daily basis), and most likely as senders too. Of all the digital marketing methods discussed in this book, email marketing is the best known, and we do not intend to dwell on what most of you already know. It is worth emphasizing that DigiMarketers must ensure that their communications do not spam consumers. As we have already seen, permission is the key ingredient for responsible DigiMarketing.

This chapter also looks at an allied and rapidly growing technique: viral marketing – the pass along from user to user of interesting digital material – and what constitutes effective viral communications.

KEY TRENDS YOU MUST KNOW

Email: The DigiMarketer's Workhorse

Over 90% of internet users access email[1], with over half of them doing so on a daily basis. Most of us spend much longer on email than on surfing the web.

Email is the 21st century evolution of traditional direct marketing. Some call it electronic direct marketing (EDM). In many ways, EDM is a direct marketer's dream. Electronic is far less costly to produce and deliver than conventional direct marketing. It's almost free and gets delivered almost instantaneously (they don't call conventional mail snail mail for nothing). It retains the strengths of a push medium, while adding the potential for automated response loops and tracking via digital channels. What's more, email is becoming increasingly accessible on portable devices. As a result, EDM *works*.

Studies peg the ROI on email marketing at anything from 900%[2] to 5,700%[3]. No wonder spending on email marketing is predicted to rise from $885 million in 2005 to $1.1 billion by 2010.[4] With 80% of marketers using, piloting, or planning email marketing programs, and 88% expecting email effectiveness to increase in the next three years[5], email has become the DigiMarketer's most used tool.

All Things to All Marketers

One of the key reasons email is such a workhorse is its versatility. It has the potential to be used at many points in the marketing process. Many companies use email as part of their acquisition or sales process, sending out email invitations to events, to highlight new products, and to make special offers. Other marketers use email as part of their retention and loyalty programs. Electronic newsletters, for example, have become a standard component of the marketing mix.

The Power of Narrowcasting

The low cost of production and delivery make segment-targeted messaging by EDM much more feasible and cost-effective than by traditional direct mail. With just a little extra time and effort, DigiMarketers can personalize their communications and speak to multiple, discrete groups of users separately and effectively.

Most marketers are still stuck at broadcast EDM, with only the crudest of personalization, but as customer relationship management (CRM) systems become embedded in corporate marketing, the resulting customer insights can be rapidly deployed into contextual, intensely relevant email marketing.

As we have already seen several times, there is a tension between narrow-casted, targeted, personalized EDM and the customer's right to privacy. Relevant EDM requires that the DigiMarketer know the customer; for customers to permit the DigiMarketer to know them requires that customers trust the marketer. Again and again throughout this book we will be returning to this theme: trust is at the heart of personalization. If DigiMarketers lose consumers' trust, they will lose the route to effective personalization.

The Spam Plague...And the Anti-Spam Backlash

Spam is the fly in the ointment of EDM!

The low cost of creating and delivering electronic messages has allowed spam to spiral out of control. As EDM has been adopted by organizations of all shapes and sizes, its misuse has become more than an annoyance. Spam is now estimated at almost 100 billion messages per day, making up an incredible 85% of all email.[6] It's no wonder that recipients protect themselves against it. Most consumers use the spam filters built into their email readers. Unfortunately, all too often users have only the slightest notion of how those filters are configured and rarely understand that they can change that configuration. As a result, spam filters inevitably block even legitimate emails. As customers re-double their efforts to protect their inboxes, the DigiMarketer's job gets that much harder.

Really these spam protection methods simply escalate the war. Currently, email filters mostly rely on keywords to identify spam. As a result, spammers are now using picture messages to evade detection. Image-based spam has exploded from less than 1% of all spam in 2005 to more than 12% of all spam in 2006. Almost all image-based spam (at least an estimated 78%) passes right through today's spam filters.[7]

Given the absence of effective self-regulation by DigiMarketers, and the supreme indifference of the spammers, most countries are now legislating limitations on spam, and criteria that EDM must meet to stay within the law.[8]

DIGIMARKETING BEST PRACTICES

Follow Permission Marketing Principles: It's a Must

Permission marketing refers to marketing communications which consumers have allowed, or requested, in some way. It is absolutely vital for DigiMarketers to follow best practice permission marketing principles (see Box Insert, Permission First, Please). If you don't, you risk contaminating the medium even further – alienating customers and losing their trust. Without trust you can learn little about your customers, and won't be able to customize your marketing. If you contact customers without their permission, they will quickly erect barriers so you can't reach them at all. As in any relationship, once the trust is gone, it's very hard to re-establish.

Permission First, Please

Best practice permission follows a six-step path. Although we refer here specifically to email, these practices apply to all DigiMarketing:

Confirmed Opt-in[9]: Emails should never be sent to recipients who have not requested them. Whenever someone does request to be added to your email list, he or she should be sent a confirmation email. The confirmation email should request the recipient to take a positive action before they are added to the list. Usually, the positive action is to either click on a confirmation link or to reply to the email and confirm that he or she really is at that address and really has requested to join the list. Unconfirmed opt-in is simply not enough. Recipients can be signed up by others without their knowledge or consent. Of course, that confirmation email can also serve a marketing purpose: don't miss any opportunity to converse with your customer.

Easy Unsubscribe or Opt-out: This is a legal requirement in some countries. Again, don't miss the marketing opportunity to gently try to find out why someone chooses to unsubscribe.

Clear Recipient Benefits: This needs to be clear in every email. It's their inbox that you are invading, their time upon which you are trespassing. Be short, to the point, with headlines – headlines that can link to additional content further down the email or to websites.

The key to successful EDM is relevance. A recent study found that 60% of those making immediate purchases from emails did so because the email focused on products they were already considering. As a result, targeted email campaigns can generate up to nine times the revenues and 18 times the profits of broadcast campaigns.[10]

Relevance is communicated right from the email subject line: the "headlines" of the 21st century. Typically, the marketer has only three or four seconds to interest the readers before they hit the delete key. Sophisticated testing methods allow for hundreds of creative variations and offers to be tested in real time.

A *Consistent, Memorable, Presence*: You have to be recognized as having permission. Consumers are increasingly lumping undesirable emails "from companies I know but that are just not interesting to me" under the same heading as spam.[1] This can have severe repercussions – even for responsible DigiMarketers. Recipients using Yahoo! and Gmail – and other similar services – have a "report this as spam" button. If consumers click that, the sender starts to get labeled as a spammer and may find future emails to all recipients rejected. The responsible DigiMarketer needs to make sure that recipients have opted-in, really realize that they've opted-in, and stay in because they really like it.

EDM insensitively implemented can rebound on the marketer with a vengeance. Jupiter Research found that 16% of consumers reported forming negative opinions about a company because of email newsletters or promotions they received.

Don't Get Too Frequent: Don't forget that the basic principles of direct marketing apply to EDM. One of the most important aspects of any direct marketing is "recency and frequency:" when the customer was last contacted and how often they are being contacted. If frequency is too high, you intrude too much and annoy the customer. If frequency is too low, your communications risk being forgotten. You will fail to establish that consistent, memorable presence. If you get the frequency/recency right, customers will appreciate you for being there at the right time.

How do you get it right? As we will see below, testing always helps. But remember the **DigiMarketing Tenet 5** (chapter 2), "consumers will initiate and direct more of the participant–marketer interchange." Let each customer select the most appropriate frequency for himself or herself. Does that customer want daily headlines? Daily detailed updates? A weekly summary? Or even an SMS of crucial items? The most effective DigiMarketers realize that their messaging can be almost costlessly re-purposed into whichever of these formats the customer would most appreciate.

It's clear that most DigiMarketers vastly overestimate their usefulness to the customer! A recent study found that fully one-third of opt-in recipients felt marketers emailed them more frequently than promised. What's more, although most excess email is simply deleted unread, about a third of the time consumers took action by either unsubscribing or complaining (reporting the email as spam). Half (54%) even went to the trouble of setting up filters to block out email from specific senders.

Maintain a Relationship: Successful email marketing helps recipients to know you, and builds trust, with a consistent, personable voice that reflects your brand. A recent survey on what drives recipients to open emails[12] found the most important determinant was "know and trust the sender" (56%); followed by (the only growing influence) "previously opened and thought valuable" (51%); and in third place the "subject line" (41.4%). It is an incautious DigiMarketer who endangers trust.

Don't Assume That Customers Use the Same Email Reader as You!

One good thing about traditional hard copy direct mail was that it would look the same way to every recipient. However, the appearance of email depends on the email reader the recipient uses. This is a good introduction to letting go for the DigiMarketer. You can't assume that your email will look (render) the same in all readers. You will need to tweak designs for the reader your customer uses.

The Email Experience Council (EEC), www.emailexperience.org, reviewed 1,000 emails and found that 21% were completely blank to readers with images turned off (a default setting for many). Another 28% showed copy but no working links. Understandably, checking for correct rendering in multiple email readers has been found to lift response rates by as much as 87%.[13]

Remember that even if recipients have images turned on, many will read the email (or at least a sufficient portion of it to decide whether to read on or not) in the preview pane, which will usually not display images.

Track Email to Determine Effectiveness

EDM is fairly easy to track. When an email is opened, embedded invisible tracking images (often known as web beacons, tracking bugs, pixel tags, or clear gifs) are accessed, allowing the DigiMarketer to record the open rate. Think of these as links to tiny empty pictures. If the email is opened, it "phones home;" that is, retrieves the (empty) picture from a server. The email sender knows that this has happened, and even which recipient has opened the email. As far as the recipient is concerned, nothing has happened (although some email readers may be configured to report the server contact, or even ask permission for it to happen).

If the recipient uses other links within the email, similar tracking can be triggered. So DigiMarketers can accurately record how each recipient behaves with the email. Of course, the effectiveness of emails that trigger delayed responses, rather than immediate responses (for example, a later visit to a website, or a call to a service representative), may not get measured.

Specific types of interaction with messages can trigger other messages, or cause future emails to be constructed differently. The intent is to create an email marketing program rather than a series of unconnected episodes. For example, a new registrant to your email list is confirmed (as we discussed above) with a nice welcome email – and hopefully a high benefit, low-cost (best spelt *free*) offer.

If the new registrant takes advantage of the offer – perhaps downloading a free report – a lead-nurturing communication can be generated. This might offer something tightly integrated to whatever has already been downloaded (a more detailed report, or a similar study, or "best practice" advice), which this time might have a price attached. If the prospect bites and pays, you send another confirmation and thanks, with a relevant upsell/cross-sell offer. Customers who receive your emails but haven't clicked on a link, or visited our website, for a while deserve a win-back or reminder email, again with an attractive (free?) offer.

Lists: Build or Buy?

Marketers must determine whether to build their own lists or rent the email lists of others. A major consideration in renting lists is the credibility and professionalism of the compiler. Remember that if the list is not really confirmed opt-in, it is you and your brand that will look like a spammer to your customers. A recent MarketingSherpa (www.marketingsherpa.com) report suggests that only about 20% of rental lists are suitable for use by reputable marketers.[14]

Built lists generally have much higher response rates since they come from consumers or those with whom the marketer has a prior relationship. But as we'll see in chapter 14, data is perishable, meaning that list maintenance is a constant headache. Whichever way you go it is clear that targeted, segmented lists are superior. Smaller, targeted, relevant lists produce higher open rates and higher click-throughs.

Use Heat Mapping or Other Modern Techniques to Improve Your Email

Heat mapping captures people's eye movements as they look at different email layouts and shows areas of high attention (hot areas) and low attention (cool areas). Marketers can then adjust layouts to get vital information into hot areas, or try to boost attention to cool areas.

Email Do's and Don'ts[15]

The do's and don'ts of email stem from a mix of direct marketing principles, technical issues related to email, and email etiquette.

DO'S

Do ALWAYS *use confirmed opt-in and provide easy opt-out* – and try to get the reason they are leaving you. Yes, we're saying it again and again because it's so important. And don't forget to use the confirmation email for an offer (preferably a free offer).

Do *use a service to check the layout* in the email reader that your recipients use. That probably means testing in

Gmail, Hotmail, Yahoo!Mail, Outlook, Thunderbird, Lotus Notes, Mac Mail, Entourage, and Eudora. There are services to do this for you (for example, www.campaignmonitor.com). You'll want to periodically update your list of email readers as new readers come on the market.

Do *make call-to-actions (CtAs) prominent* and locate them within the upper half of the layout. In a larger email, you may have multiple CtAs scattered through the email. Folds tend to be about 300 to 400 pixels south of your top border. But check in an emailing service (as above).

Do *use the subject line to get attention and show you aren't spam*: email recipients tend to look closely at the initial, or top, content and then skip through the remaining layout; keep this in mind.

Do *use a consistent send-from address* so you don't have to fight through spam filters again and again.

Do *make sure that content can be seen easily*; many readers will scroll through the email in a small preview window. Make sure that a two-inch window holds brand and main CtA.

Do *design a text-only version* that is easily read with HTML turned off, or on a mobile device.

Do *add a hosted version of the email*, so that if the images are stripped the subscriber can click through and see the entire email as an image.

Do *match 'n' mix*. Keep the look and feel of all your emails consistent, but fit the email to its purpose. Postcard emails for simple brief announcements; email newsletters of summaries that intrigued recipients can click on for more in-depth, website information; catalogue emails for product descriptions; E-press releases to the media.

Do test on a small list first. Stuff-ups on a small scale are always preferable to their large-scale versions!

DON'TS

Don't forget to get consumers to opt-in at the stage when you are doing initial customer acquisition. Many companies, even today, capture email addresses but fail to get permission at the same time.

Don't be petrified of using images, but have a healthy respect for the challenges of rendering and file sizes.

Don't have CtAs only in an image format: some recipients will have images turned off, or will not use HTML, or will make their read decision based on what they see in the preview pane. If your CtA is in image only, part of your audience won't know what they're missing!

Don't use large copy blocks. Break up paragraphs with bullet points, highlight key information; remember you're writing copy, not corporate memos (and, hey-corporate memos don't have to be boring either!).

Don't forget data collection: every time you provide something to the customer, try to obtain a little information about them. As we saw in chapter 4, data collection can be disguised as a quiz, or as something needed to provide the customer with a benefit (for example, a horoscope, or personality test).

Don't be long-winded; get the best in first. The strongest message and links should lead at the top.

Don't hound consumers: If they don't reply, especially after a few attempts, it's clear they don't want to do so. NEVER hound them! This is a critical element of good email conduct.

FUTURE TRENDS – WHERE IT'S HEADING

Rich Formats Allow Email To Do More

As email usage increases, competition for space in customers' in boxes will intensify. As a result, creative (rich) formats will evolve, further blurring the line between emails and websites. In the same way that internet display ads have evolved from simple banners to interactive, video-enhanced experiences (see chapter 4), EDM formats will evolve.

Rich email, including streaming video, will amplify users' email experience and we can expect to see more interactive email, effectively pushing the website to the (opted-in) customer rather than waiting for the customer to surf to the site.

These richer and more interactive formats will allow email to move beyond customer sales and become a customer servicing tool. Email will become more and more effective for user alerts, product updates, user confirmations, newsletters, product catalogues, consumer research, and so on.

Integrated Communications

We already discussed VOIP (voice over internet protocol) in chapter 3. It is now possible to instigate phone calls, or instant messages, to an email address.[16] This gives email an audible dimension and can deliver improved customer experience. Google's proposed call-on service (chapter 4) might allow links to be automatically opened as phone calls if the email was being read on a voice-capable device.

Spam, spam, spam, spam. Spam, spam, spam, spam

It will be just like the Monty Python song. There seems to be no end in sight to the spam deluge. The combination of near-zero costs and (amazingly enough) at least some results guarantee that spam will continue. What's more, as customers opt-in to more and more marketing, they forget which marketers they have permitted! At the same time marketers will push their luck on frequency, rich formats and interactivity, intensifying the issues around privacy and spam.

As spammers become more sophisticated at spoofing (causing the email to appear to come from someone other than the actual sender), spam takes on a more vicious form as phishing. Phishing (it's like fishing, get it?) involves sending emails – or sometimes SMSes – that appear to come from a reputable source (often a bank or online financial agency; for example, PayPal), and direct recipients to what appears to be a legitimate website. Once at the website, recipients are instructed to enter username and password details. Users, thinking they are at the genuine site of their bank or financial institution, enter the requested usernames and passwords. These are, of course, captured by the phisher and used for identity theft or other frauds.

Sometimes attacks are highly targeted – spear phishing – focusing on the members of a social network or employees of a specific company, providing highly credible communications which recipients' friends also receive, adding to the impression of authenticity. So-called voice phishing even provides phone numbers to call and uses VOIP to capture callers' details. Or the bad guys may generate VOIP phone calls which spoof the caller ID data to appear to come from a reputable caller.

As spam and fraud attempts become harder to distinguish from legitimate EDM, they have the potential to poison this marketing channel.

VIRAL MARKETING

Viral marketing persuades customers themselves to pass along your message or product to others who the customer feels would be most appreciative. As we saw in chapter 1 (Box Insert, Viral Marketing) a virus like influenza stimulates its host to sneezing which helps the virus spread. Successful viral marketing provides something, usually free, that people want to share, so spreading the marketing.

Although currently used mainly with reference to video clips, viral marketing has much wider applications. The rapid success of Hotmail, www.hotmail.com (now called Windows Live Hotmail), was one of the first viral marketing successes and owed nothing to video. Hotmail launched in mid-1996 as one of the first webmail services, and grew its subscriber base faster than any company in history[17], spending only $500,000 on advertising to recruit 12 million subscribers within 18 months – at which point it was bought by Microsoft, reportedly for $400 million.[18] A competitor at the time, Juno, is thought to have spent $20 million on ads and brand promotions while gaining only a fraction of Hotmail's subscriber base.

What was the secret of Hotmail's success? The email service was completely free, and every email sent automatically ended with an acknowledgement that it had originated from a Hotmail account, and a brief pitch for the Hotmail service.

The beauty of viral marketing is that the customer both passes on the message and identifies the target market: the susceptible others, the friends who would really appreciate that product, service, or video clip. Viral marketing is really the digital version of word-of-mouth, buzz, or network marketing.

The reach of successful virals expands exponentially. If each recipient of a viral communication passes it on to 5 friends, after 10 pass-alongs the clip has reached almost 25 million people. Using near instantaneous email as the distribution method, those 10 iterations can easily be completed within an hour or two.

DIGIMARKETING BEST PRACTICES

To a certain degree, "viralness" is out of anyone's control: that's simply the nature of it. What people want to pass on, they will. However, this doesn't imply that you should sling reams of content out there and let luck be your guide. While it's hard to predict which content will ultimately be passed most from one consumer to the next, there are indeed some basic principles that can dramatically improve your chances of success.

Compelling Content

Viral efficacy rests primarily on the quality of the content. Things that are interesting, entertaining, or informative (ideally all three) tend to get passed on. Those things that are hard-sell simply don't. The blogosphere can be as chilly as outer space if you have boring content!

A big mistake that marketers make is to assume that funny gags alone make for good viral content. Or that having something funny is a guarantee of success. The world can absorb only so many gags or funny videos before they too become hum-drum. Marketers should look more deeply at what might be interesting and compelling (and yes, humorous too, if appropriate).

"Compelling content" can come in various forms. Almost all have a hook that is interesting and intriguing to the target group a hook that members of the target group agree will be of interest to their friends. That's what gets the pass-along. A viral with a strong hook can build on communities that already exist. I know my team-mates will like this, so I pass it on.

Some companies realize they have historical footage or product information that is actually very interesting and relevant to the brand. For example, Dupont has created a *Miracles of Science* video series which tells the stories behind its different products and scientific developments.[19] These product stories provide compelling content, without it feeling like a hard-sell.

Other companies are finding that "compelling content" includes giving people special access or sneak peaks to things they wouldn't otherwise have seen. Brands that use star endorsements are shooting extra "behind the scenes" footage of these stars for use in viral videos. You don't even need big star power to draw interest. As we mentioned in the preface, Motorola in China used a viral piece featuring the Back Dorm Boyz – two college students who have attracted a following on the web for lip-synching to various popular artists. Increasingly, these micro-celebrities have sizeable fan bases that can be tapped to circulate viral content.

You should consider carefully what material you have – or could develop – to provide compelling content for viral marketing. Then give it the basic sanity check by asking "how will this viral piece help build my brand?" There's no marketing advantage in getting hundreds of thousands of pass-ons of something that isn't building your brand. Just because you're getting a consumer to pass on your message instead of sending it directly to the recipient, doesn't mean that the message should be any less relevant to your brand!

Lastly, viral content should relate to and amplify your DigiMarketing proposition. In other words, it should help you deliver on the basic "promise" you have made to your participants, via your Platform Proposition, about why they should engage with you. More of this in chapter 12.

Consider both Function and Fun

Another issue for viral marketing is whether you intend for the piece to be just for fun, or if you also expect it to serve a function. Do you want customers just to watch the viral piece? Or do you want them to keep it on their desktops, perhaps as a widget they can play with or use repeatedly for specific functions (see Widget Wisdom in chapter 3)? Is there a branded digital calendar or other item that combines brand relevancy and some degree of user functionality? Viral content doesn't have to have a specific, ongoing function, but it definitely *can* have one.

Make it User Friendly

One of the great benefits of viral marketing is that it is freed from the strictures of standard media units. If it's a video piece, it can be as long, or short, as you want. However, you still have to comply with the basic "law" of consumer interest. How long will participants really be willing to watch before they get bored?

There are also some practical issues. While it's viral, you don't want people to think it's a virus! So, you must make sure that it can get through the spam filters. Many users are now using email systems that will block all executable files. Some users will not open any attachments. Additionally, you must ensure that the file is small enough so you don't clog people's computers with the digital equivalent to sending them *Gone With the Wind*. Compression technologies are making it increasingly easy to reduce video pieces to small file sizes. However, this is another detail to get right.

Prompt the Viral Pass-On

Most web participants today don't need to be told they can pass on content; they just do. One recent survey found that well over 80% of adult US internet users had shared content with other users, over 60% did so at least once a week and 25% did so almost daily.[20] However, it doesn't hurt to make it easy for participants to pass it on perhaps via a prompt to "share with your friends" and a space to input their email addresses. This can increase the viralness of the piece.

Often, the chief purpose of a viral piece is to drive recipients to a website, microsite, or other digital destination where they can compete or participate in some form of promotional offer. This might involve rewarding consumers if their friends participate as well, so encouraging pass-on of the content. Limited time offers, special "first 100 to sign up" offers, and other participation-accelerating techniques that have been used in traditional marketing for years can be applied to viral marketing.

Use Viral Distribution Sites

There are websites that exist to host viral (or would be viral) content. These are natural starting places for your efforts – although you should definitely supplement them with email campaigns. As well as the (currently) definitive www.youtube. com, try www.viralmonitor.com, www.viralbank.com, and check for other viral portals (also known as vortals) that may be hot in your markets. Also use your own websites, or microsites, to make sure your viral catches the attention of the search engines. Pay-per-click keyword campaigns can help here too.

Give Up Control

Lack of control is often cited as a problem with viral marketing. The marketer can't control who sees the clip, or receives the product recommendation, or the context in which it is seen or recommended. As noted throughout this book, relinquishing control is something to which DigiMarketers have to get accustomed. Remember? The customer's in charge.

It does mean, however, that if you use viral marketing you had better have a scalable enterprise whose geographic coverage may grow in bizarre ways. Unlike a real-life virus, which is usually locally transmitted by touch or close contact, a viral ad can leap continents. If recipients send your clip to their friends in Afghanistan, will you be able to serve them? If you can't, the communication may be wasted. Of course, the reach didn't cost you anything, but it may create dissatisfaction in markets that you intend to enter in the future, or intrigue potential competitors and encourage imitations.

It's Viral Times

The potency of viral video clips is hard to overestimate. The most viral of viral clips have tended to be non-commercial, intensely personal, and typically extremely embarrassing for the "star." Supposedly the most viewed viral clip to date – *The Star Wars Kid* – has been seen 900 million times.[21] Made in 2003, it features a teenager using a golf ball retriever in imitation of a Star Wars light saber. The "star" later took successful legal action against his classmates who distributed it.

Viral all seems to have gotten started with the John West Salmon *Bear Fight*. This was originally an award-winning television commercial in the UK in late 2000. It then escaped to the internet and has now been viewed online some 350 million times. This seems to have given marketers the idea that viral could be big.

Burger King certainly scored with its Subservient Chicken site (www.subservientchicken.com). The site featured a person dressed in a chicken costume who would respond to typed commands by visitors (or at least to most commands[22]). Although built to resemble a live scene, the site really consists of short video clips, played according to the visitor's typed requests. The site tied into Burger King's television campaign, "Get Chicken The Way You Like It." In its first 24 hours, the site got 1 million visits;

within a couple of weeks it had reached 15 to 20 million.[23] The chicken character also has emerged in subsequent Burger King campaigns.

It Wasn't Me

Spoofs and deniable virals, which play off the brand's real communications – usually in a politically incorrect way – can lead brands to controversial positionings. Even if consumers create the spoofs, it can also provide brands with additional exposure.

Ford ran a television commercial in the UK for the Sports Ka: *The Ka's Evil Twin*. The ad featured the car defending itself against a pigeon that alighted on its hood by spontaneously flipping the hood open and knocking the bird into the road. The spot drew complaints from the Royal Pigeon Racing Association and the Royal Society for the Prevention of Cruelty to Animals. A viral version then appeared in which the car's sunroof opens, a curious cat puts its head in, and when the roof rapidly closes the cat is decapitated!

SUMMARY: EMAIL AND VIRAL MARKETING

Email and viral marketing will continue for the foreseeable future as mainstays of digital marketing. It's important to note:

- As email grows further, it's evil twin SPAM could ruin the party.

- Intelligent opt-in and smart one-to-one communications techniques can alleviate the consumer confrontation and lead to successful customer engagement.
- There's a variety of important do's and don'ts that make the difference between success and failure with email marketing.
- As with most things related to the web, consumers are taking control. Determining how to create effective viral pass-on by consumers is essential today.

Next we will go beyond the desktop to consider the channel through which most people will experience and use digital technology in the future: mobile.

END NOTES
1   www.pewinternet.org/trends/Internet_Activities_4.23.04.htm
2   www.dmnews.com/cms/dm-news/internet-marketing/35709.html
3   directmag.com/disciplines/email/marketing_email_tops_roi/
4   www.jupitermedia.com/corporate/releases/06.02.03-newjupresearch.html
5   "The Top Marketing Technologies In 2005," *Trends*, January 6, 2005; and "US Online Marketing Forecast: 2005 to 2010," Trends, May 2, 2005.
6   MAAWG estimates that 80% to 85% of incoming mail is "abusive email", as of the last quarter of 2005. The sample size for the MAAWG's study was over 100 million mailboxes.
7   www.out-law.com/page-7055
8   www.spamlaws.com provides a discussion of anti-spam legislation around the world.
9   This is sometimes called double opt-in, although for some that term has connotations of spammers.
10 www.jupitermedia.com/corporate/releases/05.08.16-newjupresearch.html
11 "Email Remains Integral for Ecommerce, yet Consumers' Active Management of their Inboxes Deepens Challenge for Marketers", *Return Path Third Annual Holiday Email Consumer Survey*, January 2007.
12 *ibid.*
13 The 2007 Rendering Report – The Past, the Present, and the Future, Email Experience Council, 2007, www.emailexperience.org
14 www.marketingsherpa.com/article.php?ident=29930
15 Several of these best practices come from the Ogilvy & Mather New York email practice.
16 www.cbronline.com/article_news.asp?guid=4F04FD06-8D2A-48E1-AA887AAD16 F5CB63
17 www.dfj.com/cgi-bin/artman/publish/steve_tim_may97.shtml
18 en.wikipedia.org/wiki/Hotmail
19 www2.dupont.com/Stories/en_US/index.html
20 www.emarketer.com/Article.aspx?id=1003796
21 news.bbc.co.uk/1/hi/entertainment/6187554.stm
22 A site actually emerged to record activities that the chicken would not perform; see dev.magicosm.net/cgi-bin/public/corvidaewiki/bin/view/Game/SubservientC hickenRequestList
23 www.wired.com/news/culture/0,63053-0.html

Chapter 6

Mobile Platforms

A t first, digital development focused around the home and the office. The hardware and software companies made certain that computing became an integral part of the workplace. Meanwhile, home computing flourished too, as the personal computer became a standard fixture in many homes.

However, the sea change over the past 10 years has been in mobility. Today we have numerous devices that can be used anytime and anywhere; digital devices have become untethered from home or office. Mobile platforms generally center on mobile phones – perhaps the most successful consumer device of the past decade. However, devices such as Blackberrys, iPods, and mobile game consoles are increasingly important components of digital conversations. In this chapter, we will look first at the mobile revolution and then at how the mobile landscape is likely to develop and its impact on the DigiMarketer.

KEY TRENDS YOU MUST KNOW

Many in digital marketing would argue that *the* platform of the future is not the computer but the mobile device, sometimes referred to as the "third screen" (the other two screens being the television and the computer, the movie screen apparently forgotten).

Seven key drivers have propelled mobile to the forefront of the DigiMarketer's priorities. The last 10 years have taken us to the first base in mobile – we could call it *Mobile* 1.0. As we will see, over the next 10 years we expect many of those same factors to drive us into the world of *Mobile* 2.0. Let's look at Mobile 1.0 first.

Mobile Driver 1: Mobile for all
Mobile Driver 2: Adding functions to the phone
Mobile Driver 3: Building bandwidth to 3G
Mobile Driver 4: Proprietary phone-centric software
Mobile Driver 5: A walled garden
Mobile Driver 6: Basic transactions
Mobile Driver 7: Driving social force

Mobile Driver 1: Mobile for All

Since 1995, mobile phones have become mass market devices. From being super-luxury items for the fortunate few, mobile phones have become worldwide communication tools, with models for all budgets. Mobile phones are by far the most prevalent digital communications channel in the world. As of early 2007, there were about 2.7 billion mobile subscribers. That's more than double the number of landline phones; more than double the number of internet users; almost double the number of television sets in the world; and more than triple the number of email users.[1]

Mobile coverage extends to about 80% of the world's population and is expected to reach 90% by 2010. Markets are at different stages of development. Luxembourg has the highest national penetration, at 164% by end of 2005.[2] Yes, that's 64% more mobiles than people. Even in the UK, there are more mobiles than people. In the US, over 50% of children own a mobile phone. China, which imported its first cell phone system in 1987, and in 1997 still had only 10 million subscribers, now has about 450 million mobile phone users[3] and expects another 50% increase by 2010. India has another 143 million, and by the end of 2006 was adding almost 5% more per month.[4] Mobile phone usage in low-income areas is boosted by the ability to rent phones by the call from the local telephone ladies. Recent research suggests that mobile phones are a crucial tool for economic development. In a typical developing country, an extra 10 phones per 100 people increases GDP growth by 0.6 of a percentage point.[5]

It is hard to overestimate the impact of mobile phones on our lives. By 2002, a global study found that mobiles were responsible for a physical change in those under the age of 25. In a reverse of the body's evolution to date, the thumb was replacing the index finger as the dominant digit! In Japan, the under-25s refer to themselves as *oya yubi sedai* – the thumb tribe. As thumbs become stronger and more dexterous, the thumb tribe is using its favorite digit for other tasks that are traditionally the finger's job, such as pointing at things or ringing doorbells.[6]

Mobile Driver 2: Adding Functions to the Phone

Near universal usage is only the starting point. Mobile phones have transformed dramatically from the mid-1990s when they were single-function, ungainly bricks. Today, mobile phones have functions that make them more akin to mobile computers than to phones. While there are functional mass market versions, there are also fashion accessory mobiles. Manufacturers no longer talk about mobile phones.

In recognition of their multi-functionality they have become mobile *devices*, or simply mobiles.

In addition to making and receiving voice calls, key functions of today's mobile devices include:[7]

Short message service (SMS), also known as text messaging, is one of the oldest and most basic functions of mobiles. Almost all mobiles are now capable of receiving and sending SMSes (short text messages). Two-thirds of mobile phone subscribers – that's 1.8 billion people – are active text messaging users. SMS is not just for the young any more. Usage is mushrooming around the world, with over 350 billion SMSes exchanged every month, about 15% of which are commercial – or marketing – messages[8]: the so-called *thumb economy*.

Some operators are already rolling out a super SMS service, enhancing current messaging services with instant messaging (IM), presence features (these provide a group with information on each user's location, availability and even mood), and the multimedia capabilities of MMS.[9] Unstructured supplementary service data (USSD) is now pre-installed in all GSM devices, allowing quicker response times for interaction than provided by SMS.[10]

Multimedia messaging service (MMS) expands SMS to include non-text items, including images, audio and video. Although now almost universally available, MMS has extremely low adoption rates, having suffered from problems of interoperability across different brands of handsets and difficulties in handset configuration.

Games are already a standard feature of mobiles. It's estimated that mobile phone gaming will go from about $2.6 billion in 2005 to over $11 billion by 2010[11] – by which time it will equal, and then go on to outstrip, the slower growing music market.

Still-image cameras are rapidly becoming standard. Research firm Gartner reports that almost 50% of mobiles worldwide had cameras in 2006, and forecasts 81% will by 2010.[12] Of all the digital image sensors made, 70% go into mobile devices, far more than go into digital cameras![13] Cameras on mobiles are becoming increasingly sophisticated, with auto focusing, flash, optical zoom, and image stabilization features, and multi-megapixel resolution.

Mobile video is growing strongly and is expected to exceed 32 million users by 2008. Innovative mobile video content applications are starting to emerge. For example, www. mobilesign.org provides a video dictionary of sign language. You enter the word to look up, and Mobilesign will send back a video viewable on your mobile demonstrating how to sign the word.

The consumer-created content boom (discussed in chapter 8) owes much to the mobile. Cameras on mobiles paved the way for sites like www.flickr.com, while mobile video has driven the emergence of similar video sites (for example, www.youtube.com).

Stereo sound and *music storage* are increasingly mobile device applications, bringing mobiles into the mp3-player space. In fact, music is currently the largest mobile entertainment genre (assuming you count ring-tones as music).

Bluetooth is almost universal on mobiles today, although not every mobile owner actually knows how to activate it. Bluetooth is a low power, short-range communications standard that can create wireless personal area networks (PANs). This allows digital devices to connect and exchange information. Today's mobiles can connect wirelessly to headsets, stereo speakers, computers, printers, and so on.

Global positioning standard (GPS) receivers are included on more and more mobiles, providing the capability to monitor and report a user's location. This is already being used to automatically add location information to photos and videos taken with the mobile. When integrated with mapping software, GPS makes the mobile a navigational device. This can also allow highly localized and targeted marketing.

The reality is that most mobile owners never use many of their mobiles' features. They simply don't know how! The complexity of today's mobile is probably the greatest single barrier to wider function usage. Most users can manage the camera and perhaps the video. Many can deal with SMS. Mastery of other features is spotty at best, and cannot be relied upon.

Some content providers report greater success with interactive voice response systems (IVR) than with SMS. Consumers are familiar with IVR from wired phone systems and are happier to simply speak their selection of menu items, rather than learn how to SMS. Univision claims to sell far more ring-tones via an IVR solution than with SMS. What's more, 85% of the IVR users say they had never bought content via text messaging. BET Mobile (another ring-tone vendor) reports similar results, with IVR doubling ring-tone sales.[14] Don't overestimate the sophistication of mobile owners just yet.

Mobile Driver 3: Building Bandwidth to 3G

All the functionality that handset manufacturers are building into mobiles would mean very little without a corresponding increase in data transmission speeds. The more sophisticated mobile functions (pictures, videos, music downloads, games, and so on) involve transmitting more and more data. As with the web, bandwidth is a critical resource of which, it seems, you can never have too much. Greater bandwidth lets digital content be transmitted faster. That makes data-rich applications much more rewarding to users. So they get used more, so users need more bandwidth. And so on it goes on.

There has been a lot of press coverage about the auctions of 3G (see Box Insert, Alphabet Soup…with Numbers, for an explanation of this term) licenses to mobile operators. Mobile operators have paid billions of dollars to secure licenses. 3G allows higher data transfer rates, meaning greater bandwidth and a boost for those data-intensive video applications – allowing video-calling and highly watchable television. 3G also allows operators to support more voice and data customers, at lower incremental costs than earlier systems.

The Mobile Ecosystem

It's important to remember that handset manufacturers are not the only players in the development of mobile; the mobile operators (or carriers), who deliver the mobile services to individual subscribers, also play a central role. Mobile devices can't be used to their fullest potential if the operator isn't providing enough bandwidth. Therefore, the operators, and the investments they make in their systems, play a pivotal role in what marketers are able to do using mobiles.

DigiMarketers need to develop mobile campaigns that will benefit all the players if they want to ensure successful implementation. Of course, users (customers) must see benefit, but so must: the network operators or carriers (who route the messages and bill users, and may own the network[15]); access providers (who operate gateways); platform providers (providing gateways and software platforms); content and application developers (who develop content and programs), aggregators and publishers (who sell content and programs to the users).

Operators/carriers look at mobile marketing as a revenue source. For many, SMSes are the #1 driver of data service revenues, with a lot of room for expansion. Operators will be extremely interested in data-heavy mobile content which they see as key to their future success.

It's also worth bearing in mind that many operators have incurred, or are about to incur, huge investments in installing 3G equipment. As a result, making a return on their investment is uppermost in their mind. Their ROI is driven by four components: building a subscriber base; building average revenue per user (ARPU); reducing churn – the rate at which subscribers defect to other operators; and optimizing traffic.

As carriers are usually undifferentiated, competition focuses on pricing incentives. Creative DigiMarketers should come up with campaigns that help carriers differentiate. And, of course, the carriers will need to be convinced that the actions of the DigiMarketer will attract, not alienate, their subscribers.

One possibility is to demonstrate that campaigns can help optimize network traffic by building off-peak usage. SMS traffic has tremendous seasonal peaks. An operator's success rests on building capacity for peaks and getting it utilized over the rest of the year. In Europe, Christmas Day can count for 25% of the year's SMSes. In China, it's the first week of the Chinese New Year. In 2007, 15.2 billion SMSes were sent in that week in the PRC alone – that's 33 per mobile phone, almost 50% up from the same period in 2006.[16]

Alphabet Soup...with Numbers

Mobile spawns abbreviations and technical complexity. Without getting into the technical aspects, simply remember that mobile data transfer speeds are exploding.

A summary guide to the letters and numbers:[17]

1G (*1st generation*): The name retrospectively attached to first-generation, analogue, voice-only, mobile phones introduced in the 1980s.

2G (*2nd generation*): Digital networks which have replaced 1G. Digital allows greater compression, packing more calls into the available bandwidth; reduces power consumption (that's longer battery life); improves security (eavesdropping is harder); and of course opens up data services (for example, SMS, email, and caller ID). Typical 2G data transmission speeds were under 20 Kbps (kilobits per second). Remembering that a dial-up modem connects at up to 56 Kbps, 2G was pretty slow.

2.5G: Is an upgrade offered by some operators, which has no official technical spec but probably allows transmission rates of 30 to 40 Kbps. So that's about as fast as dial-up. You can download ring-tones, listen to short audio clips, send MMSes, play games, and browse the web (pretty sluggishly)

2.75G: Is the label sometimes attached to systems that use EDGE (Enhanced Data rates for GSM Evolution). Again, there's no official spec, but typically speeds are up to 90 Kbps. That's almost twice dial-up speed, and gets users browsing the web acceptably, listening to streaming music (choppily), and viewing short video clips.

3G: First introduced on a commercial scale in Japan in late 2001, and now available in over 40 countries, 3G gives mobile data transmission rates of 300 to 400 Kbps to as much as 2 Mbps – that's 2,000 Kbps – from stationary systems. This level of data transmission speed opens a world of full motion video, streaming music (the radio in the phone), 3D games, and reasonably fast web browsing.

3.5G: Also known as Super 3G, or High-Speed Downlink Packet Access (HSDPA); extends 3G to as much as 14.4 Mbps.

4G: As yet, there is no established technical standard, but some have suggested that WiMAX (Worldwide Interoperability for Microwave Access) may be the basis of 4G and take transmission from 100 Mbps all the way to 1 Gbps (that's 1,000 Mbps). That gives you high-quality streaming video for calling and for watching, with on-demand movies and television. This will usher in truly pervasive computing: anytime, anywhere.

Mobile Driver 4: Proprietary Phone-Centric Software

The fourth driver of the mobile revolution is the software that resides on the phone. Along with bandwidth and hardware functionality (cameras and the like), it's the software on the device that impacts how consumers use their mobiles in their lives.

Let's look first at the operating systems of the mobile. Mobile phones have their own operating systems just as computers do. At the time of writing, there are several rival operating systems. Symbian is owned by a group of handset and consumer electronic companies, including Nokia (with 47.9%), Ericsson, Panasonic, Samsung, Siemens AG, and

Sony Ericsson. Symbian is used in some (but not all) of the phones branded by these companies.

Windows Mobile is owned, of course, by Microsoft Corporation. Windows Mobile runs on pocket PCs and smartphones, and attempts to replicate the look and feel of desktop Windows. Palm OS was originally developed for the Palm personal digital assistants (PDAs), and also provides a somewhat desktop-Windows look and feel. Some of the latest Palm devices actually use the Windows Mobile OS, and Palm also provides a Linux-based OS. In addition, there are some other operator-developed operating systems on lower-end phones.

Different types of software run under the different operating systems. Some software originates from the mobile operators, some from the handset-developers, and some is created by third parties. Software from the mobile operators and the handset developers tends, at present, to be somewhat clunky and aimed more at locking the customer into a particular operator/handset developer than providing major customer benefits.

Mobile Driver 5: A Walled Garden

As we just mentioned, many mobile operators and handset developers are still attempting to keep their users within a set of easy-to-access websites and applications. This is often called the *walled garden*. Within the walled garden, sites are easy to access (and maybe even hardwired into the device or the operating system) and display well on the device. When users leave the walled garden, sites and applications can be infuriatingly difficult to use. Often, providers have a financial interest in users staying in the walled garden.

However, operators/handset developers are gradually realizing that mobiles today don't live in isolation. They are a highly connected part of the digital ecosystem. In fact, given that most mobile users carry their device with them at all times, the mobile is capable of becoming the central point of consumer connection. If this is to happen, the operators/handset developers will have to give up some control over the content and the resulting revenues from what appears on the mobile.

Mobile Driver 6: Basic Transactions

Mobile devices already have basic transactional capabilities. In the simplest form, a nightclub can SMS barcodes to their invited guests. Each guest can then present the SMS on their mobile to be scanned at entry for verification. Specially adapted phones allowing purchases to be directly linked to users' credit cards are already under test.[18]

The mobile carrier's billing systems allow for other charging mechanisms. For example, ring-tones, call-back tones, wallpapers and so on are downloadable for today's mobiles, with a charge billed via the callers' post-paid bill, or debited from pre-paid cards.

Premium SMSes let customers be billed for calls to premium numbers. These have become the foundation for voting on television programs and gambling on sporting events. Television stations are becoming so reliant on their share of premium SMS revenues that early 2007 saw a major scandal in the UK centered around premium SMS votes in reality television shows. It appears that several shows may have encouraged further voting even after winners had been chosen.[19]

Mobile Driver 7: Driving Social Force

The seventh driver of mobile growth is the social role that mobile devices now play in people's lives. The mobile is far more personal than almost any other electronic device. In

Digital Channels

most cultures, although you can happily watch someone else's television – and might even change the channel – and often share a PC, or a game console – even close friends (*especially* close friends?) wouldn't answer one another's mobiles. Each has his or her own personal mobile. Although the PC is supposedly a personal computer – and may indeed carry a distinctive desktop wallpaper, and hide secrets – the mobile is an especially personal communication medium.

Yet at the same time, the essence of the mobile is social. It's a paradox: intensely personal *and* intensely social. Plus, it is *the* device to maintain connections. Far more than just a bundle of technology or a tool, the mobile is a highly personalized, status-revealing accessory. Look at the Boxed Insert, The Shibuya Future, below for a glimpse of a likely mobile future, already realized in Japan.

The mobile platform is so pervasive and persuasive that it already drives social trends and other digital channels. The so-called smart mob was one of the first manifestations of this power. One type of smart mob arranges (via mobile) to show up at a specific retailer at a specific time, and uses their aggregate buying power to negotiate discounts. This form of self-structuring social organization was hailed as the first sign of communication technologies empowering people.[20]

Receiving a mobile call can be seen as a symbol of one's importance. The simultaneously private–public nature of the call allows a residual communication from the person called (and calling) to others in the vicinity. The Popularity Dialer (popularitydialer.com) exploits just this aspect to allow users (in the US) to set-up fake calls to their mobile to impress their colleagues, or get out of meetings!

The emergence of well-defined (although culturally variable) mobile etiquette is a clear sign of the mobile's social impact and its centrality in consumers' lives. Quiet places (book stores, places of worship, and so on) post signs banning mobile use. In Japan, the de facto standard in public transport is "no voice, email okay." In other parts of Asia, it is commonplace for mobile device communications to take precedence over face-to-face conversations. To promptly answer one's mobile is a more important social grace than continuing a face-to-face conversation! In other countries, public transport provides "quiet cars." Some auditoriums even install wire mesh in the walls to defeat mobile use. No *Mobile* is becoming the No *Smoking* of the 21st century.

The Shibuya Future

Shibuya crossing in Tokyo has supposedly the world's highest density of mobiles. And Japan probably gives us a glimpse of the world's future as it's reflected in mobile devices. *Personal, Portable, and Pedestrian* – that's how Mizuko Ito, Daisuke Okabe and Misa Matsuda summed it up in their analysis of mobiles in Japan. [21]

In Japanese, mobiles are called *keitai*-literally "something you carry with you," suggesting "a snug and intimate technosocial tethering, a personal device supporting communications that are a constant, lightweight, and mundane presence in everyday life."

The editors of *Personal, Portable, and Pedestrian* go on to observe that mobile devices are territory machines. They can transform any space – a subway seat, a supermarket aisle, a street corner – into something personal and protected. Many digital channels (for example, web chat) deliver the concept of an intimate stranger, someone with whom experiences can be shared with vividness and immediacy, but without physical presence. But the mobile channel evolves that concept with immediacy and much greater intimacy. As it is always on, the mobile creates a state of wireless closeness: a tele-cocoon zone of intimacy to help maintain relationships.

DIGIMARKETING BEST PRACTICES

Recognize that the Customer is in Control of this Very Personal Device

As outlined above, the mobile is an intensely personal device – and the customer is in 100% control. Customers' exposure to mobile marketing is voluntary. The customers' needs, goals and expectations must drive everything the DigiMarketer does.

The best practice rules of customer engagement on the mobile – the how, where, when, and how often that marketing is permitted to intrude – have yet to be determined. What is already clear is that permission is of the essence. The mobile is not an interrupt-driven medium.[22] Blocking marketers from the mobile device is all too easy. Therefore, DigiMarketers must act with caution and respect. But those who get it right can definitely tap into a vibrant new channel.

For example, Nike Airmax built on a conventional media campaign, showing athletes getting up early and working out, by adding a simple mobile twist. Mobile users could sign up for a recorded wake-up call from a famous athlete such as Maria Sharapova. Participation in the first week exceeded that expected for eight weeks by 300%. Some users set up multiple wake-up calls; coaches and team managers signed up their entire roster.[23]

Use the Personal Addressability of Mobiles

As noted in chapter 1, every digital device is individually addressable; your mobile identity is unique. For just that reason, many users prefer to call their friends' mobile numbers to avoid parents, secretaries, and so on. Most of us answer our own mobiles, although increasingly only to names we recognize. This assures marketers – once they have gained the customer's trust, and have secured permission to communicate – of direct contact with a unique, recognizable individual who deserves personalized communication. Background profiles of mobile users are gold. For example, BMW China used highly targeted mobile ads to promote test drives on 3 series cars. The campaign included a mobile website which allowed visitors to customize virtual cars.[24]

Unfortunately, some marketers think that addressing a person by name in an SMS birthday greeting is personalization. DigiMarketers need to get at least as far as horoscopes, biorhythms, or (better) age-related health advice or location-related weather forecasts. An automated SMS birthday greeting from someone I don't know is scarcely a relevant use of personalization, even if it does come on the right day and carries my name.

Build on Mobile's Location-specific, Out-of-home, Capabilities

In the US, Starbucks already offers a service whereby potential customers SMS an area's zip code to MYSBUX and get a list of nearby Starbucks stores. Burger King ran a Chicken Fries promotion with a mobile code on the packaging. When customers SMSed the mobile code they had a chance to win trips to the Super Bowl. The aim was immediate gratification, targeting consumers out-of-home and at the point of purchase.

This is likely to be far more effective than a similar offer on in-home television, which would require customers to go to a store, or to recall the offer when next in-store.

Identify Real-time Information that Really Matters to Consumers

We can't overstate the positive brand impact of ongoing contact with consumers, particularly using benefit-laden topical news. For example, Novartis offered pollen-count alerts via SMS to promote its new allergy nasal spray for hay fever. Consumers who signed up received personalized, up-to-date, location-based pollen counts and special alerts on high-count days. The company also used SMS to send hay fever management tips; 56% of users agreed they would sign-up again – even if the service was fee-based.[25]

    Most news services already provide headline SMS alert services, often on a fee-paying basis. Yahoo! Alerts provides free SMS alerts on topics chosen by the user, including news, weather, sports, stock market, even horoscopes. Some banks are even offering SMS alerts about any account activity. Textmarks (www.textmarks.com) has a product to allow any blog or website to offer their own SMS alerts system.

    MasterCard Nearby (www.mcnearby.com) lets Mastercard cardholders use their cell phones to find the nearest ATMs when in the US, Canada, Australia, and much of Europe.

Take Advantage of User Down Time

Mobile devices have come to be used as breaks – as ways to pass the time or ways to disguise waiting – like a healthful cigarette. As a result, the mobile user is susceptible: turned on, tuned in, attentive, waiting for relevant information.

If there is any time that we can seize a modern consumer's undivided attention it is with the mobile. Again, the Japanese have a word for it – *nagara* – while-doing-something-else. And that is the essence of the mobile device; it is always there. Whatever else may be happening, the mobile is grabbing some of the customer's attention. Most mobile users are looking at or listening to their devices when they use them. Given the current screen size, competitive offers and distracting clutter is unlikely. A message accepted by the mobile user is a message received and attended to by the user in person.

Realizing that the crowd at sporting events has a fair amount of down time, American Express promoted a contest at Wimbledon. Members of the Wimbledon audience could SMS guesses at the winners of the next day's event, thereby entering a contest pool. AmEx not only got brand awareness, but claimed a meaningful number of card applications.

Don't Contribute to SMS Spam

Unlike the web – but like email – the mobile has push potential. The marketer can initiate the message. Already, several hundred million advertising SMSes are sent out every month in Europe alone. Metrics are solidifying, and ad formats are becoming standardized, although pricing models still vary between cpm (cost per thousand) and cpc (cost per click), and there are as yet no gold standard third party tracking mechanisms.

Unlike email, however, access to the mobile has gatekeepers – usually the mobile carriers, the companies that manage the networks over which the signals are transmitted. Carriers have thus far been fairly successful at maintaining a relatively pristine, spam-free environment.

But the plague of spam still threatens the mobile. Every untargeted, irrelevant or low benefit SMS lowers the effectiveness of the vehicle and squanders users' trust.

DigiMarketers should always avoid anything that consumers might interpret as spam. The easiest way to do that is to consult, and strictly abide by, a code of conduct established by a reputable, professional association. For example, the Mobile Marketing Association, a global US-based organization with 400 members in over 20 countries (www.mmaglobal.com), has a clear, concise code.[26] So too does the Interactive Advertising Bureau (www.iab.net) and other similar organizations.

These codes of conduct generally dictate strict customer opt-ins for any mobile marketing communications – with confirmation – and with the ability for the consumer to opt-out at any time, usually by simply sending the word STOP via SMS.[27] All opt-ins are non-transferable (that is, opt-ins to one list cannot be sold or passed to another list without additional opt-in). In addition, for effectiveness, be sure to follow the basic points in the Box Insert below.

Effective Mobile Marketing

Get to the Point QUICKLY

The mobile consumer wants immediate relevance. A recent IDC survey found mobile users had very limited tolerance for pre-rolls of more than 8 to 10 seconds. To be successful, a mobile marketing campaign must engage users in the first few seconds. Mobile users are not a captive audience.[28]

Simplify the Desired Response

We have already discussed IVR (interactive voice response) as a way to make customer action easier. For alternatives, see the Boxed Insert QR Codes later in this chapter. Until the mobile interface is itself redeveloped, such devices will be essential.

Deliver Real Benefit

Again and again studies find that customers will do a lot if they gain a lot. And if they gain a little, they will do nothing. Like all digital media, mobile is essentially interactive, and a moment of fame is a tremendous motivator. A recent Nike promotion in Times Square in New York City managed to integrate many of the tips here. Passers-by used their mobiles to SMS a custom shoe design and receive a free pair of Nike IDs. Selected shoe designs were then posted live on the Times Square jumbotron – right in front of the SMSer. Reportedly, users were at least as excited by their designs appearing on the billboard as they were by winning free footwear!

Create Clear User Flow Diagrams

Thinking through exactly how different types of users will work through any system of information, offers, web links and so on is absolutely crucial. Given the impatience of the mobile user, it will be foolhardy to trap them in the sort of automated response hell that mired automated telephone response systems in the 1980s. In the US, mobile operators already require detailed flow diagrams to allow mobile marketing.

Test, Test, Test

Web usability studies have shown that even small samples can identify 80% of usability problems. The tracking possible with mobile marketing allows the marketer to experiment with even small changes in the offer, its wording, and its presentation, and almost immediately see the impact on open rates, response, and effectiveness.

> ### Build on What Customers Already do
>
> The more marketing can reflect what the customer already does, the more successful it will be. Most consumers are comfortable with the camera feature on their mobile. Pontiac used this in a promotion for their G6. Those who photographed a G6 and sent the image from their mobile were entered into a draw to win $1,000,000.
>
> Axe deodorant, building on its playful girl-catching positioning, provided a "little black book" applet. This allowed users to assign different ring-tones to different contacts. This provides a benefit to the consumer while reinforcing brand associations.
>
> Use of additional phone features can be introduced slowly as customers become more comfortable both with the features and with mobile marketing.

Consider the Full Range of Mobile Options

Mobile marketing options are expanding all the time, limited only by the creativity of the DigiMarketer. We can already see:[29]

Text and win: These contests are often related to on/in-pack codes. Customers SMS the code and may win prizes. As consumers are highly likely to SMS as soon as they consume the product, in-pack codes can give insights on consumption timing.

Voting and Quizzes: are great ways to feed databases. Successful SMS campaigns often ask for little fragments of data about the customer for each benefit offered. The benefits – maybe a quiz, a horoscope, an intelligence test, a personality profile or a compatibility rating – are the sugar on the data-provision pill. Collated, coordinated, and data-mined, this database then allows personalized offers – increasing customer benefit, yielding more customer information and better personalized offers – the virtuous circle of DigiMarketing!

Mobile content: Pictures, ring-tones, video, all of which can be brand associated and build brand relationships. The movie *Mr Bean's Holiday* was the first UK use of a mobile technology called Snap Happy. A mobile user photographs a Mr Bean poster bearing the Snap Happy logo and MMSes the picture to a specified number. The Snap Happy technology automatically identifies the user's type of phone and delivers them free ring-tones, wallpaper or video, all formatted for their particular phone.[30]

Mobile games and other mobile applications: These can be as simple as a biorhythm system or as complex as an instant messaging service. Again, be sure to offer branding and involvement possibilities.

CRM (*customer relationship management*): Mobile can actually deliver customer service and support, complementing other service channels. IDEA Cellular Ltd implemented an SMS-based self-service solution aimed at prepaid mobile subscribers in India. Prepaid customers are extremely price sensitive and very prone to churn (switching suppliers) to get the best deal. Call centers tend to get overloaded, creating waiting time, and potential buyers leave. Therefore, a user can simply SMS the word CARE to a designated number, and they receive a return SMS which guides them through the different deals. Other keywords trigger more specific SMSes. The whole thing is totally automated, available 24/7, and is free to the consumer. This relieves call-center traffic and actually enhances customer service.

Direct response ads: typically via codes and keywords. A mobile component, as simple as a number in a print ad to which to SMS a keyword, adds tracking, interaction, and the ability for personalized follow-up to a print ad. This can be particularly effective for ads that are read on the move. Consumers can SMS the keyword immediately, rather than having to remember the ad until they get to their home or office. Other campaigns use direct SMS responses to post consumers' comments on their television spots or billboards.

Text-to-buy services: Allow mobile device users to SMS to buy print advertised products instantly, often at a big discount. The service also integrates with mobile PayPal.[31]

M-coupons: SMSed barcodes and coupons which can be redeemed on sight in-store.

Bluetooth/infra-red: Bluetooth and infra-red technology can be used to link to electronic tags in outdoor poster ads. In the UK, Hypertag (www.hypertag.com) places electronic tags in outdoor poster advertising, displays, or even on other users at promotional events. A customer who points their mobile at the tag and clicks can receive additional content via infra-red or Bluetooth. Bluejacking sends unsolicited messages to Bluetooth-enabled devices in the immediate vicinity. For example, HSBC's branches in London have trialed delivering messages to nearby Bluetooth-enabled devices to ask users if they would like to receive a promotional message. Such communications need to be used with great care so as not to alienate users. In this case, the system was smart enough to remember devices they had already queried, so the same device was not queried twice.

Mobile search: As we saw in chapter 3, mobile search is potentially the killer app for the mobile device. To date, DigiMarketers are a long way behind the curve. A recent study[32] in the UK found for searches using the company's name, 93% of FTSE 100 companies fail to get their homepages on the first page of mobile search results! And only 5% get their page as the first listed result on mobile, versus 90% for online searches. Clearly DigiMarketers are neglecting mobile search optimization.

Integrate with Other Marketing

Mobile must be part of the whole marketing mix – a component of an integrated media strategy. In what is often called *ad convergence*, mobile works well to add additional features to existing media. As we have seen, mobile components in other ad media can add interaction, tracking and personalization to print, television, and billboards.

NBC's *Deal or No Deal* television game show uses mobile within the show (and the website) to let the audience into the experience. Viewers of the television or on the website can SMS their guess at the lucky case numbers and win prizes if there's a match. The website also sells downloadable wallpaper for the mobile, not only increasing viewer involvement but also reportedly providing sufficient revenue to cover the entire show's production costs.[33]

The Dove "Campaign for Real Beauty" was one of the first to integrate SMS with electronic billboards. Dove erected a large billboard of a happy, fresh-looking older woman, alongside a text-to-vote number. Passers-by could choose between describing her as "wrinkled" or "wonderful." The billboard summarized SMS and online voting in real time.

Ford Fiesta went a step further in Europe by combining personalizing billboards with content from SMSes. The billboard displayed a short code. Passers-by who SMSed the code and their name to the displayed number were entered in a draw. The billboard, in turn, displayed a "good luck" message personally addressed to the person, and sent him or her another SMS with a question. If answered correctly, the billboard reacted like a winning pinball machine.

Lipton Ice Tea

Teenagers in Japan are perhaps more comfortable interacting with their mobile phone screens than they are watching their television screens. As a result, the key metric for brand building – particularly when it comes to youth – is migrating from impressions to involvement.

In Japan, Lipton wished to capitalize on the growing potential of mobile marketing, so they created a site for young drinkers of its ready-to-drink tea product. The resulting I-mode site, created by Ogilvy & Mather Japan, was unique from the start. The site used the core concept that tea relates to people's moods and stimulates their moods in different ways. The Re-Fresh! site allowed users to check their personality type and then do daily mood checks. This activity, not just around the product but around the consumer in relation to the product, generated natural consumer involvement. After all, nothing is as fascinating to consumers as themselves!

Having established the site as a beachhead for mobile promotions and CRM initiatives, Lipton then decided to experiment with new types of messaging that would touch this young target emotionally and eventually elicit a response and further involvement. As this was a young audience, the majority of them had entered the web-based promotion via their mobile phones.

The program was called "Chatty," a play on the words "Cha" (tea) and "chatty" meaning talkative. The idea of the campaign was to send daily emails that provided a little daily pick-me-up on the go – just like the Lipton product. The tone of the "Chatty" email was casual and friendly, and the mobile email was personalized with the users' nickname, just as if they had come from a silly pal. The emails followed a specific calendar; that is, Monday's contents were focused on refreshment to recover from the weekend; Tuesday focused on tea, and every other week included specific Lipton product information; Wednesday focused on silliness with a funny picture; Thursday offered specific seasonal advice; and Friday recommended weekend activities and events. While the campaign was well mapped out, from the users' perspective it felt "unscripted" and a bit random at times.

Work with the Other Players in the Space

As we have seen, the attempts of mobile operators to hold users within walled gardens are breaking down. Nonetheless, successful DigiMarketers should take care to create campaigns that offer benefits to all the parties in the mobile ecosystem.

Don't Assume that Content that Works on Another Channel will Work on Mobile

It's necessary to understand the essence of the communication and the essence of the mobile device. For example, although ring-tones were already a $2.5 billion market by 2004, and can provide the marketer with excellent branding opportunities, the reality is that the ring-tone rarely plays for more than 10 seconds. The message has to be encapsulated into this window.

Nor can video content created for television always be successful on the mobile: UK Operator 3 bought rights to video broadcast Premier League soccer games to mobiles, only to find that the widescreen shots that work on televion were unwatchable on mobile. Baby clips and viral ads are more in tune with the device.

The DigiMarketer must make sure that their communications look good on *all* mobile screens. This may be a lot more difficult than it sounds. At the time of writing, there is no emerging standard for mobile screen size, resolution, or layout. As a result, it may be necessary to develop several versions of mobile communications and to serve the right version to the right device.

FUTURE TRENDS – WHERE IT'S HEADING

At the beginning of the chapter, we outlined seven drivers that have created Mobile 1.0. As we look forward at the next 10 years, we see those same key drivers taking mobile into its next phase of evolution: Mobile 2.0. We believe the impact of these same drivers will be qualitatively distinct. We can expect to see much more sophisticated mobile content across the board, and much more sophisticated consumer-created content (this will be the focus of chapter 8). The vision is one of mobile as the major platform: bigger and more vital than the web is today.

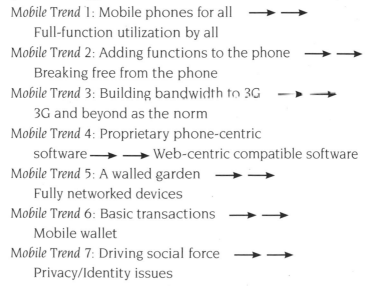

Mobile Trend 1: Mobile phones for all $\longrightarrow$ $\longrightarrow$
    Full-function utilization by all

Mobile Trend 2: Adding functions to the phone $\longrightarrow$ $\longrightarrow$
    Breaking free from the phone

Mobile Trend 3: Building bandwidth to 3G $\longrightarrow$ $\longrightarrow$
    3G and beyond as the norm

Mobile Trend 4: Proprietary phone-centric
    software $\longrightarrow$ $\longrightarrow$ Web-centric compatible software

Mobile Trend 5: A walled garden $\longrightarrow$ $\longrightarrow$
    Fully networked devices

Mobile Trend 6: Basic transactions $\longrightarrow$ $\longrightarrow$
    Mobile wallet

Mobile Trend 7: Driving social force $\longrightarrow$ $\longrightarrow$
    Privacy/Identity issues

Mobile Trend 1: Mobile Phones for All $\longrightarrow$ $\longrightarrow$ Full-Function Utilization by All

Mobile phones are already in the hands of customers around the globe. The next phase will see global customers really getting access to the multiple features of their mobiles. We have achieved penetration by the mobile; next we will see penetration of the mobile's capabilities.

Already, the fastest growth in mobile penetration is in Africa, growing at twice the rate of Asia.[34] As in many emerging markets, subscribers are technology skipping. They are not only leap-frogging wired phones, they are also adopting the mobile as their first, and probably only, internet-capable device. Many of these users will never own a PC. The primary way they will surf the web will be through mobile devices.

As the mass of users becomes more comfortable with the entire functionality of their mobile device, we can expect to see more cross-functionality – using, for example, the device's camera to control, or enhance, a mobile game, just as the Eye Toy did for the PS2.[35]

For the DigiMarketer, this means a move from the high reach but low richness of the mobile phone of 2007 to the truly rich reach of the mobile device of the future. This broadening of mobile mastery will be significantly aided by the Mobile Trend 2, a paradigm shift in user interface.

Mobile Trend 2: Adding Functions to the Phone $\longrightarrow$ $\longrightarrow$ Breaking Free from the Phone

Whereas the last 10 years has seen functionality added to the phone, we believe that the next 10 years will see the phone-ness being removed from that multi-functionality! Not that we won't still be able to make voice calls. We will, but will probably do so less and less in favor of asynchronous communications (that is, communications that don't depend on all parties communicating at the same time). But the mobile interface will finally give up its reliance on the traditional phone keypad. The phone's interface has hardly changed since the rotary dial was supplanted by the keypad. It's salutary to note that the keypad was first pitched extensively at the 1964 New York World's Fair – alongside Bell's ill-fated Picturephone video telephone system! The keypad is basically a numeric input device with an alphabet slapped on to it! It lags far behind the device's new functionality and contributes a lot to perceived complexity.

Already in early 2007, Google has reputedly entered an agreement to become a virtual mobile network operator in the UK[36], and has confirmed that it is developing a mobile[37] – reportedly a mass market device.

On June 29, 2007, in what AT&T CEO Stan Sigman described as "the largest commercial product launch in the history of electronics"[38], Apple launched its iPhone, which interestingly does not have a traditional keypad of buttons, although it can show a graphic representation thereof. In early 2007, Microsoft acquired Tellme Networks (www.tellme.com), variously described as a "voice portal"[39] and a "provider of voice services for everyday life."[40]

Google, Apple, and Microsoft seem to be racing towards the creation of a voice-driven user interface for their mobiles. At the moment, the aim seems to be to create a natural voice/vision interface: so-called Dial-Tone 2.0 With an improved interface, we can expect to see more and more convergence, with the mobile taking the lead role in data access, perhaps at the expense of the PC.

Challenging the Computer Form Factor

The mobile is literally changing the shape of computing. While conventionally a computer has had a base (housing CPU, connections, memory, and so on), a screen (rigid and preferably large), and a keyboard (similarly rigid and almost as large), design of each of these three elements is dramatically challenging the limits of the current form factors, creating new shapes for the future computer/mobile device.

Already, memory miniaturization has dramatically shrunk the base unit; for example, a micro-MMC (micro MultiMedia-Card, one of the standard memory forms for mobiles) can contain at least a gigabyte of storage, and it's smaller than a thumbnail.

Meanwhile, Polymervision: The Rollable Display Company (www.polymervision.com), a spin-off from Phillips, has already developed a fully functional prototype mobile with a rollable display, packing a five-inch display into a regular-sized mobile.

Other solutions project screen information onto any flat surface (or even use special spectacles to float the information in front of the user). The keyboard is harder to deal with as there are tremendous user benefits in standard-sized keys. One solution, already available, laser projects a virtual keyboard onto any flat surface. The user then "types" in the normal way. The device even issues simulated key clicks! Finger movements are monitored and passed to the mobile device by Bluetooth. The result? A full-sized keyboard for any mobile device. Alternatives may see non-keyboard interfaces (for example, voice commands), or screens that double as keyboards (for example, the iPhone).

For the DigiMarketer, breaking free of the phone keypad promises consumers who – for the first time – can enjoyably use the full features of their mobile device. This sets the stage for the mobile to become *the* digital device.

Mobile Trend 3: Building Bandwidth to 3G ⟶ ⟶ 3G and Beyond as the Norm

As 3G becomes ubiquitous (see Boxed Insert, Alphabet Soup... with Numbers) and carriers move to even higher bandwidths, video calling will become commonplace. NTT DoCoMo expects to launch Super 3G by 2010, improving network speeds by a startling 260 times![41] Beyond 3G, we can expect to see a full better-than-DVD-quality moving picture on our mobile device. Just as the jerky cinema of Charlie Chaplin morphed into the lush high resolution of Imax, so the 15 fps of 2G will give way to photorealistic movies, and television, on the mobile screen.

McKinsey is already predicting that mobile television will be a 24 billion euro market in Europe alone, reaching almost 200 million users.[42] The implications of this are discussed in more detail in chapter 10.

Mobile Trend 4: Proprietary Phone-Centric Software ⟶ ⟶ Web-Centric Compatible Software

As handset producers abandon the phone as the shape of the user interface, so will they abandon their attempts to impose their own proprietary software on users. As of 2007, almost every brand of phone carries its very own proprietary software for almost every function. To play your music on most mobiles today entails re-indexing your music into the proprietary interface of (usually) the handset manufacturer, and probably recreating playlists, favorites, and so on. This only adds irritation for the customer! It is inevitable that the benefits to consumers of being able to use the same software on all their digital devices will compel web-centric compatible software.

We are already seeing web browsers developing specifically mobile versions. Opera (www.opera.com), although free for the PC, sells its mobile browser, which it claims to be the most secure on the market. ZenZui, www.zenzui.com (formed by ex-Microsoft researchers, partly owned by Microsoft, and using Microsoft licensed software), offers quicker, clearer mobile web access via an on-screen zoomable user interface (ZUI – get it?). This features clickable tiles, each offering access to partner sites that the mobile user has explicitly allowed to their device. Meanwhile, Yahoo!Go (mobile.yahoo.com/go) uses a carousel interface with widgets to simplify mobile browsing.

These developments suggest that anything web-based will shortly be integrating mobile components. We can expect that the social networking communities already springing up across the web will rapidly become connected mobile communities, harnessing the mobile's video and audio capabilities into community sites. For example, Twitter (www.twitter.com), the mini-blogging application launched in 2006, allows short messages to be blogged directly to the web from the mobile – insiders have made this the most talked about app since Flickr (www.flickr.com). Elsewhere, widgets are appearing aimed at the mobile device, allowing seamless access to specific web communities.[43]

The mobile gaming platform will likely expand with cross-platform mobile games, linking mobile and online versions of the same game. The Korean mobile massively multiplayer online game (MMOG, see chapter 9) *Path of a Warrior* already offers some continuity between online and mobile. Its sequel is expected to build on this parallel gaming between platforms.[44]

This suggests a web-centric future in which DigiMarketers no longer create separate campaigns for each medium, but will need to integrate their marketing across all the digital media. For example, in Motorola's "House of Blues" campaign, consumers can send photos from their mobile device cameras to an LED billboard in real time. They can also blog their images online.

Mobile Trend 5: A Walled Garden ⟶ ⟶
Fully Networked Devices

As mobile software becomes web-centric, so we can expect to see the abandonment of any remaining attempts at restricting users to a walled garden. Seamless web access and increasing bandwidth will dramatically enhance mobile applications of existing web software and development of new mobile-oriented software. This is likely to build on the unique capabilities of the mobile, especially its GPS (location tracking) capabilities. As we saw in chapter 4, mobile search has the potential to explode.

Others are working on a system of augmented reality that would combine aspects of GPS, image recognition, and factual databases. So a tourist could point their mobile device at a building and the device would display additional information about the landmark on its screen. Or a customer might point the device at a restaurant and the menu (and e-coupons) might appear on the screen. Or you could find your friends in a store or stadium, with directions to them appearing on the screen.[45]

There are clearly privacy problems involved, but few question the use of mobiles to monitor employees, or at-risk family members. Some dating sites already use services that locate nearby facilities and facilitate communication based on user proximity. These side step privacy concerns by informing users of their relative position to the other rather than their absolute position, and of course are strictly opt-in, fee-paying services.

The most used location systems at the moment are navigational. These relate where you *are* to where you *want to be*, and use built-in maps to compute a route to your destination. These navigation systems can provide transit information and even predict the time to a destination, and of course can help users access local information based on their position. So the mobile can display stores and restaurants in a particular area or provide information on local history, culture, weather – all updateable in real time to reflect changing weather and traffic conditions.

This offers the prospect of highly localized marketing: publicizing new outlet openings, special sales in specific locations, or very localized offers (for example, SMS coupons for impulse purchases at a specific adjacent outlet). For the DigiMarketer, we can expect a move from static, display marketing on the mobile to dynamic, interactive, tightly personalized problem-solving mobile marketing.

Mobile Trend 6: Basic Transactions ⟶ ⟶ Mobile Wallet

As we have seen, in most countries mobiles can only handle the most basic of financial transactions. Where basic payments can be made each carrier has its own independent system. This is likely to impede widespread usage, just as multiple gauges slowed down the railroads.

In some of the most advanced digital societies in the world (for example, Japan or South Korea), payment chips embedded in mobile phones provide detailed and sophisticated financial applications. South Korea already has more than 12 million mobile payment–enabled handsets in circulation, with 80,000 terminal payment machines in shops, restaurants and cafes. Japan is at least two years ahead in the development of the *keitai* wallet: the mobile device as a payment method. Already, by early 2007, NTT DoCoMo has signed up 1.3 million customers for its mobile credit card[46] service, and its m-commerce is at $400 million per annum. However, even in Zambia, where Coca-Cola now tells its 300 Zambian distributors to pay for deliveries not in cash but by sending text messages from their mobile phones, mobile payment is growing.[47]

Forecasters are already expecting the worldwide value of mobile commerce to climb from just $3.2 billion in 2003 to over $37 billion by 2008.[48]

Next Generation E-commerce: Micro-Payments

What's missing in most markets is a mechanism for mobile devices to transfer small payments in a way that is easy and convenient, while being secure, trustworthy and cost effective. On the web, payments are routinely made (in most countries) using credit cards, PayPal[49], Amazon honor system,[50] or Click-and-Buy[51] type accounts. These are hard to extend to mobile, and at best their transaction fees (typically a minimum 50 cents US) make them useful only for mini-transactions. To support micro-transactions — say a 50 cent ring-tone, or 10 cents of advice on where to eat — requires a system with much lower fees, but which is equally widely accepted, safe and transparent to buyer and seller.

The GSM Association's "Pay-Buy Mobile" initiative aims to move directly to contactless payments using near field communications technology. Prepaid smart cards have already gained wide acceptance as a payment method (Oyster, the London subway prepaid smart card, is used on 75% of trips). It is a small step to implant the smart card chip into the SIM card of the mobile device. This is exactly what Sony's FeliCa chip allows (see Box Insert, FeliCa Chips, below).

FeliCa Chips

The Felicity Card (usually known as FeliCa) is a contactless RFID (radio frequency identification) chip smart card developed by Sony and widely used in electronic money cards. This has been modified into a Mobile FeliCa for use in mobile phones and is at the heart of the DoCoMo mobile wallet in Japan.[52]

The result will be a secure, interoperable and transparent service for mobile customers, financial institutions and the banks. The device is on trial in South Korea in late 2007.[53]

As the mobile device moves to the fore of ubiquitous computing, we can expect to see consumers allowing their mobile to link directly to an increasing number of sensors and displays embedded in the everyday environment. These links will require permission from the user initially (an opt-in to recognizing that sensor or device), but will be thereafter unnoticed by the user These links will widen the application of mobile micro-payment systems.

For example, consider the growing unattended point of sale (UPOS) sector. Cashless car parking would give each parking meter a proximity chip. If you park, the meter talks to the smart card chip in your mobile device and registers the time you parked. When you leave, the meter collects its parking fee from your mobile's smart chip. This increases convenience, reduces your need to carry cash, and reduces opportunities for fraud.[54] The system could easily be extended to offer warning SMSes when your parking time was about to expire or when the fee was about to jump. Of course, as with all DigiMarketing, that parking fee could be custom determined. It might depend not only on how long you parked, but how much you used that company's meters each month, or even the size of your car, or its energy efficiency (did we mention that the meter might chat to the RFID in your car too?). These opportunities are discussed further in chapter 9.

M-*banking*, M-*brokerage*

There is even the potential to conduct banking and brokerage transactions from the mobile. The mobile device offers security superior to any card: it can be deactivated remotely, it can request input of additional data (PINs, for example), and can even execute its own visual ID (see below).

Digital Channels

A recent survey of more than 450 potential customers and over 50 banks worldwide found that 92% of all survey participants were willing to conduct banking transactions via mobiles. Nearly 60% were even willing to pay an extra fee to utilize mobile remittance facilities.[55] Mastercard already allows remittances to be sent as text messages.[56]

For the DigiMarketer, the mobile has the potential to break free from simple transactions, and combine brand image building and immersive offers with a direct purchase device.

Mobile Trend 7: Driving Social Force ⟶ ⟶ Privacy/Identity Issues

Of course, among all this optimism there is a potential downside too. That downside is consumer rejection of the increased pervasiveness of the mobile, and especially its use by careless marketers.

To maintain the mobile channel's fairly pristine nature will require real restraint on the part of DigiMarketers, with a respect for privacy and a care not to be intrusive: rarely characteristics of marketers, some would say.

Continued relevancy and permission are absolutely vital for DigiMarketing. It is already clear that financial incentives to customers (free calls, reduced bills, and the like) are effective ways to sugar-coat the marketing pill. In a survey of over 11,000 US mobile subscribers, 41% of those who view or intend to view mobile video say they would watch ads to get free content, and another 20% would watch ads to get reduced-fee content.[57]

Identity and Security

In many ways the flipside of privacy is security. We have already seen web identity as a key issue for the future development of the web (chapter 3) and noted identity theft problems.

Unless the environment is truly secure, with wire-lined walls to prevent leakage of radio waves, it is simply impossible to guarantee that transmissions will not be capable of being received by others. Indeed, breaking into businesses' wireless networks is the new trend in computer hacking. A hacker used to dial thousands of phone numbers to find a modem to communicate with (so called war dialling); today the hacker drives around with a laptop sniffing for insecure wireless networks (war driving).

Those Other Mobile Devices

It is worth noting that, at the time of writing, the mobile phone is not the only mobile device. Standalone personal digital assistants (PDAs), dedicated email devices (especially the Blackberry), personal stereos (notably the iPod), and portable game players (PSP, and so on) are all part of the total mobile platform.

Our crystal ball is hazy so we cannot tell you whether these devices will ultimately be subsumed within a single mobile device! What we *can* see is that for separate devices to exist there must be a strong customer benefit delivered by each device. Perhaps the iPod will always be valued for music (and video) in situations where even the smallest mobile phone device cannot go. On the other hand, it may be totally eclipsed by the more versatile iPhone, or subsequently developed devices.

The developers of Blackberry hope to position the device as a CRM tool, receiving data from central servers with an interface less cluttered than that of the mobile phone device, and with greater security. The aim is to create an executive information and decision-making tool. At the same time they are pursuing agreements with PDA manufacturers.

Whether these devices become permanent parts of the mobile landscape, or are finally seen as evolutionary dead-ends, at the moment they deserve consideration in the DigiMarketer's plans.

Move On QR Codes

Mobiles are increasingly being used in conjunction with non-digital devices such as standard televisions and billboards, bringing them many DigiMarketing advantages. This is usually accomplished by a code on the non-digital media which when entered into the mobile device triggers a connection to digital media.

The simplest form is the qtag, www.qtags.com, used in radio ads to boost response rates. Drive time ads encourage listeners to SMS a keyword – a qtag – to a short number. Those who do receive a reply including a link to a web page where they can learn more about the advertised product/service. Keywords in print, billboard, or television can be SMSed and trigger a variety of behaviors.

A higher tech version is the QR code (we already met these in chapter 1). These turn any "flat" space, such as a billboard or print ad, into a direct response mechanism that can automatically link a viewer or reader to the web.

Adidas put QR codes on retail tags and clothing imprints. Customers who photographed the code with their mobile were automatically taken to the mobile version of the Adidas website. In tests in Korea, 60,000 people participated and the Adidas site got over 2,000,000 page views.

Qode, www.qode.com, from NeoMedia Technologies offers a similar functionality, and has found applications in print publishing, creating interactive textbooks. Readers can download the Qode app to their mobiles, scan the qodes in the text, and automatically access additional information including videos, games, and updates. A qode on the book's cover even allows the authors to pitch the text direct to the potential buyer!

Mobile identity solutions are at hand. As early as 2007, NTT DoCoMo adopted software from Neven Vision (now owned by Google) that uses the mobile's camera to recognize the user. The mobile device itself can then automatically allow (or not) access to the mobile and its data without contacting any remote server.

For the DigiMarketer, privacy concerns recur across all digital media. Personalization and privacy will generate a whole new set of complex trade-offs which must be managed to the complete satisfaction of the customer if the mobile device is to realize its marketing potential.

THE ULTIMATE DIGIMARKETING PLATFORM?

When you add up the outcome of these seven drivers of the future – full-function utilization by all; breaking free from the phone; 3G and beyond as the norm; web-centric compatible software; fully networked devices; mobile wallet; and, despite, the inevitable privacy/identity issues – the result is a tantalizing platform for DigiMarketing.

No wonder mobile marketing is exploding. Like all DigiMarketing, marketing via mobile channels is now here to stay and will be increasingly mainstream. Globally, mobile ad spend is forecast to go from $1.4 billion in 2006 to

$11.7 billion in 2011 – an over eight-fold increase. Mobile multimedia ad spending is forecast to explode with a twenty-fold increase from just over $100 million in 2006 to over $2 billion by 2011. Worldwide, mobile ads will go from 5.4% of total ad spend in 2006 to 21% by 2011.[58]

In 2007, mobile commercial messages had a 95% open rate: that is, almost every message sent was actually opened by the recipient. In contrast, email marketing aims for 20% to 30% open rates. And the immediacy of SMS means that response can be measured and campaigns adjusted almost in real time.

The key question then for marketers is what do you want to achieve using the mobile platform. Mobile devices provide an unparalleled window into customers' lives. As always on and always near devices, they fit into virtually all consumer lifestyle modes. They are there when consumers are simply killing time. They are there on the bus, train, or plane ride. They are with the consumer in the supermarket aisle, and at the register, and at the point of consumption. Consequently, mobile phones can scale to a variety of roles in the marketing mix from general information to specific transaction.

It's worth stressing that this doesn't always mean something functional. The mobile is not just a third screen: it is not just one more display medium. The real potential of mobile marketing is the ability to create a new marketing experience. An experience, as a recent IDC report puts it, that is "in some cases, on-demand, that delivers information to you when it is directly relevant, and one increasingly based on your individual needs, interests, aspirations and behavior."[59]

SUMMARY: MOBILE PLATFORMS

The mobile platform offers numerous benefits to DigiMarketers and merits a role in most marketers' digital plans:

- The price-point of mobile devices makes them the great mass device around the world.
- Mobile devices are the new computers, now residing in people's pockets and purses.
- The constant march towards more mobile bandwidth means that video on the mobile will eventually be a mainstay in most markets.
- Mobile platforms are becoming transaction and search-driven too, adding further momentum to these mass consumer devices.

Next we will look at games – another area that is garnering a great deal of attention given its growing scope and influence in people's daily lives.

END NOTES
1   Ahonen & Moore (2007) quoted in mmaglobal.com/modules/wfsection/article. php?articleid=796
2   en.wikipedia.org/wiki/Mobile_phone
3   *Wall Street Journal*, January 5–7, 2007, p4.
4   *Financial Times*, January 5, 2007, p12.
5   www.economist.com/opinion/displayStory.cfm?story_id=3742817
6   observer.guardian.co.uk/uk_news/story/0,6903,673103,00.html
7   Potential DigiMarketing applications of these features of mobiles are discussed below, under Consider the Full Range of Mobile Options.
8   www.netatlantic.com/products/sms/about-sms.html
9   www.mobilemarketingmagazine.co.uk/
10 en.wikipedia.org/wiki/USSD
11 shopping.guardian.co.uk/games/story/0,,1536050,00.html
12 www.gartner.com/it/page.jsp?id=498310
13 blogs.zdnet.com/ITFacts/?p=12492
14 www.wirelessweek.com/article.aspx?id=78584
15 Although increasingly we see the emergence of virtual mobile operators, like Virgin, who simply lease space on other operators' networks.
16 *The Asian Wall Street Journal*, March 5, 2007, p29.
17 This discussion is based on en.wikipedia.org/wiki/4G; reviews.cnet.com/4520-11288_7-5664933-2.html?tag=arw; and en.wikipedia.org/wiki/3G
18 *The Economist*, February 17, 2007.
19 www.ofcom.org.uk/tv/ifi/prsinquiry/ayrereport/
20 Howard Rheingold, *Smart Mobs: The Next Social Revolution*.
21 *Personal, Portable, Pedestrian: Mobile Phones in Japanese Life*, edited by Mizuko Ito, Daisuke Okabe and Misa Matsuda.
22 www.ecommercetimes.com/story/dUNaKjF4rRE7yj/US-Ready-for-Mobile Marketing.xhtml
23 www.christine.net/2006/11/top_mobile_mark.html
24 *The Wall Street Journal*, January 4, 2007, "Cell Phone Ads are Easier Pitch in China", or online.wsj.com/article/SB116787863206166699.html.
25 www.e-consultancy.com/knowledge/events/download/beauty-parade-2004-02-mobile-marketing/flytxt.ppt
26 www.mmaglobal.com/modules/content/index.php?id=5
27 The guidelines can be accessed at www.mmaglobal.com

28 www.fiercemobilecontent.com/node/2941
29 Based in part on technokitten.blogspot.com/2005/12/what-is-mobile-marketing_
    08.html
30 www.netimperative.com/2007/03/26/Mr_Bean
31 money.cnn.com/2007/02/12/magazines/business2/anomaly_lucky.biz2/index.htm
32 www.mobilemarketingmagazine.co.uk/
33 www.christine.net/2006/11/top_mobile_mark.html
34 www.timesonline.co.uk/tol/news/world/article737130.ece
35 news.bbc.co.uk/2/hi/technology/6445617.stm
36 www.vecosys.com/2007/05/24/google-mobile-phone-powered-by-02-confirmed/
37 business.timesonline.co.uk/tol/business/industry_sectors/technology/
    article1536776.ece
38 www.macnn.com/articles/07/05/16/att.on.iphone.launch/
39 en.wikipedia.org/wiki/Tellme_Networks
40 www.tellme.com/about
41 *Financial Times*, January 5, 2007, p12.
42 "Understanding Europe's Market for Mobile TV", Jacques R Bughin, *McKinsey
    Quarterly* Web Exclusive, April 2006.
43 www.widsets.com/index
44 news.bbc.co.uk/2/hi/technology/6445617.stm
45 *The Wall Street Journal*, March 26, 2007.
46 *ibid*.
47 www.developments.org.uk/articles/loose-talk-saves-lives-1/
48 *The Economist*, February 17, 2007
49 www.paypal.com was sold to eBay for about US$1.5 billion.
50 www.amazon.com/honor/
51 clickandbuy.com
52 en.wikipedia.org/wiki/FeliCa
53 www.gsmworld.com/news/press_2007/press07_21.shtml
54 A simplified version of this is already offered in Dublin. www.nccmembership.
    co.uk/POOLED/articles/bf_webart/view.asp?Q=bf_webart_113353)
55 www1.uni-hamburg.de/m-commerce/banking/presse/eng/PR20060119.html
56 www.finextra.com/fullstory.asp?id=16497
57 According to a study performed by M:Metrics and released in 2007 by the Mobile
    Marketing Association Mobile Marketing Association. mmaglobal.com/modules/
    news/article.php?storyid=91
58 eMarketer, January, 2007, *Mobile Marketing and Advertising*.
59 technewsworld.com/story/56071.html

Chapter 7

Games: The New Hollywood

D igital games are no longer limited to teenage nerds hunting dragons, stealing cars, or generally creating digital mayhem. Instead, digital games are already widely used and well-accepted as mainstream entertainment, and even teaching aids. In this chapter we look at the development of games into networked, connected activities, creating an interactive, personalized, and dynamically updatable communication channel.

DigiMarketers can, of course, use this game environment to communicate to potential customers. But games are moving beyond being just a communication medium. They are actually becoming a consumption arena in their own right. DigiMarketers can choose to encourage consumption activities, and sales, within the game itself. The growth of massively multi-person online games (MMOGs) is creating new virtual worlds in which customers are spending increasing amounts of time – and money. Marketers need to understand how to use such virtual universes and how to anchor them to the "real" world.

KEY TRENDS YOU MUST KNOW

Repeat after me: "bigger than Hollywood, bigger than Hollywood." Yes, many of you will need to think again about what is quickly becoming one of the largest and most influential digital platforms around. As audiences for broadcast television dwindle, and movie-going stalls, digital games are the fastest growing media sector worldwide. The value of the global games industry has been predicted to surpass the film and music industries combined, increasing revenue from US$25.4 billion in 2004 to US$55 billion in 2008.[1]

This growth isn't simply a function of more game makers releasing more titles, although there are undoubtedly more games available today than ever before. We believe there are four interconnected drivers behind the growth of games.

Key Drivers of Game Growth:

Games Driver 1: Everybody's doing it

Games Driver 2: Games get connected

Games Driver 3: Games become more varied

Games Driver 4: Games become Hollywood

Games Driver 1: Everybody's Doing It

If you want to understand games, you have to go beyond the juvenile, male stereotype that many people attach to the platform. Already by 2005, more adults played games than kids. More than one-third of players are women. In the US, there are 30% more women over the age of 18 playing digital games than there are boys aged 17 or younger.[2] *The Sims*, http://thesims. ea.com, the biggest selling game to date[3], is played more by women than by men.[4]

Game consoles are increasingly becoming part of the family's home media center. Game consoles are right there, alongside the television, digital recording device, digital music player, and PC. As of 2007, 41% of US households with televisions owned a game console[5]; 25% of Americans over the age of 50 played video games, an increase from 9% in 1999. In Japan, digital games are heralded as "brain training for adults."[6]

About six million US households have at least one power gamer: that's someone who spends as much as 20 hours per week and $50 per month on games. There are more than 15 million active players of casual games (which as we will see are usually free ad-supported games – think *Tetris* or *Patience*).

While Microsoft's Xbox 360 and Sony's PlayStation 3 tend to dominate the hard-core gamer market, Nintendo's Wii (with its innovative motion-sensitive controller) positions itself as a family friendly, feature-rich console that's at home in the ordinary living room — further widening ownership of game playing devices. Game devices are predicted to grow by 40% every year from 2005 to 2010[7], while handheld consoles are exploding, with growth expected to be over 90% per annum from 2005 to 2010.[8]

Asia leads the way, as it does in so many aspects of digital. In South Korea, 60% of those aged 9 to 39 consider themselves frequent online game players. As digital games widen their appeal, and take over more and more consumer leisure time, they become an ever more effective medium for advertisers.

Games Driver 2: Games Get Connected

Mainstream digital games originated in the early 1970s in the form of arcade games, played on standalone coin-in-the-slot machines. These found their way into the home as game consoles – capable of playing a single game. These rapidly morphed into multi-game consoles, often using cartridges to switch games. At the same time, as computers entered the home, we saw the development of PC-based computer games. Now we see convergence as the latest consoles

(PlayStation, Xbox and Nintendo, and others) become superior computers, offering better graphics and sound than most PCs.

Innovations in game consoles diffuse much faster than in PCs, because new consoles are almost universally sold at a loss. Manufacturers need to get consoles into the market rapidly in order to sell games, recouping their console losses from the $5 to $10 royalties they take on every game sold. As a result, the financial barriers to adopting the very latest technology in consoles are lower than for that same technology in PCs. What's more, the benefits of the latest game technology – like those dramatic 3D photo-realistic graphics, the surround sound, the force feedback controller, with motion sensor – are extremely visible, immediate, and socially experienced.

However, the single most dramatic step in gaming development from the DigiMarketer's perspective is that almost all game playing devices are now connected. This even applies to portable, hand-held consoles. This means that games can now reside on, or be connected to, the web rather than locked on a single, standalone machine. Networked games can have the key features of any website, allowing for dynamic interaction and the ability to upgrade a game almost instantaneously. From the game players' perspective, the most relevant benefit is the ability to communicate with, and/or compete against, other players in real time. This shift from a static, solitary (or at best small group) format to dynamic, large group format means that games now emphatically have a social dimension.

And when we say "large group format," we mean large. Almost 1.5 million players go for the multiplayer shoot-'em-up games on websites like Microsoft's Xbox Live (www.xbox.com/live).[9] By March 2007, subscribers to *World of Warcraft* (www.worldofwarcraft.com) – a massively multi-person online game – had reached 8.5 million worldwide, with each participant paying about $10 to $15 a month to be able to play. By the same time, the user-created world of *Second Life* (www.secondlife.com, secondlife.com, and see Box Insert on p.217) had been joined by 5 million people, with 33% of them having visited the world in the last 60 days.

Games Driver 3: Games Become More Varied

It is important that DigiMarketers appreciate that digital games does not mean a single activity – or even a single reason for playing. As with most things in digital, games have evolved a great deal over the past decade. Older readers are likely to associate digital games with *Pac-Man* or *Pong* – simple applications that ran primarily on a desktop.

However, the range of digital games, and range of experiences they offer, is now so broad that DigiMarketers need to match their marketing with the type of game and the experience it offers. Even the term *games* is increasingly outdated. Some call the market interactive digital software, and one of the industry's trade associations recently renamed itself as Entertainment Software Association.

There are many ways to categorize and classify games, none of which are definitive. A simple classification for marketers is: casual games, advergames, video games, and MMOGS (massively multiplayer online games) with related MMORPGs (massively multiplayer online role playing games). Here's a brief overview of these different game types.

Casual games: Are the most game-like of digital games, often based on traditional board games and card games. The Microsoft incarnation of *Solitaire* (or *Patience*, depending on which flavor of English you speak) claims to be the most-opened application on the computer ever. Quizzes, polls, self-assessment surveys can all be classed as casual games.

Casual games make up about half of all games played online[10] and are now a $1 billion market worldwide, with an increasingly diverse audience – 60% to 66% of which are female.[11] Although often played on PCs, casual games with their low processor load and small screen footprint are ideally suited for mobile devices.

Casual games are the most frequent entry point to the world of digital games, leading the charge in opening up the demographics of gamers. At www.pogo.com – a casual game website – gamers aged 50 and over make up about 28% of visitors[12]; what's more they play for longer and so account for over 40% of total time spent on the site. Women tend to play 35% longer each day than men, and the site finds that the women "come for the games but stay for the community…it's a kind of MySpace for seniors."[13]

Marketing in these types of games still tends to be very basic, generally limited to product placement at the beginning or end of the game, or on the game packaging, or logo (usually static) on the screen during the game.

Advergames: Are a halfway house between entertainment and marketing. Typically played on a PC, downloadable advergames offer DigiMarketers the possibility of creating a custom game built around their products or brands. The challenge, of course, is to find the right combination of brand exposure and entertainment value to ensure consumers find the advergame sufficiently engaging.

Most advergames come as free downloads, but some have been sold with products. Burger King's *King Games* for the Xbox, for example, sold for $3.99 each with a value meal and became the best-selling games of the 2006 holiday season. The advergame industry, estimated at $83 million in 2004, is forecast to reach over $300 million by 2009.[14]

There are a number of reasons DigiMarketers are getting into advergames. First, stickiness – time spent with the game – is measured in minutes, or tens of minutes, not in seconds. Consequently, there's plenty of time to develop brand identity and for the player to interact with and experience aspects of the product or brand. Second, advergames lend themselves to integration with the brand's website or with other

DigiMarketing activities. Third, advergames can incorporate additional features and levels that can be unlocked using on-merchandize codes. This provides a critical link to sales and the point of consumption. Fourth, development costs are far more manageable than for video games. An advergame costs from $15,000 to $100,000 to develop, depending on its complexity. Well-developed advergames can take on a viral aspect and gain huge circulation, especially if they have a non-dating, seasonal theme (for example, snowball fighting with Santas). Finally, many advergames are based on Flash or Java and consequently port well to mobile screens, an increasingly important game platform.

How successful can an advergame be? M&Ms advergame *Flip the Mix* (http://mms.kewlbox.com – don't go there now, you'll never get back to finish this chapter, let alone the book) reportedly cost about $40,000 to produce and users have logged over 25 million hours of playing time – an incredible value![15]

Video games: Traditionally sold in boxes and usually played on a console, sometimes on a PC, video games are currently the heart of the games industry. In fact, hard-core players tend to call these real games, and definitely play them on a console. Video games have a high degree of user engagement and absorption. Their players don't only spend long periods playing, they reportedly average nine hours a week in activities "around the game" sharing tips, cheats and tricks.[16]

The problem for the DigiMarketer used to be that the development lead time for video games is typically six to 18 months. To make the most of the marketing opportunity, the DigiMarketer needed to get in at the start. This used to lock the marketing down six to 18 months before the game was released and leave the entire process static, and potentially dated.

However, once games became web-connected this all changed. The DigiMarketer can now update the in-game advertising to parallel up-to-the-minute changes in the rest of the marketing effort. Video game producers can even slot new advertisers into existing games.

Massively multiplayer online and role-playing games (MMOGs *and* MMORPGs): As noted earlier, the era of standalone video games is giving way to networked games. This has led to one of the most exciting digital developments from both a marketing and societal viewpoint: massively multiplayer online games, or MMOGs (sometimes called massively multiplayer online role-playing games, MMORPGs).

MMOGs let participants – who are more than simply "players" – compete against each other and react in real time to what others are doing. As the name suggests, massively multiplayer games can involve enormous groups of participants, numbering in the tens or even hundreds of thousands. Each MMOG game has its own setting, or virtual reality (sometimes called a *metaverse*), that participants enter when they join the MMOG.

Participants collaboratively create or follow a story that may or may not have an objective. Increasingly MMOGs do not have clear objectives, but are simply virtual worlds in which participants hang out as they wish.

A common feature of MMOGs is that participants assume the identities of fictional characters (avatars). Avatars are well-suited to MMOGs as these games are a bit like life – but life in a kaleidoscopic, 3D world where characters have super-powers. Avatars can fly, glide, teleport or do just about whatever their owner wants.

MMOGs have been around since about 1997, but it is only in the last few years that the confluence of broadband, faster computer processors, and photo-realistic graphic chips have allowed virtual worlds to really take off. In 2007, some estimates put the total number of subscribers to such worlds as high as 10 million people, many spending 40 hours a week in-world.[17] Typically MMOG and MMORPG users pay monthly subscriptions to enter their realms. Worldwide subscriptions already exceed $3.6 billion a year.[18]

MMOGs tap into strong social influences – especially the herd mentality, or the wisdom of crowds, or network effects, or whatever you want to call it: the coolest place to go is where the coolest people go. As a result, only a very few hit MMOGs ever exist at one time. In North America the MMOG market has typically been dominated by a single product. First, it was *Ultima Online* (www.uoherald.com), then *Everquest* (www.everquest.station.sony.com), then *World of Warcraft* (www.worldofwarcraft.com). Although there are estimated to be more than 50 potentially viable metaverses (virtual realities) in development or in testing around the world, only a handful will rise to the top.

The growing importance of brand presence in MMOGs is one of the key concerns for DigiMarketers. The connectivity that enables participants to communicate with each other also potentially enables DigiMarketers to communicate with participants. This means that games, updates, and marketing can be digitally distributed, almost instantaneously. It also enables participants to link directly with brand websites. However, few participants want to leave the gaming environment. So, the most common question for DigiMarketers is how to embed their brands in the game, without becoming too obtrusive and annoying.

This Increasing variety in games can be viewed as steps in a progression from casual games to the deeply immersive virtual worlds of MMOGs (as shown in Figure 7.1). Generally, as you go further along this continuum of game types, from casual to virtual worlds, the level of consumer immersion increases. So too does the level of brand immersion, as DigiMarketers embed themselves further into the networked virtual worlds that games are becoming.

Game Types

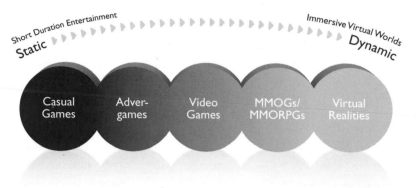

Figure 7.1: Summary of Game Types

Games Driver 4: Games Become Hollywood

Digital games *are* movies. As digital games achieve ever higher levels of graphic realism – and movies increasingly rely on computer-generated special effects – the distinction between movies and games is blurred as never before.

Leading actors, directors, and crews are now working across both the game and movie worlds. Oscar-winning actors are laser-scanned for 3D character models. Oscar-winning lighting, music and sound people retouch their finest work to create a game that improves on the movie.[19] Digital games now average $10 million to produce – and another $10 million to market. Atari's *Enter the Matrix* game, launched in 2003, reportedly cost over $20 million in production alone.[20] However, it sold one million copies in its first 18 days of release, 2.5 million over the first six weeks, and eventually five million copies.[21] The Activision game *Spider-Man 3* cost over $45 million in development alone.

In early 2005, Microsoft announced that it would self-produce the movie version of its *Halo* game franchise (which had already grossed $600 million as games) rather than entrusting the job to Hollywood.[22] Global sales of *Halo* 2, for Microsoft's Xbox, reached $125 million in its first day – better than *The Incredibles* movie from Pixar did in its entire first weekend.[23]

The big difference between this new Hollywood of games and the old Hollywood of cinema is interaction. Whereas viewing motion pictures is pretty much a passive experience, today's games are far from passive. While movies are lean-back, games are very definitely lean-forward experiences. The gamer interacts constantly with the game, and is in many cases totally responsible for the development of the storyline and the outcome of the game. This ability of digital games to involve, immerse and actively engage participants makes them a vital channel for the marketer. Yet marketing in games lags far behind games' importance in players' lives. In-game advertising was estimated to account for less than 1% of total ad spend in 2006.[24] This will undoubtedly change as DigiMarketers come to recognize what a massive and important platform digital games really are.

DIGIMARKETING BEST PRACTICES

Try Something Simple First

Although virtual worlds may be cool, technically complex, visually effective, absorbing and immersive, it doesn't follow that they are right for your brands. Casual games reach a wider, and older, demographic; their players are just as dedicated – and generally considered to be more accepting of advertising intrusion.

Ads in casual games are probably the closest to traditional media of any in-game marketing. This makes it a good place for the DigiMarketer to start. Brand logos can be placed within the context of a casual game, and can remain on screen throughout the game. The size and position of the ad can blend in with the game environment. For example, Degree antiperspirant sponsors a free online *Texas hold 'em* game on MSN Games (www.games.msn.com). In return Degree gets on-screen ads, and the Degree for Men logo prominently displayed on the game table and card backs.

Most casual games are downloaded or played online. This means the user has a live internet connection and the ad can be clickable, pausing the game and opening the advertiser's website. Video ads can be run at the game's start and end, and at natural game breaks (during re-sets, or level changes), minimizing intrusion and disruption.

Make Sure the Marketing Improves the Game

Games are highly involving experiences. The marketing needs to build upon that environment, not disrupt it. At the moment, most gamers are encouraging marketing. But their permission is conditional. Once marketing intrudes too much, once it breaks the game's spell, the gamer will take steps to cut that marketing out. As with all DigiMarketing, that customer is in control and the marketing must strictly be in non-interrupt mode.

Consider In-game Placements, Sponsorships, Licensing and Static Display Ads

These are probably the simplest and most prevalent forms of advertising within games at the moment.[25] This marketing simply treats games like movies or popular television shows. In-game placement carries all the values of movie placement (that is, awareness, brand building, capturing the brand values of the game to your product, and so on) with the advantage that in the game the consumer actually interacts with the product in an active, involved – and potentially meaningful – way, over a prolonged period.

Games also allow marketers to showcase the real benefits of their products, often in ways which might not be appropriate in television advertising. A car in a simulation can be driven at high speeds, and can give the "driver" a real experience of its performance – performance that can't even be alluded to in ads. Volvo worked with Microsoft to feature the S40 in the Xbox *Rallisport Challenge* 2 game. The vehicle fits the game and enables participants to experience its performance literally (well, almost) hands on.

The key is to make sure the placement makes sense for the game. Don't choose to place in games, choose the game in which to advertise. Fit is vital, both with the game and with the gamer. It won't work well if the placement isn't relevant to the game and to the brand. A good placement fits seamlessly into the game – and actually improves the gaming experience – while exposing the brand in a suitable context, and allowing the gamer to interact meaningfully with it, in a way that reveals true brand benefits. Often this is accomplished by demonstrating the brand's impact on a character in the game.

For example, when *The Sims* characters consume McDonald's products, they gain nutritional points. The Adidas Hyperride shoe is featured in a handheld PlayStation Portable game called *Freerunning* (freerunning is a sort of obstacle course jogging). The Hyperride shoes actually improve players' in-game performance.[26]

The product can also promote the game. Volvo S40 ads show nothing but footage from the Rallisport game. The music-based games *Frequency* and *Amplitude* were very innovative in their play and both featured popular recording artists. Later, the promotion went the other way when the band P.O.D. included a scaled-down version of the game bundled with its latest record release.[27]

Consider Micro-Sponsorships Too

In a virtual world, DigiMarketers can even sponsor individual items used by individual gamers – corporate-sponsored micro-transactions. If a player wants new gear for his or her avatar, he or she could send a message to the brand's avatar and ask if the brand would fund it that new avatar outfit. Whether the player got their free stuff might depend on a quiz, or on real-world purchases, or on a real-world loyalty or referral program. These sort of creative arrangements have the potential to create highly positive, brand-centered interchanges with customers, on a very personal, individual basis.

Try Licensing Your Brand to a Game

Brand licensing makes a lot of sense, provided the brand identity fits the game. So Ferrari has licensed its brand to System 3's racing games. Static in-game display ads can build awareness and allow transfer of game values to the brand itself, and can be stepping stones to more dynamic interactive ads that really exploit the strengths of this digital channel.

Reach Gamers Through Game-Related Sites

The Unilever brand, Axe, is a deodorant body spray positioned as a lifestyle product with a seductive fragrance that increases men's luck with the ladies. The brand needed to reach the increasingly elusive 18- to 24-year-old male market. Therefore, Axe designed a promotion around a series of "amateur" films involving two young men, Evan and Gareth, touring America and writing the book on "getting the girl."

Axe used the games site www.xfire.com to distribute and promote the videos. Xfire is a free tool that makes it easier for gamers to find and play online games with their friends, locate patches and updates, and chat live in-game. The site claims a community of 2.5 million gamers worldwide, playing almost 200 person-years of gaming every day on the site!

Reportedly, Xfire drove a significantly higher number of downloads than the other channels that were also contracted to host the videos; 51% of the Xfire's audience stated an intention to purchase an Axe product. And when asked, "Do you think Axe will help you get the girl?," 38.7% of Xfire users were certain it would.

Consider the Opportunities of MMOGs, and be Willing to Experiment in Order to Stand Out

These are probably the cutting edge for DigiMarketing at the moment. An intensely immersive, massively involving, emerging vehicle whose rules we are only just starting to grasp. It seems possible however that as people spend more time in virtual worlds, that they will want to better integrate their presence in such worlds into their real lives. So over time we can expect to see the real world and metaverse blending, and key elements of the environments – friends, pastimes, even brands – mingling together; what has been called the *gravity of reality*.[28]

As one of the blogs devoted to *Second Life* puts it, "What if the real world came in, and no one really noticed?"[29] And this is largely what has happened. At present, real-world companies and organizations are having very little impact on *Second Life* as a whole. Branded sites associated with real-world companies are as yet not figuring among the most popular locations. Nissan in *Second Life* has a set of connected islands, a race courses, auto-stunts and a multi-storey vending machine that delivers free cars. But the Need 4 Speed dealership, where you can configure your own fantasy car, developed by a *Second Life* resident amateur, attracts more visitors.

Remember that for the participants, MMOGs are superior worlds. The game worlds are not the real world, they are beyond our grey reality. Remember that's why people go to them: to escape! It's not clear that participants will really want to play at shopping in the mall! So the real-world communication may not fit well. A recent survey reported that 70% of *Second Life* residents were disappointed with the marketing they saw in their metaverse. It was seen as too traditional (billboards and all); too much linear extensions of existing real-world marketing.

Maintain and Build Upon Your In-Game Presence

The same survey found that marketing efforts tended to be launched with over-hyped fanfare, and then all but abandoned – very frustrating for residents looking for interaction. Almost half of the respondents were skeptical as to whether these brands would ever return to their stores and sites.

To build the brand you need to be around for the long term; to treat the MMOG as a world in its own right – a world that will need an annual plan, where your brand is expected to give back, to contribute to the community.

Involve Participants in Collaboration for Your Brand

Virtual worlds are at heart a collaboration between creator and customer – for example, *Second Life* is a customer-created world. If marketers are to create exciting experiences and involve their brand in the world, they need to allow an interactive collaboration, which weaves the brand into the world. Just sticking a billboard on a thoroughfare invites passers-by to collaborate by defacing the billboard! Which is a fine interaction only if that's what the marketer intended.

Try Not to Offend Metaverse "Residents"

Take some time to acclimatize to how residents behave and what annoys them. Real-world companies claiming to be the first PR agency, or the first radio station, when other similar activities have long been available in these metaverses are doomed to annoy the natives – who presumably are why the DigiMarketers are there in the first place!

Take Your Community With You

One approach is to build a space within a virtual world and take your existing community to it. In *Second Life*, many companies are buying their own islands to use for corporate training, meetings, and so on, as a more exciting, more social, more open way (with no travel costs) to do what they are already doing. These brand islands become adverworlds.

IBM is one of the biggest "land" owners in *Second Life* with at least 24 islands, each of 16 acres. The company uses this land to facilitate real-world activities.[30] In November 2006, 2,000 IBM employees met in Beijing, while another 5,000 watched by webcast. CEO Sam Palmisano logged onto *Second Life*, and sent his avatar to attend a virtual IBM meeting attended by IBMers from around the world.

By early January 2007, more than 3,000 IBM employees had *Second Life* avatars, and about 300 were routinely conducting company business inside the "game." Palmisano calls 3D worlds such as *Second Life* the "next phase of the Internet's evolution" and says they may have "the same level of impact" as the first web explosion. After meetings in *Second Life*, participants often gather and mingle to chat informally. They form the water cooler networks and bonds just like in real life, but closer and faster.

Make Sure it's Measurable…and Test, Test, Test

Online games have the potential for sophisticated performance metrics that can capture just how the gamer interacts with the marketing and even develop ROI measures. It also offers the potential for real-time testing and refinement.

What's more, the virtual world environment may give you insights into participants' real-world dreams and fantasies. After all, the virtual world is a graphic illustration of your customers' fantasies. Look at how your products are being used, and adapted; where your brand appears already, and in conjunction with what. Apparel and furniture manufacturers are already using virtual-world creations as models for real-world products.

Consider the Game Rating

Nielsen already have a rating system – GamePlay Metrics – to monitor video game consoles, and record which games are played, along with player demographics, internet behavior, and so on. The video game rating system is also intended to offer insight into what television and internet trends the players follow. The ratings are aimed at both the game industry and the game advertisers, who are seeking data on how to pinpoint their audiences and assess the best game vehicles.

Don't Forget to Register any URLs You Mention in the Game

In Tom Clancy's *Rainbow Six* 3 game, at a certain level a URL appears written in large letters across a wall. However, the game's developers never got around to registering the address, and apparently forgot about it when the game was released. Shortly after, an Xbox player noticed the URL, registered it, and loaded it up with links to hardcore pornography. Let that be a lesson for you.

FUTURE TRENDS – WHERE IT'S HEADING

The future of games will be a continuation of the core trends we've just reviewed. In particular, as the connectivity of games increases – with even more immersive participation as a result – DigiMarketing will shift from primarily brand presence and sponsorship into more diverse and embedded virtual-realities marketing and sales strategies (as shown in Figure 7.2). These three issues will define the gamesphere of the future:

Games Trend 1: 24 x 7 connectivity

Games Trend 2: Immersion leads to parallel lives

Games Trend 3: Virtual realities marketing

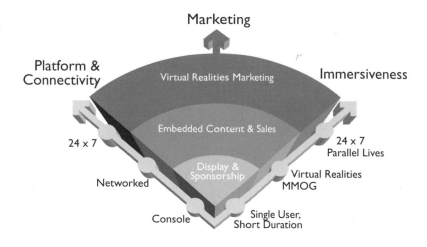

Figure 7.2: Roadmap of Games in the Future

Games Trend 1: 24 x 7 Connectivity

The gaming experience of today is increasingly connected via networked games. However, that connection will go into overdrive in future years. As all games reside on the internet, the physics of involvement will continue to change dramatically. Games are merely one component of a massive digital lifestyle trend. So, the effects of Web 2.0 and 3.0 will impact upon the way people treat games too. In particular, the power of agent activity (via avatars) will shape future game playing.

Already MMOGs run 24 hours a day, with different people joining at various points to participate. Whether it is to beat all those others, or (as is increasingly the case) to simply interact with all those others, social context becomes the reason for playing the game. Heavy gamers may spend well in excess of 40 hours per week. However, this desire to stay connected is likely to extend beyond the time an individual spends personally in the game. This will happen as avatars follow instructions to continue playing, even when the "real" participant is asleep or engaged in activities.

Participants will also choose to stay constantly connected to an MMOG or parallel reality (such as *Second Life*) through both fixed line and wireless connections. Wireless connectivity will allow a participant to play from home, then seamlessly continue to participate as they head outdoors, ride on a train, or sit in the doctor's reception area.

Games Trend 2: Immersion Leads to Parallel Virtual Lives

This constant connectivity is immersing consumers in MMOGs not just as games, but rather as persistent, 24 x 7 parallel universes – what their proponents call *metaverses*.[31] There are some critical aspects to these metaverses that need to be well understood by any aspiring DigiMarketer.

First, virtual may mean escapist, but it doesn't mean unreal or unimportant. The enthralling, absorbing reality of the game players' virtual world is one of the big attractions for marketers. Game players don't leave the room part-way through the game! In fact, it's the reverse: they will do all they can to remain in the game. And the chief reason is that they derive pleasure and validation for their "successes" in these metaverses, just as they experience pleasure and success in their physical world.

Second, although non-participants may regard these virtual worlds as shallow, 2-dimensional representations of the real world, participants in metaverses often consider them an *enhanced* version of reality! MMOGs provide realms in which one's avatars have special powers above and beyond the normal physical world. Plus, as Philip Rosedale (an MMOG pioneer) has speculated, the artificial barrier of the computer screen actually enhances the communication process rather than hinders it.[32] Within these worlds, avatars are willing to interact with strangers in a way that they would not in real life – a manifestation of the "intimate stranger" syndrome. This makes MMOGs one of the most vital of the new social networking environments.

Third, those who enter these virtual worlds willingly suspend disbelief and enter into a mutually agreed pretence, but participants are not simply blowing up dragons or killing cops – they are buying and selling virtual real estate, building virtual homes, buying virtual fashion, and even making virtual friends. In these worlds, virtual spouses even spy on each other. Corporate espionage is a problem too: rivals place bugs in each others' offices. Essentially, all the human motivations – both good and bad – of the physical world are now present in these metaverses.

We should note that there is an increasing societal toll of metaverses in the form of "video game addiction." The problem is so acute in places such as Korea that game addiction counseling centers are springing up as a result. In 2005, the Chinese government imposed limits on the hours each day that students could play MMOGs. This was in response to a group of *World of Warcraft* players committing mass suicide! However, this was a bloodless protest because it took place within the game; the players' digital manifestations (their avatars) martyred themselves. Wired magazine called them "virtual suicides in response to a crackdown in a virtual universe," and went on to point out that "virtual isn't the same as unreal."[33] The irony, of course, is that the increasing attention metaverses are receiving, and even the problems of game addiction, are further signs of the real power and relevancy of metaverses, making them all the more appealing to DigiMarketers.

Games Trend 3: Virtual Realities Marketing

The big question for DigiMarketers is what they should do in these immersive, constantly connected metaverses. There is no right answer. However, there are some trends we see today that, when projected into the future, provide some guideposts. The big implication of these guideposts is that marketers will need to think beyond a few tactics; instead, they will need to have well-rounded brand-building and sales plans within these virtual worlds. Here are some of the likely key features of virtual realities marketing:

All in-game signage becomes clickable: Signage and billboards of all types has become a standard fixture in games, particularly in sports simulation games. Interestingly, sports simulation gamers generally accept in-game ads as making the overall game experience more realistic[34]; 37% of heavy gamers – playing at least 16 hours a week – and 27% of medium gamers – playing less than 11 hours a week – agree that featuring actual products or companies in games increases realism.[35] The developers of games also welcome ads as an important source of additional revenue.

However, in-game signage is no longer about just brand visibility. Once the game is connected to the internet, those banners and billboards become clickable. Now marketers have some interesting options. For example, the billboard advertisement for pizza in the game can be linked to the local pizza store, allowing the gamer to order online without disturbing their play. In addition, marketing can be aimed at consumption within the game environment, where participants do virtual ordering and then receive physical world delivery of goods.

In-game incentives and information: The pizza example just mentioned could lead consumers to a purchase. However, equally, clicking on the branded signage could lead to information, promotional videos, incentives or coupons – all aimed at stimulating real-world activity and sales. All forms of in-game brand signage can potentially be used as a direct response vehicle for a brand. The issue, as always, is whether the interaction proves too disruptive to the game environment to be successful with participants.

In-game advertising and video: One trend that doesn't appear too disruptive in metaverses is the use of in-game advertising, such as showing commercials on participants' virtual televisions in their homes in *Second Life*. Just as branded billboards around sports stadiums make a sports simulation game more realistic, so too does the inclusion of advertising in virtual worlds. Virtual advertising is becoming more inventive and morphing into new forms. For example, we are already seeing videos – many ad-supported – being created within the virtual worlds using the graphics engines from games. There's even a name for it, *machinima*. Some of the early efforts (for example, *Zinwrath*, and: *Illegal Danish Super Snacks*) have been viewed millions of times. This trend provides an interesting choice for DigiMarketers between creating videos reflecting activities in the "real" physical world or potentially focusing instead on reinforcing the in-game environment.

In-game shops: Another development that parallels the physical world is the establishment of real-world businesses in virtual realities. Famous brands are now regular fixtures in metaverses, so it's not unusual for game participants to stop by a virtual Coke machine or check out the latest IBM products in a virtual shop.

More real-world companies are establishing in-game storefronts in order to leverage a virtual-world presence to improve their real-world brand preference. This is not limited to companies simply selling goods; the service industry is blossoming online too. Real-world banks, movie makers, even advertising agencies are increasingly playing a virtual world role. However, they have competition. Metaverse entrepreneurs are cropping up in a number of businesses. Their focus is not on leveraging the virtual world back to the physical world. Instead, they seek to take advantage of new business models such as virtual item sales. These sales – conducted for real money – are now so high that so-called gold farmers, many in China, have full-time jobs creating in-game artifacts, or accumulating in-game skills/scores which can then be sold to other gamers. The first metaverse millionaire – who made one million real US dollars – is a virtual real estate agent from China.

In-game sales, endorsements, and promotions: The issue of in-game sales is an interesting one that deserves any DigiMarketer's consideration. Even if you don't have an interest in selling virtual goods, you will still want to think about how product trials and sales in virtual realities could impact your real-world business. This is because in-world shopping can be highly social and can provide you with exposure to potential new customers. Of course, the bystanders in an in-world product trial are avatars, but there is still a heavily social element since avatars frequently comment on each others' purchase decisions. In fact, personal connections between in-world avatars (the virtual world manifestations chosen by players) form far more rapidly than relationships in the real world between the players themselves.

This leads to a second issue that merits consideration – creating virtual realities influence. Marketers will increasingly seek to build influence and exposure in virtual realities. Consequently, more real-world marketing tactics will be replicated in virtual worlds. Virtual promotions, virtual product launches, even virtual endorsements will become the norm. Given the role of avatars, a virtual version of Richard Branson can be constantly scouring the virtual landscape promoting Virgin products, even attending virtual events. The mind boggles!

Virtual and physical world links: "Today, virtual worlds are where video and VCRs were in the early 1980s, or where the web was in 1993," says IBM Vice President for Technical Strategy Wladawsky-Berger.[36] So, over the next several years, there are likely to be a number of developments that marketers can't even foresee. There are already plans to link virtual worlds, and replicate all the marketing infrastructure of the real world across these virtual manifestations. Over time, it may well be that different MMOGs confederate and interact, just as the nations on earth interact for global trade. This will make having a coherent virtual realities marketing plan an utter necessity.

Second Life

Second Life, created by Linden Labs, is probably the purest version of a digital world as of 2007. *Second Life* provides a brightly colored, 3D world that resembles *Grand Theft Auto* crossed with *Lord of the Rings*, all completely created by users. Users' create their own bodies (avatars) and meet people in wildly varying contexts. Text chat was the original interaction, with voice conversation introduced in mid-2007.[37]

Consider the following about *Second Life*:

- It has its own currency (the Linden), that is exchangeable in the real world against the US dollar.

- By September 2007, spending in the metaverse already exceeded $1 million per day (that's real, well as real as they are, US dollars).
- It has almost 10 million residents as of September 2007 (that is, real people who have opened accounts and operated an avatar at the site); up from about 20,000 in 2005, and 1 million in October 2006.
- 1.5 million of those residents visited within the past 60 days.
- At least one *Second Life* resident is already a dollar millionaire, employing 20 people in the PRC building things and improving the "land" they own.
- Over 60 companies, employing about 350 people, are operating inside *Second Life* to serve real-world customers working on projects worth at least $10 million.[38]
- It has learning centers set up by universities and non-profits to take advantage of the dispersed learning environment.
- It was the launch market for Calvin Klein ck N2U perfume (unfortunately no avatar can experience the product – the metaverse has no smells).
- There is an interactive *Second Life* mall (AOL Pointe) created by AOL, where visitors can shop for clothes for their avatars, watch videos, skateboard, and so on; AOL sees this as the next step towards a 3D web, and an important learning exercise.[39]

Second Life has its own addresses (like the web's URLs) called SLURLs. These are clickable hyperlinks that take the user right into *Second Life* (provided they already have a *Second Life* account), teleporting to the advertiser's chosen location. As one commentator puts it, "Instead of just going to another web-page, when you click one, you dive into the Net."

Some industry observers think that *Second Life* is the new Microsoft, with the same ability to spawn new businesses: "In two years I think *Second Life* will be huge, probably as large as the entire gaming community is today."[40] When Toyota Motor Corp wanted to market their Scion to young buyers, they hired Millions of Us (a *Second Life* design company) to build Scion City — a futuristic island, with a car dealership selling Toyota Scions, and a racetrack where the avatars can try them out! It took about 10 weeks to build Scion City — and reputedly about $100,000 with $10,000 per month upkeep. Although the reach is not that of a website, the quality — and duration — of the brand interaction is probably much higher.[41]

SUMMARY: GAMES

- Games represent one of the newest new media for marketers.
- Games are a new media that is simultaneously a new marketplace. As we have seen, the virtual realities of the metaverses are venues not only for advertising and brand-building but for selling items for in-metaverse consumption.
- As more consumers routinely switch between virtual reality and real reality, the worlds will collide. The boundaries between the physical world and the metaverse will blur.
- Every DigiMarketer will need brand-building strategies that are integrated across metaverses and game platforms.

END NOTES

1 www.businessweek.com/magazine/content/05_09/b3922094.htm?chan=search
2 www.theesa.com/facts/top_10_facts.php
3 The original *The Sims* base game has sold over six million copies. The
   entire Sims franchise of games sold over 70 million units worldwide as of
   January 2007. See "Why There are no Indie Video Games," Luke O'Brien, *Slate
   Magazine*, www.slate.com/id/2142453/
4 "Video games: Hollywood's New Art," *Special Reports, Guardian Unlimited*.
   www.guardian.co.uk/computergames/story/0,11500,1515016,00.html#article_
   continue
5 news.yahoo.com/s/zd/20070306/tc_zd/202426
6 www.nintendo.com/gamemini?gameid=Y9QLGBWxkmRRzsQEQtvqGqZ63_CjS9F
7 blogs.zdnet.com/ITFacts/?p=12367
8 *ibid*.
9 "Game Wars", www.businessweek.com/print/magazine/content/05_09/b3922094.
   htm?chan=gl
10 www.theesa.com/facts/sales_genre_data.php
11 news.com.com/Casual+games+get+serious+-+page+2/2100-1043_3-60714652.
   html?tag=st.num
12 As of February 2007, www.nytimes.com/2007/03/30/arts/30seni.html
13 *ibid*.
14 news.digitaltrends.com/talkback172.html
15 In its first five months, the game was reportedly played for up to 2.5 hours on
   averge about 6 million times, www.kewlbox.com/news/news.aspx?NewsId=28
16 www.imediaconnection.com/content/11088.asp
17 Paul Hemp, "Avatar Based Marketing", June 2006, *Harvard Business Review*.
18 www.nytimes.com/2005/12/09/technology/09gaming.html?ex=1291784400&en=a
   723d0f8592dff2e&ei=5090
19 www.guardian.co.uk/computergames/story/0,11500,1515016,00.html#article_
   continue
20 "Video Game Makers Go Hollywood. Uh-Oh." www.nytimes.com/2004/08/22/
   technology/22games.html?ex=1250913600&en=ecbfdd1fb0465b49&ei=5088&
   partner=rssnyt
21 www.gamesindustry.biz/content_page.php?section_name=pub&aid=3409
22 "Game Wars", www.businessweek.com/print/magazine/content/05_09/b3922094.
   htm?chan=gl
23 *ibid*.
24 "3D Video Game Insertions Raise the Bar on Recall", www.clickz.com/showPage.
   html?page=3553106
25 www.igaworldwide.com
26 www.brandrepublic.com/News/233650/
27 www.gamespot.com/ps2/puzzle/amplitude/news.html?sid=6091835
28 Attributed to *Second Life* avatar SNOOPYbrown Zamboni, aka Jerry Paffendorf
29 nwn.blogs.com/nwn/2006/10/why_mixed_reali.html
30 *ibid*.
31 A word coined by Neal Stephenson in his 1992 novel, *Snow Crash*.
32 Counterterrorism Blog: MetaTerror: The Potential Use of MMORPGs by
   Terrorists, counterterrorismblog.org/2007/03/metaterror_the_potential_use
   o.php
33 www.wired.com/wired/archive/14.04/law_pr.html
34 "In-game Ads Work, Study Says", CNET News.com, news.com.com/In-game+ads
   +work%2C+study+says/2100-1043_3-5887880.html
35 www.wired.com/gaming/gamingreviews/news/2006/10/71899
36 "It's Not a Game", February 5, 2007.money.cnn.com/magazines/fortune/fortune_
   archive/2007/02/05/8399120/
37 blogs.zdnet.com/social/?p=269
38 "It's Not a Game", February 5, 2007.money.cnn.com/magazines/fortune/fortune_
   archive/2007/02/05/8399120/
39 "*Second Life*: Virtual Stores, Real Customers", Innovation, MSNBC.com,
   www.msnbc.msn.com/id/17284628/
40 Mark Anderson, author of the *Strategic News Service* newsletter.
41 "*Second Life*: Virtual Stores, Real Customers", Innovation, MSNBC.com,
   www.msnbc.msn.com/id/17284628/

Chapter 8

Consumer-Created Content

T he common refrain in digital circles these days is that the "consumer is in control." Given the amount of power in consumers' hands (or on their desktops), it's hard to argue with this. We have moved rapidly beyond the time when people would simply view or access material. The web has gone beyond its role as library. Instead, consumers have started writing in the library books…and not just writing, but posting photos, videos, and recordings!

Today, consumers want to – and do – modify, edit, and change existing material as well as create a wide variety of their own material. As we saw in chapter 3, this is an integral part of Web 2.0, and it's having a profound impact on marketers today. It's also one of the key issues you will have to think through as you put together your own digital plans. How comfortable are you with giving consumers control?

Actually, it doesn't matter too much how comfortable you are. If you don't give consumers control, they will simply take it – as the programmer, using personal video recorders (such as Tivo) to time shift, or as creators, actually generating their own content by webcasting, podcasting, and videocasting. However, marketers can also harness consumers' creativity to mutual advantage. This new world of consumer content and "consumers in control" is the phenomenon we address in this chapter.

KEY TRENDS YOU MUST KNOW

Some have called it consumer-generated media, online buzz, and online word-of-mouth, but we prefer consumer-created content (ccc) to reflect the fact that the content goes well beyond conventional media, and well beyond conventional word-of-mouth. Some talk not of consumers but of *prosumers*: producers *and* consumers. At a minimum, it's important to recognize consumers today as participants not passive targets. The following are the key issues that have been driving the growth of ccc:

CCC *Driver* 1: Revolution of the media model
CCC *Driver* 2: Explosion of formats
CCC *Driver* 3: Social networks provide the platform
CCC *Driver* 4: Turbo-charged word-of-mouth

CCC Driver 1: Revolution of the Media Model

In *The Cathedral and the Bazaar* (first an essay and later a book by Eric S. Raymond[1]), the author contrasted the cathedral of conventional software development with the bazaar of the open source movement. In the cathedral, the few – skilled and wise – work quietly and reverently to build the perfect edifice. In the bazaar, the masses babble away at solving their own specific problems and somehow the whole confusing bazaar works – the market clears. Each works at what is important to him or her, and by doing so helps others solve their problems.

Although originally focused on software, the analogy also describes the changes in media creation.[2] Historically, media content was developed by relatively few creators. The content they created was filtered and edited by publishers. Publishers then distributed their publications through a network of outlets: bookstores, news stands, movie theaters, television, radio stations, and so on. To become a publisher took access to considerable capital. Those printing presses, television broadcast stations and movie studios were expensive. The masses were passive receivers of media content, which they generally paid for in cash or by exposure to advertising. Most of the money generated by the media went to pay for the distribution network, and the publishers and their editing. A small amount trickled back to the creators.

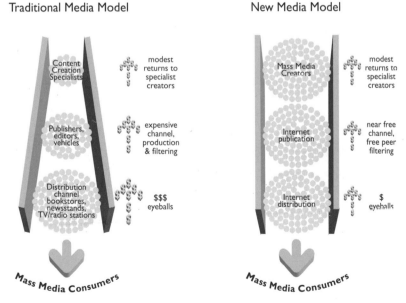

Figure 8.1: Change of Media Models

In contrast, the internet makes a different publication model very feasible (as shown in Figure 8.1). In the bazaar model, everyone can be a creator. The cost of becoming a creator is close to zero. And creators have direct, almost free access to publication vehicles via the web. Plus, web-based communication is instantaneous and global; anyone with an internet connection can access YouTube (if it hasn't been censored where they live!), or can access Flickr, where they can post their videos or pictures respectively. Notice there is almost no filtering or editing of content, though some sites (like YouTube) may have an option for users to flag content as offensive. Rather than the funnel of conventional publication, we have the unfettered tube of the internet (see diagram).

Wired magazine called it "The Age of Peer Production"[3], identifying "people power" as the number one trend driving the global economy. Just as the printing press revolutionized publishing over 550 years ago, so the latest breakthrough – amateurs doing it on their own – is revolutionizing media now. According to Cisco CEO John Chambers, 2007 marks the first time that consumer internet traffic will surpass business internet traffic.[4] This is due to the tremendous explosion in consumer-created content.

Even *Time* magazine – never renowned for being on the cutting edge – declared that the Person of the Year 2006 is *you*. It was awarded for "community and collaboration on a scale never seen before," and the "many wresting power from the few and helping one another for nothing."[5]

In early 2007, Jupiter Research reported that 75% of internet users aged 18 to 25 were using (reading or writing) online content of some sort, and almost half had done so in the last month. Nor is this solely the province of the young: one-third of those over 55 years old had participated in consumer-created content.[6]

CCC Driver 2: Explosion of Formats

One of the reasons ccc (consumer-created content) has grown at such a tremendous rate is the variety of formats within which consumers can express themselves. Figure 8.2 gives an overview of the most common formats consumers use today.

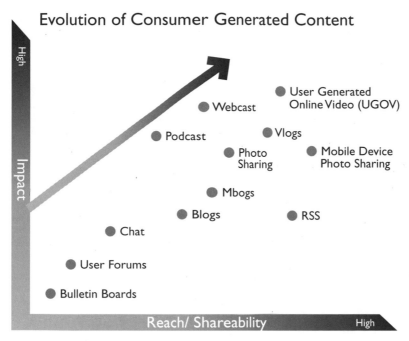

Figure 8.2: Most Common Formats Consumers Use Today

Text postings: Consumer-created content was a key feature even of the internet's precursors (notably CompuServe, later acquired by AOL). Consumers created text, and sometimes pictures and files, to post on discussion boards, forums and Usenet newsgroups. These were, and are, often industry or interest specific. Most social networking sites include extensive message boards. Most product categories have several websites associated with them, devoted to candid consumer reviews and reports. Many brands have bulletin boards run by their supporters – and their detractors.

Most corporate websites include feedback opportunities, and as many as 70% of consumers who post to corporate sites also post to other sites. Complaints on your corporate site give you a chance to stem problems quickly before they escape to wider, harder to monitor, platforms. There are many third-party sites, designed to collect complaints, reviews and customer feedback.

Wikis: A wiki is a website that allows visitors to add and edit content, and has become the basic tool for mass collaborative authoring. The word *wiki* comes from Hawaiian for *quick*.[7] Initially many felt that wikis were too susceptible to vandalism, deliberately introduced errors, and other disruptions: known as *trolling* in the online community. However, for most wikis there is a system of registration and a waiting period before it is possible to generate content. Wikis were an early driver of consumer-created content, getting opinion leaders accustomed to participating through wikis.

The best known wiki is Wikipedia (www.wikipedia.org), an online encyclopedia which was initially completely based on volunteer efforts by the general public. Although sometimes accused of a populist bent – the entry on the Flintstones is twice as long as the entry on Homer[8] (that's the Greek Homer, not Homer Simpson, who has a reasonably long entry) – Wikipedia has developed an editorial hierarchy based on the number and quality of contributions made.

In late 2005, the journal *Nature* sampled scientific entries and declared that Wikipedia was about as accurate as the *Encyclopedia Britannica*.[9] It was soon pointed out that as the Wikipedia sample entries were about 2.6 times longer than *Encyclopedia Britannica's*, that gave Wikipedia a lower percentage error rate![10]

By 2007, Wikipedia was the number one educational reference website in the US with an over 26% share of visits for the category. Wikipedia was visited some 3,400 times more that Encarta (www.encarta.msn.com), Microsoft's encyclopedia.[11] The English language version is in the top 10 sites worldwide by traffic.

Blogs: Blogs have mushroomed as free software, and hosting, allowing anyone to set up a professional-looking blog. About 40% of web users under 29 read blogs, while 20% actually write and publish their own blogs.[12]

Although a blog was initially intended as a log – an online diary – in fact most are indistinguishable from websites. The vast majority of the blogs currently in existence are operated by private individuals on a hobbyist basis. Some, however, have become highly influential in a range of fields. The success of these blogs has led many companies and other organizations to implement their own blogs (but be careful, and see below under "Flogging").

By 2007, Technorati (www.technorati.com) – originally a search site for blogs, now monitoring almost all consumer-created content – was already tracking over 95 million blogs (and 250 million pieces of tagged social media[13]). Technorati adds over 175,000 new blogs every day, and a total of about 1.6 million new posts daily. Although only about 20% of bloggers are active, blogs now make up 22% of the top 100 websites, with some evidence that readers often don't know that they are reading a blog.[14]

Blogs really are a global phenomenon, with over a third written in Japanese, the most popular blog language. Blogs provide an efficient way to get at the extremities of the long-tail; there are blogs on esoteric topics from cut-glass chandeliers (www.chandeliers-info.com, sponsored by an online chandelier store), through to weird things for auction online (www.weirdonlineauctions.blogspot.com), and to sources for conspiracy videos (www.conspiracyvideos.blogspot.com).

Splogging: As with so much on the internet, spam follows consumer interest. Splogging is the automated posting of comments on blogs – comments which are often totally unrelated to the blog and are intended only to provide links into the spammer's website, in an attempt to boost its search engine rankings. Most blogs now force posters to prove they are not spambots before they can post comments.

This is usually done by asking the user to identify a series of distorted letters and numbers. Those protective codes are called captchas (Completely Automated Public Turing Tests to Tell Computers and Humans Apart). Of course this becomes a disincentive for legitimate posters, and reputedly spammers are hiring people in low-wage countries to enter the captcha codes! Google recently experimented with an audio-based form of human check. But again the bazaar mentality is coming to the rescue with software like Akismet (akismet.com), which first attempts to identify spam and quarantine it, and then uses feedback from blog users to identify spam that has got through, remove it, and improve its filters.

RSS: Real simple syndication, as we've discussed, creates "feeds" of headlines and/or summaries to which internet users can subscribe. Users can see a dropdown list of the headlines (automatically updated) in their browsers, and select which items to read further. Services such as the Australian developed Particls (www.particls.com)[15] even provide RSS feeds as scrolling tickers in the browser, with a prototype smart agent selecting items that should interest the user.

Photo sharing: This enables consumers to post and share photos with selected groups, or with the world. It is also possible to "tag" photos, one's own or those of others, to make them easier to search. Tagging and folksonomies are discussed below. Most photo sharing sites are free, being either advertising supported (Flickr, Twango, Ringo, and others) or online photo finishing sites where the photo sharing is aimed at selling prints or merchandize bearing the photos.

One of the first demonstrations of the power of consumer-generated video was iPod's Dirty Little Secret (see Box Insert).

　　　　　　　　　　　　　　Digital Channels

Revenue models for sites housing user-generated video have yet to solidify. But it seems likely that advertising will eventually provide the needed revenue support for the vlog posters, with pre- or post-roll ads, or sponsored video players, or ads alongside the player. A few sites are already generating advertising-driven revenue streams (Rocketboom, www. rocketboom.com, claimed to generate $250,000 in 2006). In early 2007, YouTube announced that it would put some of its most popular independent creators on a par with its media partners like CBS.[17]

iPod's Dirty Secret

In late 2003, Casey Neistat found that his iPod battery could no longer hold its charge. The Apple store told him they didn't do battery replacements, and that it would be better to buy a new iPod. Casey called the Apple Care 800 number and was told the same thing. So he mailed his iPod to Steve Jobs, and was phoned with the same message again: no battery replacements.

Casey bought a third-party replacement battery and the iPod failed completely. So he and his brother made a short video of their experience and posted it on the internet. Within six weeks the video had been downloaded over 1 million times.[16] Within days Apple announced expanded warranties for new iPod owners and a mail-in battery replacement service. This didn't stop the print media from picking up the story and using it as a hook on which to hang an analysis of iPod margins.

And by the way the video is still there (www. ipodsdirtysecret.com). And if you do a Google search for "iPod battery" it will still show up. The web has a long, long memory.

Moblogs: These are mobile-enabled blogs that allow users to easily post photos and video (easier to post than text!) from mobile phones – turning the world into an army of roaming reporters. Some call it mobile vlogging, which uses the mobile device to take video and upload it to a website, a one-click procedure with many mobile devices.

Overall, it's important to recognize that blogging is moving in two directions simultaneously. On the one hand, blogs are becoming more elaborate through video and other enhancements. At the same time, they are becoming simpler. Twitter.com, for example, consists of one- or two-sentence blogs from time-starved participants – mostly using mobile devices – who still wish to have a say.

Webcasting: A webcast distributes sound, or sound and visuals, over the internet using streaming media technology. Essentially, webcasting is broadcasting over the internet. Almost all major broadcasters from the non-digital world now have their own webcasts (BBC, CNN, Al Jazeera, and so on), as do many small organizations and private individuals. Webcasts are usually streamed (that is, delivered continuously rather than as downloadable files), making recording more difficult and offering some degree of intellectual property protection.

Podcasts and video podcasts: This is transfering audio, and video, via files which can be downloaded. Although the name refers to playback on a portable player (perhaps an iPod[18]), in practice podcasts are often played on a computer. Typically users choose the podcast they want to hear and subscribe to it, automatically receiving regular updates. iTunes maintains a top 100 list of podcasters, with top-ranked podcasts exceeding 150,000 downloads a week. Video podcasts are sometimes called *vodcasts*.

Machinima (muh-sheen-eh-mah): This is perhaps the cutting edge of consumer-created content. Machinima is created by using the graphic engines of real-time interactive games to make movies! That's making movies within the real-time, 3D, virtual world of the game – using only the tools and resources available within the game. It is the latest example of emergent game play using game tools for purposes for which they were not designed…that is, not just for playing the game.

In many ways machinima[19] epitomizes the digital world: conducting highly involving, highly time-consuming, real-world activities within a virtual world, for enjoyment in the real world. Take a look at www.machinima.com; it's an eye-opener.

CCC Driver 3: Social Networks Provide the Platform

Generally, far more people read than write content. "Visits to media upload ratios" – the percentage of site visitors that actually create (upload) content – are typically small; something like 0.16% for YouTube, 0.2% for Flickr, 4.59% for Wikipedia. The characteristics of content creators vary depending on the site. For example, Wikipedia users aged 35 to 55 are much more likely to be content creators, with the younger users being readers. However, YouTube has a wider creator group aged 25 to 54.

Social networking sites and networked games are different. Both of these require participants to be creators – either by virtue of creating (and perhaps adorning) their own home page or by creating their own avatar and controlling its actions. These socially driven digital watering holes have attracted large audiences who become accustomed to content creation through participating on such sites.

CCC Driver 4: Turbo-Charged Word-of-Mouth

Traditionally word-of-mouth communications moved at a snail's pace, simply from one individual to the next. An individual who happened to be a content creator, or a media celebrity with fame and attention, could transmit one-to-many. Most of us were not in that group. Email and the web changed all that.

Via digital channels, consumers suddenly have a massive platform with tremendous reach. Every user's communication now has the potential to be amplified across the web. And this digital soapbox can be used by brand advocates and brand critics alike. Indeed, digital advocacy in an era of instant information and viral messaging is a power to be reckoned with. Plus, peers have become the new source of influence and authority.

As noted in the example of the Neistat brothers and Apple (Box Insert), consumers today can express very strong opinions via consumer-created content. However, one of the most important ways in which consumers express their opinions is also the most simple: voting. Consumer voting and polling is now a huge growth area. Television shows (for example, *American Idol*, which has been replicated around the world) capitalize on this consumer voting. "Voting" extends naturally to consumer reviews and opinions. As a result, on the web you can find consumer reviews of everything, from books, to cars, to hotels in popular holiday destinations.

DIGIMARKETING BEST PRACTICES

Consider Consumer-Created Content on Your Own Site as well as on Consumer-Created Sites

As well as getting presence on consumer-created content sites, DigiMarketers can expand the consumer-created content on the marketers' own sites. All it takes is a clear consumer-created content strategy. This is a key part of the DigiMarketing planning process, which we will cover in the final section of this book.

Make Sure You are Really, Really Authentic

That's the key to success on consumer-created content sites! The content on these sites is typically a highly targeted labor of love – created by independent, passionate amateurs. If DigiMarketers are to fit in, it's critical they sound authentic and harmonize with the true voices of consumers. The last thing consumers want – on their own sites remember – is a heavy-handed huckster. And yet, all too often that's what marketers give them. There's already a word for it: not blogs and blogging but flogs and flogging (see Boxed Insert).

Flogs and Flogging

Flogs are fake (or flack) blogs created by marketers masquerading as real people! The outcome is also known as *blog backfire*.

Although apparently created by enthusiastic amateurs, these blogs are really corporately financed and scripted. The European Union recently banned flogs, product reviews, and websites created by businesses without revealing their identity on the grounds that businesses are banned from "falsely representing oneself as a consumer."[20] In the US, the FTC reportedly adopted a similar stance.[21]

In 2005, in the UK, Cillit Bang, a range of cleaning products from Reckitt Benckiser, ran a series of television ads starring a fictional pitch man, Barry Scott. The television ads were followed up with a Barry Scott blog campaign. The fictional "Barry" even placed comments on others' blogs: one was appended to a real blogger's description of an emotional family reunion.

Within the same day, the real blogger had identified the source of the comment, and noted that it came from a company owned by a major advertising agency. A general

---

revulsion rippled through the blogging community, the web and the press[22], culminating in a Cillit Bang apology. Scarcely a successful branding relationship.

In December 2006, Sony was caught as the author of a flog (www.alliwantforxmasIsapsp.com). The site purported to be a fansite: a blog run by a teenager trying to help his friend convince family members to buy him a PlayStation Portable for Xmas. Real bloggers suspected the style and voice of the blog. A quick search showed that the site was registered to a marketing company associated with Sony. Sony pulled down the site and its postings…and squandered the most valuable resource of the DigiMarketer: trust.

The digital trail left by postings, and the tone taken by cavalier marketers, makes it almost certain that fake posts will get found out, and generate massive adverse publicity, almost instantaneously. Those generating consumer content seem rather good at spotting the fake from the real thing.

As we have seen, there is a need across all the digital channels for the marketer to accept that they are no longer in full control. This is especially true in the context of consumer-created content. Top-down command and control simply will not work. The marketer risks coming across as crude, impolite, domineering, and simply inappropriate.

The best way to sound authentic is to *be* authentic. Whether it is Levi's stressing the brand's Gold Rush heritage[23], or Dove undermining the beauty makeover culture (see Boxed Insert, "The Campaign for Real Beauty," following), brands that speak from positions of truth automatically sound more authentic.

Back in 1999, *The Cluetrain Manifesto* (www.cluetrain.com), written by experienced marketers, predicted that "in just a few more years, the current homogenized 'voice' of business – the sound of mission statements and brochures – will seem as contrived and artificial as the language of the 18th-century French court."[24] It seems as though that time is already here.

Understand the Nature of the Site, then Create a Dialogue

Successful DigiMarketers take time to understand what is going on the consumer-created content site. Then they carefully match the tone and the topics. Notice that most postings are short and to the point, not verbose ad-speak.

Try to develop a two-way relationship. One major consumer electronic goods manufacturer, having set up sites to house comments on their products, was aghast to find that some users were posting negative comments. The legal department sent out cease and desist warnings, which (of course) the writers immediately posted online, bringing down a firestorm on the brand. More subtle marketers intervened to hold focus groups with the complainants, and develop solutions to their problems.

The best way to create dialogue is to tell – and provide support for – the truth. As with offline PR, if the bloggers are wrong, get your side of the story out fast. Provide high-level contact information and respond promptly to enquiries. Guide, don't try to force.

Remember that most traffic finds consumer-created content via search engines. You can always get your side out by Google AdWords and other paid search ads (see chapter 4). You can even create micro-sites specifically to refute rumors or false information. The DigiMarketer needs to integrate the full range of digital marketing channels.

Consider Consumer Co-Created Content for Your Brand(s)

Early attempts to harness consumer-created content focused on consumers competing to create advertising. In late 2006, Frito-Lay announced a competition to make a Doritos commercial to be screened during the Super Bowl: a slot worth over $2 million. Soon after, Dove drew over 1,000 entries in a competition for consumers to make a Dove Cream Oil moisturizer ad, to be screened on Oscar Night 2007: a $1.7 million slot. These have become known as *viewer created ad messages* (VCAMs).[25]

Right now (late-2007), enabling consumers to create brand commercials seems to be the flavor of the day. And getting the consumer involved in creating advertising content certainly promotes a very high level of customer engagement, builds interaction and helps put the customer in charge. But this isn't necessarily the most meaningful way to engage consumers with your brand, and keeping the brand's focus while unleashing customer creativity is no easy task. If brand control is too strong, consumers will rebel; if it is too weak, the brand message will become diluted and confused.

A different way to involve consumers is to give them an opportunity to create an actual product. An example of this is a Grand Tourismo promotion which encouraged consumers to do their own online detailing of a vehicle. The person who did the best detailing job then won the actual vehicle – detailed as they had created it on the website.

It is vital to keep participation credible. There needs to be a focus on consumer feedback, and it needs to be more pervasive than just creating one ad. Consumer involvement and feedback opportunities need to be seen across the full spread of the brand's activities, with the brand evidencing a sincere desire to listen.[26]

Of course the DigiMarketer can create events which are particularly suitable for consumers to create content around. Late in 2006, Target (the US discount store) suspended a magician above Times Square for two days; almost 20,000 videos of the event were posted on YouTube. The Dove "Campaign for Real Beauty" (see Boxed Insert) is a particularly successful example of creating a platform for authentic, credible feedback.

And the DigiMarketer can create forums to help focus and structure consumer-created content and to provide impartial, unbiased, expert advice to users. See for example the gardening forums presented, very gently, by Miracle Gro (forums.lawncare.com).

The Campaign for Real Beauty

The *Evolution* viral video (showing a model's transition from the ordinary to the billboard sublime based on make-up, hair-styling, and digital retouching) is highly emotional and involving. The video, created by advertising agency Ogilvy & Mather, got a million views on YouTube alone. And remember that views at YouTube itself are the tip of the iceberg. As we saw in chapter 3, the YouTube widget allows the video to be embedded right in consumers' blogs, which is exactly what happened.

Evolution resonated with consumers, and became an authentic part of consumer-created content around the globe[27], even stimulating spoof consumer-generated videos (imitation is the sincerest form of flattery).[28] But the process didn't stop there. The blogs featuring *Evolution* also had comment space, generating another round of consumer-created content: blog readers commenting on the *Evolution* video – and commenting on each others' comments – often with considerable emotional intensity.

The Dove "Campaign for Real Beauty" also extended consumer-created content to its website, with a Share Your Views section.[29] The campaign even used digital billboards to tally consumers voting and feedback by SMS. All those YouTube widgets, comments, discussions and spoofs will provide persistent links for the search engines – googling "Evolution Dove" yields over 1.4 million results – and help form the Dove brand persona as genuinely caring about women and real beauty.

Don't Think of Consumer-Created Content as "Free"

Some marketers lick their lips at the thought of harnessing consumers' efforts – and for free! The reality is that consumer-created content isn't' "free." It will take resources to monitor consumer content on your site to make sure it isn't indecent or defamatory. If you want to run a promotion, it will take time – perhaps lots of time – to review the various entries and make selections. In its Super Bowl ad campaign, Doritos received over 1,000 videos that had to be screened and then voted on to select the winners. Then there is the cost to advertise and run the consumer-created content promotion. Doritos spent $1.3 million on advertising in October 2006, while the promotion was being advertised.[30]

Utilize and Answer Consumer-Generated Feedback

Consumer-created content can be an invaluable source of market research, not only on your brand but on your competitors, the whole product category, and consumer problems and concerns. You have the chance to observe a free, candid and completely natural focus group – with the option to gently intervene if you see misconceptions, rumors, or a need for better information arising.

DigiMarketers need to be aware of where their brands are being discussed, and what is being said. The tone of the postings, the sentiments and emotions expressed provide a valuable barometer of brands' true standing in the marketplace. Consumer internet discussions can identify emerging issues and themes, and give a unique insight into consumers' vocabulary and your brand's reputation. And, of course, consumer-created content, as with the rest of the digital media, leaves a highly measurable trail.

Identify and Use Micro-Celebrities to Endorse Your Brand

As we have seen, there are various micro-celebrities who may have a following that is directly relevant to your brand, product or service. Do some online research to figure out who these people are. Then consider innovative ways to either weave your product into their content or involve them in your DigiMarketing platform.

Use Consumer Voting as a Simple Way to Engage with the Brand

Don't overlook the incredible power associated with giving consumers a voice through a vote. While at first sight this doesn't look like "content," giving consumers simple mechanisms to be participants and not just viewers – to make their opinions (literally) count – can encourage involvement with your brand.

FUTURE TRENDS – WHERE IT'S HEADING

As we look to the future, we see important developments in a number of areas that have their foundation in the key trends we've just covered:

        CCC *Trend* 1: Evolution of consumer content –
                      Everyone's TV
        CCC *Trend* 2: Micro interests proliferate
        CCC *Trend* 3: New forms of networking

CCC Trend 1: Evolution of Consumer Content – Everyone's TV

We're really at the start of consumer-created content, so it's hard to predict how it will develop. However, using previous media developments as a guide, as well as considering the implications of a few initiatives today, one thing seems certain: consumer-created content will definitely get richer as it goes. Video is now the medium of "everyman" (and everywoman): we live in a video age. So you should expect that people will increasingly develop multimedia content.

Consumer-content creators will ignore some of the structures of "traditional" media created by the old barons of content, and will respect others. One of the things they already ignore (and will continue to ignore) is the strict time limitation of traditional media. For years, commercial creators have been required to force their creative ideas into fixed units, typically of 15, 30, and 60 seconds.

Consumer-content creators have no such worries. They simply time the content to fit the natural length of their message. This trend will continue as consumers create multimedia mash-ups that we can't envision today. Interestingly, this has also liberated marketers who, at least in digital channels, are now experimenting with longer (and shorter) video content, since they aren't buying media as a "unit."

One area where consumers seem to be respecting traditional strictures is in the format of the programming. From years of television consumption, consumers are acclimated to the comfort of television hosts and presenters. As consumers move past the "funny video" approach that has been a hallmark of early content creation, many are attempting to build a following for themselves on a regular basis. Bloggers, as the new generation of authors and editors, have already grown accustomed to thinking about their audiences, many of whom give immediate feedback that guides blogs' contents. Some video-bloggers (like www.rocketboom.com) have already built a regular audience. Fast-forward this trend into the future and you'll see more people (as individuals and in small groups) in the business of building their own video channels on the web. And you can well expect that MySpace pages will become richer in content and format too. Everyone will effectively be in the television business. Perhaps Andy Warhol's quip about everyone having 15 minutes of fame was right after all…or perhaps it will last longer.

CCC Trend 2: Micro-Interests Proliferate

Micro-niches: Consumer-created content is especially well suited to niche hobbies, interests and concerns, providing the DigiMarketer with one more highly targeted weapon.

Micro-niche sites are now starting to become more marketer friendly and systems are starting to emerge to facilitate marketing through these sites. For example, www.mothersclick.com was created by a first-time mother in San Francisco as a parenting advice site aimed at new parents. Users answer each other's questions and can take part in private discussion groups on any topics to do with parenting. Within about 18 months, the site had 10,000 members and some small ads. It is now evolving to include more marketing, without alienating users.

Many blogs, podcasts, and video podcasts are already using services like FeedBurner, www.feedburner.com (purchased by Google in 2007), or Podtrac, www.podtrac.com, to manage their feeds, make them easier for users to receive, provide RSS capabilities, analyze users' metrics and generally add professionalism.

These news feed management services typically include an advertising networking component, with the service aggregating advertising across a variety of consumer-created content sites which attract similar audiences. The feed manager then sells advertising space on channels of similar sites, providing a Google AdSense-type service for consumer-created content feeds. Pricing currently is cost-per-thousand (cpm) based. Advertisers are also able to prevent appearance of their ads if the feed content contains keywords that the advertiser has deemed inappropriate for the brand. By late 2007 about 66% of FeedBurner's feeds carried ads.

Micro-celebrities: As we have seen, one of the interesting by-products of the rise of consumer-created content is the rise of individual consumers as micro-celebrities. We use this term since these people aren't celebrities in the sense that they would stop traffic or be mobbed on the street for their autograph. In fact, they might well not be noticed on the street at all. But, through their blog, vlog, or other content, they have a "following." And successful micro-celebrities today might have a following that numbers in the hundreds of thousands, or possibly millions. Perez Hilton, a "gossip king of the web," is a blogger who has 5 million readers a day on his site.[31] Instead of splashing out millions for "star" endorsements, some marketers are turning to these infinitely more affordable micro-celebrities for product involvement.

CCC Trend 3: New Forms of Networking

One key element of the Traditional Media Model (see figure 8.1) which is missing in the New Media Model is filtering and editing of content. Traditionally this role was played by publishers and those hired by them. On the web, anyone can (and frequently will) say anything, as in the famous *New Yorker* cartoon[32], where one dog tells another, "On the internet, nobody knows you're a dog."[33]

Interestingly enough, the web is dealing with this filtering problem in its own ways. First, to help classify and categorize consumer-created content, we have *tagging* and *folksonomies*.

Tagging and Folksonomies

Tags are not new. Tags are simply a few descriptive words assigned to an asset (a photo, web page, article, person, book) to make it easier to find in the future.[34] Tags are metadata – data used to describe data. The tagging we see today differs from traditional cataloging in that it is no longer the sole domain of expert librarians and indexers. Now anyone can tag. And (usually) there is no controlled list of tags that must be used. Consumers can spontaneously tag as they see most descriptive.

This bottom-up generation of tags has been called a folksonomy.[35] By relying on consumers' own language, rather than arcane cataloging terms, it is argued that retrieval will be better. Some systems (for example, the website bookmark tagging site Del.icio.us, http://del.icio.us) suggest tags a consumer might find relevant – based on the tags others have assigned, and on those the consumer has already employed. This helps standardize the folksonomy somewhat.

Folksonomies, along with our next trend, crowd wisdom, promise to play the editing and filtering role previously played by publishers, and tame the stampede of consumer-created content.

Crowd Wisdom

As well as the searchable metadata provided by folksonomies, the new media model is creating methods of filtering for quality – a role of publishers and reviewers in the past. Several models are emerging based on variants of collaborative filtering. As we mentioned in chapter 3, collaborative filtering helps customers help each other by pooling information about behavior.

Sometimes called *crowd wisdom*, the idea is that multiple heads are better than one! So information can be organized and its value predicted by the actions of masses of customers. The idea is that the most interesting, most relevant items will float to the top of the consumer-created content. "Floating to the top" will be signaled in some way by recording crowd wisdom.

This can be done most simply by consumers' explicit ratings. So, for example, Digg (www.digg.com), "the digital media democracy," allows anyone to submit a posting. Readers can then either "digg it" or "bury." As a story gets more diggs it attains greater prominence on the site. The process is claimed to be somewhat susceptible to the undue influence of a few high-ranked "diggers" and abuse of the "bury" option, which was designed to combat spam but can be used to suppress dissenting opinions!

Spotplex (www.spotplex.com) lists postings from participating blogs, ordering them according to how many times they have been read. Participating blogs include some code on their sites, which monitors what's being read. The more times a story is read, the higher it appears in Spotplex. Very popular stories will make it to the Spotplex home page.

Other sites attempt to do more than simply follow the herd. Amazon (www.amazon.com) tells users what "consumers who bought this item also bought," the idea being that customers that have one purchase in common with us will be more likely to lead us to other things we will like.

StumbleUpon (www.stumbleupon.com) uses the same concept for websites. Based on your reaction to a site compared to the reactions of others, StumbleUpon will suggest other sites that people who seem to share your tastes also like.

This brings us to a more sophisticated filtering of importance, using *reputation scores*.

Reputation Scores

Reputation scores are all about knowing who to trust. Part of the shame of marketing is that consumers are far more likely to trust one another than to trust marketers or media! Forrester Research found that "recommendations from consumers" were the most trusted form of advertising – with trust levels roughly double those of paid advertising.[36]

The tipping point for blogs came in late 2004 when a segment on 60 *Minutes* aired on network television provoked a firestorm of criticism in blogs. The bloggers, including typeface experts, pointed out that crucial letters used on the show probably could not have been produced by a secretary on a typewriter. Dan Rather, the show's presenter, finally admitted that he no longer had confidence in the authenticity of documents he had used.

As the democracy of the web grows, people will turn to new ways to determine who to trust. Reputation scores add sophistication to crowd wisdom by weighting actions of individuals with good reputations. In small towns, an individual's reputation is built by visual, verbal, and behavioral cues gleaned from face-to-face interactions. In big cities, reputations might rest on more formal approaches, including elections, appointments, and a judicial system.[37] Online, most interactions have very few of the informal behavioral cues used to assess reputation offline. As a result, formal reputation measurement systems are starting to emerge.

eBay (www.ebay.com) invites buyers and sellers to rate each other, and aggregates those ratings.[38] Slashdot (www.slashdot.org) – the self-described "News for Nerds. Stuff that Matters" site – gives contributors a *karma score* which is shown beside every posting. Karma derives from tags (on a 6-point scale) assigned to that contributor's postings by moderators, from story postings, and even from meta-moderation (that's scoring the scores of moderators!). Moderators have a limited number of votes; when these are exhausted the moderator reverts back to a regular contributor.

Already these reputation systems are being abused with negative feedback blackmail on eBay (that is, threatening to rate negatively if the seller/buyer doesn't accept a better deal); sock puppets (that is, fake identities created to praise the real identity); anonymous cowards (that is, posters who give no identity); and trolls (that is, posters who pretend to be community members, but are really intent on disruptive mischief and confusion in their postings).

Reputation is likely to become key in the future of the web. Our smart agents will filter information based on reputation scores, feeding users what the agent has learned will be the most reliable information in that particular user's eyes. There is a fundamental tension between reputation and privacy. Reputation is built around identity carrying over multiple transactions; privacy is protected by decoupling identity from those multiple transactions.[39] The way in which this tension is resolved will be a key development in the future of the web.

We will come back to this critical issue of digital influence and online reputation management when we cover DigiMarketing planning at the end of this book.

Google Bombing

As we saw in chapter 4, part of the Google algorithm for ranking web pages depends on the anchor text used in links to that page. The thinking is that links will likely use words descriptive of the content to be found on the page to which the link points. A Google bomb exploits this by arranging for a large number of links to use text which has no relationship to the content on the linked page.

One of the first Google bombs made the search phrase "more evil than Satan himself" bring up the Microsoft homepage as the first result. Probably the most famous was the association of "miserable failure" with the official George Bush biography on the US White House website.

Typically Google bombs have a short life span, rapidly becoming written about too much in highly regarded sites, and in fact generating content which knocks the bomb off the top spot. Searches for "miserable failure" now show pages and pages of sites about the Google bomb rather than the Bush biography. Changes in the Google algorithm over time have also invalidated most Google bombs.

An adapted version of Google bombing is spamdexing. This involves posting links to a website in internet forums, and other accessible consumer-created content sites, including phrases with which the site hopes to be associated.

As we mentioned in chapter 4, search engine bowling is a very controversial technique, which some argue is not actually possible. The aim is to make a competitive site (or one carrying unfavorable reviews of your product or service) look like it is trying to game the search engines. Typically this is done by introducing thousands of links into that site, often from low reputation, spurious sites, over a very short duration. So the links might all appear over a 48-hour period. This may cause the search engine to demote the targeted site to a very low rank, or even eliminate it completely from search results.[40]

SUMMARY: CONSUMER-CREATED CONTENT

- Consumers creating content is probably the most remarkable and far-reaching of all the changes discussed in this book.
- The idea of consumers as separate from producers permeates marketing and business. Yet now consumers are producers – and doing a very good job at it.
- DigiMarketers will need a delicate hand to steer consumer-created content along lines that support the brand, without being felt to interfere or exceed their rights in the democratic space of digital media.
- This is probably the area where marketers have the most to learn: to learn let go, to let consumers contribute, to let consumers take charge, while still building a brand. Delicate sensitivity and marketing have not traditionally gone hand-in-hand. Well, in the future, if the marketing is to succeed, they will have to!

END NOTES

1 www.catb.org/~esr/writings/cathedral-bazaar/
2 In fact the book version of *The Cathedral and the Bazaar* was the first complete, commercially distributed book published under an open source document license – allowing and anticipating modifications to the original document.
3 "People Power", Chris Anderson, *Wired*, July 2006. www.wired.com/wired/archive/14.07/people.html
4 Bobby White, "Cisco Says Sales Growth to Cool in Current Quarter", *The Asian Wall Street Journal*, May 10, 2007, page 30.
5 www.time.com/time/magazine/article/0,9171,1569514,00.html
6 blogs.zdnet.com/ITFacts/?p=12835
7 Or alternatively "What I Know Is".
8 "The Ignorance of Crowds," Nicholas G. Carr, *ENews*, Booz, Allen, Hamilton, May 31, 2007.
9 news.bbc.co.uk/1/hi/technology/4530930.stm
10 science.slashdot.org/article.pl?sid=05/12/15/1352207&from=rss
11 www.hitwise.com/press-center/hitwiseHS2004/web20.php
12 *Pew Internet & American Life Project*, January 2007.
13 www.technorati.com/about/
14 www.readwriteweb.com/archives/web_20_expo_data.php#more
15 www.particls.com
16 www.washingtonpost.com/ac2/wp-dyn/A16540-2003Dec19?language=printer
17 newteevee.com/2007/05/03/youtube-starts-paying-star-users/
18 In late 2006 Apple attempted to assert rights to the word pod, but soon withdrew any challenge to podcast.
19 The word comes from the combination of machine cinema or machine animation.
20 www.timesonline.co.uk/tol/news/politics/article1361968.ece
21 www.qj.net/FTC-to-viral-marketers-disclose-your-corporate-connections/pg/49/aid/76037
22 www.plasticbag.org/archives/2005/09/on_cillit_bang_and_a_new_low_for_marketers/ news.bbc.co.uk/1/hi/magazine/4326446.stm www.guardian.co.uk/uk_news/story/0,3604,1585687,00.html www.plasticbag.org/archives/2005/10/an_apology_from_the_cillit_bang_team.shtml
23 www.clickz.com/showPage.html?page=3625715
24 www.cluetrain.com/
25 www.current.tv/make/vc2/vcam shows a selection.
26 notetaker.typepad.com/cgm/
27 www.blogpulse.com/trend?query1=dove+beauty&label1=&query2=&label2=&query3=&label3=&days=180&x=36&y=9
28 www.youtube.com/watch?v=7H07hwxtjRI&eurl=
29 www.campaignforrealbeauty.com/share.asp?section=share
30 "Doing What with Ketchup? Consumers Create ads", Louise Story, *International Herald Tribune*, May 28, 2007, page 11.
31 Jac Chebatoris, "A Gossip's Golden Touch", *Newsweek*, June 4, 2007, page 53.
32 www.cartoonbank.com/item/22230
33 Apparently, the most reproduced cartoon for the *New Yorker*. Its appearance, in 1993, is an index of just how fast the internet permeated our consiousness. See www.nytimes.com/2000/12/14/technology/14DOGG.html?ex=1186459200&en=404acb8cb00af597&ei=5070
34 www.adaptivepath.com/publications/essays/archives/000695.php
35 The term was invented by information architect Thomas Vander Wal, see www.vanderwal.net/about.php
36 www.nielsenbuzzmetrics.com/cgm
37 en.wikipedia.org/wiki/Reputation_management
38 Reputation scores also act as a switching cost tying vendors and buyers to a particular site: having built a good reputation score at eBay, I have an incentive to stay with that site.
39 www.windley.com/essays/2006/reputation_principles
40 This at best dubious, and perhaps impossible, technique is discussed in www.forbes.com/2007/06/28/negative-search-google-tech-ebiz-cx_ag_0628seo.html

Chapter 9

Digital Signage

I f there is a "sleeping giant" of digital marketing, then digital signage is it. Increasingly, digital signage is a street-level reality, supplanting more of the traditional signage and billboards that currently dot most city landscapes. Plus, in-store digital signage – sometimes also referred to as digital point-of-sale – is growing too. Both forms will eventually make digital signage as important a force in digital marketing as any of the other trends we've covered so far.

To simplify things, throughout this chapter we'll simply use the term *digital signage* to refer to the broad array of in-market and In-store options (see Box Insert, Types of Digital Signage). We should also note that, because of the growing importance of digital signage, some industry pundits are even calling it the *fourth screen* – the other three being the television, the computer, and the mobile.[1]

In this chapter we'll look at the forces driving the growth of digital signage, and why it is destined to be a more pervasive part of our lives. We'll also outline some of the emerging uses of digital signage, so you can be sure to maximize its potential as part of your DigiMarketing plans.

KEY TRENDS YOU MUST KNOW

As we examine the massive potential of digital signage, let's start with some basics. Two forces are propelling the growth of digital signage. First, marketers want to access consumers closer to the point of purchase. Although e-commerce is growing, enabling people to buy as easily from their bedrooms as from store aisles, there are many marketers who are not – and possibly won't ever be – e-commerce enabled. The next best thing for them is to prompt consumers using digital technology at locations where consumers can already buy.

Second, technological advances, coupled with rapidly declining costs of that technology, are making digital signage more practical and affordable. As we'll see, the economics of digital signage make more sense everyday. Consequently, more digital signage is getting into stores, malls, and other venues.

The coupling of demand (to get closer to consumers) and capability (the availability of cost-effective digital signage solutions) is spurring digital signage growth. Let's look a bit more deeply at the key drivers of digital signage:

Digital Signage Driver 1: The push for connectivity
Digital Signage Driver 2: Changing economics of digital
        signage
Digital Signage Driver 3: Mega retailers build in-store
        signage networks
Digital Signage Driver 4: Outdoor signage replaces
        traditional billboards
Digital Signage Driver 5: Technology-enabled targeting
        and segmentation

Digital Signage Driver 1: The Push for Connectivity

Over time, every roadside stop, billboard location, rooftop, and store front can potentially be "connected" (for a list of digital signage options, see the Box Insert, Types of Digital Signage). As noted already, part of the impetus for digital signage is to find ways to get "closer" to consumers, particularly in the face of declining consumer attention to traditional media. To date, research results seem to indicate that advertising at points of sale is having an important impact on product selection. In fact, a Forrester study suggests that in-store advertising receives a higher rating for "how much each (channel) influences your perception of a brand or company" than do brand websites and television advertisements.[2]

Another study, conducted by TNS for the company that manages Wal-Mart's digital signage system, concluded that "advertising on Wal-Mart TV drives significantly higher motivation levels than advertising for similar brands on in-home TV."[3]

This research has raised some questions.[4] However, the research seems to substantiate the general marketing sentiment that more brand selection decisions are happening at points of purchase. As products (like media) continue to proliferate, the "war for attention" at retail will intensify, encouraging digital signage.

Connectivity of digital signage has some clear operational benefits. Digital content can be updated quickly and efficiently from a central location. Marketers don't have to wait weeks for material to be printed and distributed. This is particularly important for marketers who compete in highly price sensitive categories where competitors frequently change prices or bundling strategies. Marketers using digital signage can move quickly to counter competitors' pricing on a site-by-site basis, all coordinated from a central location. What's more, signage content can be richer and more involving.

More marketers are questioning why they should have a static image on a poster when they can have a video, or even customized messages if the digital screen has the ability to recognize individual customers.

Types of Digital Signage

We are using the term *digital signage* as an umbrella term to describe several types of in-market and in-store signage, including:

In-Market

In-lift screens: Digital screens in lifts are multiplying as marketers seek captive audiences happy to watch a screen for the time it takes to reach their chosen floor.

Taxi-cab seat backs: Taxis are a bit like lifts, in the sense that people are generally a "captive" audience for the duration of the ride. However, unlike lifts, taxis drive around, making location-based information, particularly if the seat-back display has a touch screen, all the more important.

Petrol station monitors: Petrol stations generate large consumer traffic, which is also "captive" for a period of time while they fill up. Digital displays are appearing on the petrol pumps.

Track-side and in-carriage/in-flight: Trains, subways, and planes attract large, captive crowds. Already, we are seeing screens in departure terminals, at track-side, and in carriages. Airline in-flight entertainment is fiercely competitive, providing a prime advertising vehicle for luxury goods, financial services, and tourism marketers.

Roadside screens: Roadside screens of varying sizes allow for video and other multimedia content to be displayed, often in interactive formats, linked to mobiles (as we saw in chapter 6).

Large spectaculars and JumboTrons: Megascreens are appearing, particularly in large physical nexus points in major cities. Stroll around the shopping districts of Shanghai, Tokyo, or New York City, and you will see this type of signage.

Moveable digital signage: Attached to the sides of trucks, these offer the ability to go where the crowds are, and change messaging by location. IBM used these types of moveable digital signs during its US Open tennis sponsorship.

ATMs: The primary function of an ATM is not as signage. But banks are realizing that ATMs, usually placed at high traffic points across a city, can be used to show brand messaging to captive customers while providing banking services.

Vending machines: Again not primarily signage, but vending machines are starting to build in more digital features such as electronic payment and screens.

Kiosks: We mention this last as kiosks straddle in-market and in-store (plus in-mall locations).

In-Store/Malls

End-aisle displays: Digital screens in stores, particularly at end aisles (usually the highest traffic locations), are proliferating. Many of these screens are interactive, with either touch screens or some type of loyalty card reader.

Shelf-screens: These are mini-screens taking the place of traditional "shelf-talkers" (the messages that are sometimes attached to shelves).

> *Electronic menu boards*: Many retailers, particularly in the fast food business, are changing from standard menu boards to electronic boards which can be quickly and easily updated with promotional items and prices.
>
> *Radio frequency identification* (RFID): While not visual signage, RFID chips will play an increasing role in store (see Future Trends, below).

Digital Signage Driver 2: The Changing Economics of Digital Signage

One of the factors spurring the growth of digital signage is their increasing cost-effectiveness. Global plasma display revenue is expected to rise to $8.6 billion this year, up 11.8% from $7.7 billion in 2006. But increased competition and continuing price drops are expected to cause the market to contract to $8.7 billion by 2011.[5] LED screens are also projected to show 10% to 15% price drops.[6] And according to outdoor firm Watchfire, prices of LED panels have dropped by as much as 60% in recent years.[7] The implication of this is simple: a key component of digital signage is getting steadily cheaper. At some point in time, the economics will make digital more cost-effective than the old-fashioned methods of printed paper or plastic signage.

The software to manage the screens is a critical component of digital signage, be it a single screen or a network of screens. Today, there are a number of major competitors in the software development area, including Scala (www.scala.com) and Wirespring (www.wirespring.com). Marketers generally don't need to worry about the details of the software options, unless they are considering building and running their own retail digital signage network (see Box Insert, To Build or Not to Build). However, it's worth noting here that as the software side of the business continues to develop, companies who operate the networks – and the marketers who advertise through them – will gain more power and control over scheduling and message management. This will be particularly true as systems become internet connected.

Today, companies spend billions of dollars for temporary posters, hanging mobiles, shelf-talkers, and assorted other marketing material to highlight their products. This material frays, fades, and becomes outdated as new promotions and prices come into effect. A key part of the financial equation is the cost and quality trade-off of traditional point-of-sale material versus using digital content and screens.

To Build or Not to Build: The Digital Signage Question

There are several models at play when it comes to digital signage networks:

Retail signage – company owned: Some retailers want to leverage the valuable real estate they own to better promote their own products. This type of retailer – for example Nike – uses digital signage to boost sales or better service customers in their own stores. Retailers who go this route will need to assess the cost and complication of maintaining a digital signage network in their stores. They will also have to determine how to best architect digital signage into their store design, noting the current footfall patterns.

Retail signage – company owned, with third-party advertising: Other companies – most notably large retailers such as Wal-mart, Tesco, and Carrefour – build digital signage networks with a primary focus on leasing the advertising space to other marketers, generally companies that make the products displayed in their retail space. Some of these companies may operate their own networks, although more are outsourcing part or all of the process to specialist providers.

Third-party space: Not all companies will be in a position to consider installing digital signage. Many, most notably packaged goods companies, don't own the retail space in which their products are sold. So, for this type of marketer the key decision is how to best deploy their marketing through digital signage networks in the retail spaces where their products are sold. This is akin to simply buying time on the television networks; the marketer only buys '"slots" on someone else's network and doesn't have to worry about owning or maintaining the digital signage.

Digital Signage Driver 3: Mega Retailers Build In-Store Networks

The companies with the most to gain from digital signage, and who are also best placed to install digital signage, are the large retailers. For this reason, they are leading the in-store signage field. Wal-Mart TV in the US, with approximately 125,000 networked screens, reaching about 127 million shoppers per week[8], has the most extensive retail network. In terms of market reach, Wal-Mart TV is a credible rival to the television networks.

And there are many others around the world of companies: Banesto Banks in Spain[9], Pharmacy TV in Poland, Carrefour in China, and Tesco in the UK. Tesco is a large retailer whose network is considered the most extensive in the UK. They recently re-launched Tesco TV as Tesco Screens.[10]

While retailers have the "real estate," they don't necessarily have the programming know-how. For this reason, retailers are working with media companies to run these substantial networks. In Mexico, Televisa, which dominates the Mexican television scene, reportedly invested $20 million to install 5,000 screens in Wal-Mart de Mexico locations.[11] In the United States, Wal-Mart TV is operated by Premiere Retail Networks (PRN), a business unit of Thomson. In mid-2007, PRN and NBC Universal hooked up in a strategic alliance to partner on ad sales and to develop customizable content for PRN's supermarket network.[12] Given the growing interest in this area, it's certain there will be further deals and partnerships as the digital signage ecosystem develops further.

Digital Signage Driver 4: Outdoor Signage Replaces Traditional Billboards

It's not just the large retailers and media conglomerates who are eyeing digital signage. Traditional outdoor companies, and a host of new entrants, are looking to become substantial players in outdoor and in-market digital signage as well.

One of the widely touted new entrants is Shanghai-based Focus Media. The NASDAQ-listed company started out targeting affluent professionals in China with 30-minute loops on television screens in elevator lobbies. However, through a string of acquisitions, Focus has expanded its model to supermarkets, mobile phones, and movie theaters.[13] Today, streetside digital signage has become common in Shanghai. This sector will grow further as Focus Media and its competitors have their eyes on connecting lifts and other locations across Asia. However, at the time of writing this book, it is yet to be seen whether these companies will fully justify the sometimes lofty valuations they currently enjoy in the stock market.

In the US, out-of-home advertising is expected to remain the second-fastest growing medium (in terms of advertising revenue growth) in 2007, behind only the internet.[14] This growth is being spurred in large part by the growth of digital signage.

Companies such as Clear Channel, CBS Outdoor, Lamar, and JCDecaux are looking for aggressive growth in digital signage. This is no surprise, since they generally derive more revenue from digital signage as they can rotate advertising creative on the same screen, unlike traditional billboards that feature just one, fixed advertiser for months at a time. However, outdoor digital signage players must contend with regulatory control (this varies a lot by market around the world) on the number of outdoor signage locations. In this regard, in-store signage operators have more leeway.

Digital Signage Driver 5: Technology-Enabled Targeting and Segmentation

A key advantage of digital screens (whether in-store or outdoors) is that they can be used for targeting and segmentation. When Wal-Mart TV started out in 1997, it was mostly a "dumb" system. Content was on a unified loop, so all shoppers saw the same advertising. However, the upgrade of Wal-Mart TV from satellite broadcast to an internet-based system means advertisers can now deliver messages to different store departments, plus they can target individual screens.[15] This upgraded system will increasingly be the norm, meaning that the signage networks – whether company-owned or run by a third party – will work just like the internet, allowing different material to be served to different locations.

This will have a profound impact on marketers' ability to target appropriate material to different screens, with obvious segmentation applications. Imagine a chain of 100 pizza restaurants that operates across a major city. Not all of those locations will be performing the same. There will be top stores, average stores, and a few stores that are relative laggards. A marketer might, therefore, decide to serve more aggressive promotional offers (pending legality in a given country) to spur consumer traffic to those poor-performing stores.

Alternatively, the marketer might have local area promotions and serve different content promoting special pizzas that cater to different ethnic neighborhoods. Once signage is digital and networked, there will be endless targeting and segmentation applications.

DIGIMARKETING BEST PRACTICES

Create Material Appropriate for Digital Signage

As digital signage is still in its infancy, marketers can be forgiven for not knowing exactly what type of material best suits this channel. However, simply repurposing television commercials or other marketing material is unlikely to be effective. This channel will probably need purpose-made content. Most shoppers will not stand in an aisle to watch a 30-second television commercial. Marketers need to use shorter, punchier, action-oriented messaging. This means a combination of direct marketing, activation, and sale enablement techniques to craft appropriate digital signage content. Good digital signage content will direct the consumer – for example, prompting shoppers to enquire about a new product or to request a product demonstration. Digital signage content will be more akin to point-of-sale than brand advertising, and should be treated as part of the sales-closing process.

Exploit the Dynamic Potential of the Channel to Keep Content Fresh

Marketers should exploit the ability of internet-based systems to serve new and targeted content. Messages can be constructed for different days of the week, or even dayparts. Dynamically generated messaging – such as alerting shoppers when there are only three units of a given item left – can help spur consumer action.

Use Local Area Marketing Planning

Depending upon the location and capability of the signage (namely, whether it's two-way or not), marketers can develop local area marketing strategies. For example, you can tailor directive messages to build traffic to individual store outlets. Effective outdoor advertisers do this already, to a degree, but they lack the ability to dynamically serve new content to traditional outdoor signage.

Time-based elements of a local area marketing plan can also be implemented using digital signage. For example, if your store outlets have a low period in the afternoon, and you want to drive store traffic during that time, your outdoor and in-store digital signage can be coordinated around promotions where there are giveaways or surprise items in the afternoon. Digital signage can be used to feature a changing array of items, depending perhaps on inventory situations.

Consider Digital Signage for Product Education, not Just Sales

Particularly when digital signage is two-way, marketers should consider how to use the screens to inform and educate consumers, not just sell to them. On the internet, participants tend to research and compare products, and search. This can be mirrored at in-store kiosks. Participants can enter questions for the kiosk screen to answer; complex information can be simplified with visuals or short videos. This might include side-by-side comparisons of your product with competitors, or even comparisons of different sizes within your own range of products, so consumers can make better decisions. Ultimately, this leads to sales, but it does so through using information, not just offers.

Integrate Digital Signage Content with Other Digital Channels

One of the game-changers that we noted in chapter 1 is the interconnectivity of digital devices. Your digital signage content should be integrated with the other digital channels you are using. For example, Nationwide Insurance in the US took clips consumers had contributed to their "Life Comes at You Fast" website (www.lifecomesatyoufast.com) and streamed them to a digital sign in Times Square.[16] As marketers get better at linking their digital assets, digital signage will need to be treated as part of overall digital strategy, not as a separate channel.

...Especially Mobile Devices

In particular, marketers should leverage the natural, symbiotic relationship between mobile devices and digital signage. The key question is how to coordinate the two when a consumer is walking down a street or is in a shopping aisle.

Even if the digital signage doesn't allow direct interconnectivity (for example, by a touch screen or keypad), marketers can still prompt a consumer link by displaying offers, codes and an SMS number (we saw some examples of this in chapter 6). In markets where QR codes are prevalent, the signage could display a QR code; consumers who use their mobile to photograph the code will be linked to a website. Response-enabled digital signage might read a loyalty card or connect with a chip in the phone (such as the FeliCa chips in DoCoMo phones in Japan) to allow for individual interaction.

FUTURE TRENDS – WHERE IT'S HEADING

> *Digital Signage Trend* 1: More screens
> *Digital Signage Trend* 2: More flexible technology

Digital Signage Trend 3: Being there – tele-immersion and more

Digital Signage Trend 4: Consumer control, personalization, and privacy (yes, again)

Digital Signage Trend 1: More Screens

The first Digital Signage Trend is simple: there will be more screens. It's still early days for digital signage and the market is a long, long way from being saturated. There is a lot more upgrading of existing billboards, posters, bus shelters, and other "traditional" locations to be done. Additionally, there will be new locations to be connected, particularly off the back of the substantial growth of office buildings and shopping malls in developing economies around the world. For this reason, some research suggests the digital signage market could be $14.6 billion by 2011.[17]

Digital Signage Trend 2: More Flexible Technology

Not only will the number of screens grow, the screens themselves will change in shape and capability. Current technology developments indicate that the future of digital signage will be both rich and flexible – in the literal sense. Sony is among the companies developing digital paper, which is super-thin and flexible, just like normal paper, yet able to display images and video from digital sources.[18] This will lead to a variety of handheld digital screens, which can be rolled and stuffed into a person's pocket. As digital paper eventually comes into commercial use, imagine every train station column or curved tunnel capable of displaying a video message. Or imagine store fronts "wallpapered" in digital paper, with different tiles of digital paper noting the specials in the store – or possibly dynamically generating price offers depending upon purchase patterns and stocks in the store.

Crystal ball gazing about the applications of new technologies can be fascinating. However, the technology is likely to unfold in ways that can't yet be foreseen. Suffice it to say that technology will create digital signage in more formats than just flat screens. This will lead to more interesting and engaging uses of digital.

Digital Signage Trend 3: Being There – Tele-immersion and More

Digital signage is also likely to take on a more life-like quality. New technology developed by Cisco and HP already promises to bring the benefits of "tele-immersion" or "telepresence" to commercial use. The technology being rolled out from both companies is aimed at turning video conferencing into an experience where all parties feel they are really in the room together. This includes state-of-the-art audio and visual technologies that eliminate time lag and add photo realism to the displays. While teleconferencing is currently seen as a corporate activity, there are likely to be interesting marketing applications of this technology as well. For example, a star endorser could appear in a photo-realistic display, and – as this is a digital, two-way technology – consumers could interact with the star, as if they were in the same room. As always, much will depend upon marketers' creativity and their ability to deploy the technology in ways that amplify their brands.

It's worth noting that the "being there" experience could well wind up being three dimensional. For example, Light Blue Optics of Cambridge (UK) has developed groundbreaking holographic technology which could result in a new generation of pocket-sized digital video projectors and projection displays incorporated into handheld devices.[19] With holographic technology, the star endorser we just mentioned might show up in the middle of a shopping mall as the 3D representative of your brand. Remember too that all things digital are on the same standard, and can be "ported" across devices; it could be your CEO's avatar from *Second Life* who shows up in the hologram projection in the shopping mall. Or, given the power of consumer-created content, it could be the hologram of a "brand fan" who is then projected into venues around the world to support your brand. The potential implications of connecting digital channels are truly mind-boggling.

Digital Signage Trend 4: Consumer Control, Personalization, And Privacy (Yes, Again)

Our last trend brings us back to three intertwined and recurring themes throughout this book: consumer control, personalization, and privacy. These issues are likely to be important factors in the long-term development of digital signage (and DigiMarketing as a whole).

Let's start with the issues of consumer control and personalization. Most marketers, even when they think about video-rich signage of the future, still think primarily as one-way marketers, showing consumers images or messages chosen by the marketers. However, as with other digital channels, consumers are looking to have some input and control. This doesn't necessarily mean consumers will create all the content on the digital signage – although as we saw with Nationwide Insurance (in Best Practices above), that can be the case. Instead, consumers – using motion recognition technology – might want to arrange and contribute to the information that they see. Recall for a moment the scenes of Tom Cruise in *Minority Report* arranging information on an electronic board with hand gestures. This isn't science fiction; it's already there at Chicago's O'Hare Airport, terminal 3, courtesy of Accenture.[20] This is the potential future of digital signage as consumers choose to rearrange displayed material to incorporate their own information in a digital signage mash-up.

Another *Minority Report* scene you might recall is the talking billboard that delivers personalized messages to people that walk past. In the movie the billboard uses iris recognition to identify customers. While we don't know of a billboard doing this (yet), iris recognition is in routine use at airports and borders.[21] Given the advancements in technology we've noted already, digital signage is likely to recognize individuals probably via their mobile phones or (smart) loyalty cards, rather than by irises (which as you may recall, Tom Cruise defeats by eyeball transplants). FeliCa-chip enabled billboards may usher in an era when digital signage is both personalized and a new point of transaction. For example, a billboard touting an airline's new route and promotional fare to Majorca could then prompt you to book and buy on the spot.

This vision of personalization and control leads us back to the inevitable tension between customization and privacy. While auto-personalized signage would have its benefits, do consumers really want signage to monitor their movements, not to mention their shopping habits and personal needs? Whether or not marketers manage to walk the fine line with consumers is yet to be seen.

The tension of privacy and identification can already be seen today in regard to radio frequency identification (RFID) tags. This technology, originally developed to be used in tracking and identifying palettes of products in the shipping process, transmits a unique serial number from a tag which can be placed on a box or embedded in a piece of clothing. RFID technology has already caused controversy and boycotts by consumer privacy advocates who worry about the technology being used to monitor consumers, potentially without their knowledge.

As digital moves in-market and in-store, surrounding consumers with data and personalized information, will this create a more enjoyable, efficient shopping experience, or an enveloping barrage of personalized offers? It will be up to DigiMarketers to deploy new signage technologies with intelligence and care.

SUMMARY: DIGITAL SIGNAGE

Digital signage can (and should) fit into the plans of most marketers – especially those that have a large retail presence. Overall, some of the key applications of digital signage that you should remember are:

- Digital signage can be used effectively to cater to the different traffic patterns and different neighborhood locations of a marketer's various stores or outlets.
- In-store digital signage can work in combination with other technologies – particularly mobile phones – to help with "customer activation" to prompt sales.
- In-market signage can also be used to support local area marketing.
- Marketers will increasingly be able to use response and loyalty technology in order to maximize the potential of digital signage to act as more than one-way screens.

Next, in the final channel chapter, we will look at how the largest and most venerable of the marketing channels – television – is set to change forever.

END NOTES

1   www.digitalsignagetoday.com/article.php?id=17117. Of course the pedants
    (see thefourthscreen.blogspot.com/) point out that historically screens go: 1st
    cinema, 2nd TV, 3rd computer, and 4th mobile device. Which would make digital
    signage the 5th screen. Whatever.
2   Forrester's NACTAS Q2 2006 Survey
3   www.lexdon.com/article/Premier_Retail_Networks_Announces_Results/20264.
    html
4   www.wirespring.com/dynamic_digital_signage_and_interactive_kiosks_journal/
    articles/Is_Wal_Mart_s_in_store_TV_network_really_more_effective_than_TV_-
    255.html
5   www.informationweek.com/news/showArticle.jhtml?articleID=201400240
6   www.purchasing.com/article/CA6465139.html
7   www.watchfiredigitaloutdoor.com/NewsStory.aspx?Story=20070129_01
8   www.usatoday.com/money/industries/retail/2007-03-28-walmarttv-tim-mcgraw_
    N.htm
9   www.scala.com/news/banesto-bank.html
10 www.digitalsignagenews.blogspot.com/2007/07/tesco-tv-to-become-tesco-
    screens.html
11 www.digitalsignagenews.blogspot.com/2006/04/televisa-to-deploy-digital-
    signage-to.html
12 www.thomson.net/EN/Home/Press/Press+Details.htm?PressReleaseID=1fb980d
    5-5c90-4f45-aaf3-a0f60f489709
13 Laura Santini, "Focus Media's Growth Prospects Spur Divergent Views on
    Shares", Heard in Asia Section, *The Asian Wall Street Journal*, November 6, 2006,
    page 19.
14 www.watchfiredigitaloutdoor.com/NewsStory.aspx?Story=20070129_01
15 www.usatoday.com/money/industries/retail/2007-03-28-walmarttv-tim-mcgraw_
    N.htm
16 www.hoteldigitalsignage.com/news/2006/06/21/emerging-outdoor-digital-
    signage-ads-engages-consumers-with-technology-and-creativit/
17 www.1888pressrelease.com/rocsearch-report-says-digital-signage-market-up-to-
    us-14-6-b-pr-0iou60v32.html
18 www.associatedcontent.com/article/258706/sony_develops_electronic_paper_
    video.html
19 www.gizmag.com/go/3087/
20 news.softpedia.com/news/The-Screen-from-Minority-Report-is-Hosted-by-
    Chicago-039-s-O-039-Hare-Airport-22792.shtml
21 www.en.wikipedia.org/wiki/Iris_recognition

Chapter 10

Television Reinvented – IPTV

For decades, the devices we know as "televisions" have been central features of homes around the world. Couch potatoes have enjoyed the passive activity of watching television programs, sports, and news. Traditionally, the vast majority of television programming has been financed by paid advertising messages interspersed throughout the programming. Particularly for fast-moving consumer goods, these television commercials have become a staple of marketing.

In this chapter we review the changes that are impacting the traditional television model and trace the developments of television as a digital channel. This will have considerable, lasting repercussions, particularly for consumer-packaged-goods marketers. As we will see, it is not that television programs are no longer of interest to consumers – they most definitely are. Consumers will continue to appreciate interesting programming. But as that programming becomes digital, it will be enjoyed on the full range of digital devices, and will take on all the features of digital content, including addressability (and therefore personalization), interaction, and consumer control and creation. Television will never be the same again.

KEY TRENDS YOU MUST KNOW

The Broadcast TV Model Collapses

In the traditional model of television, programs were created by the major television networks, or by studios that then sold programs to the networks. Marketers paid the networks – and their related affiliate stations – to run standard-length advertisements at breaks in the programs and in between the programs. These so-called "pods" of advertising reached a general mass audience, and to some extent could target particular demographics, based on program content. Commercial airtime was sold based upon the notion that consumers who watched the program would also watch the commercials. Viewership of programs was validated by consumer panels whose behavior was then extrapolated to the universe of potential viewers.

Advertising during programs shown in the evenings at a time when most people were watching – prime time – fetched the highest rates, along with advertising in some special programs, usually sports. Consumers generally understood and followed the program schedule. Consumers actually altered their lives to be in front of the television when the programs they wished to watch were scheduled.

Virtually every single element of this television model has collapsed, or is in the process of collapsing.

Channel Surfing

Maybe the beginning of the end of the traditional television model was the remote control. The television remote meant that the couch potato, with a languid press of a button, could change the channel when the ads came on. The first (albeit wired) television remote is claimed to be the Zenith "Lazy Bones," launched in 1950[1]; this developed into wireless versions during the 1950s. The assumption that program viewers equaled advertising viewers came into question. By 1986, the Wall Street Journal was already using the expression "channel surfing."[2]

The First Pass at Time Shifting

Or maybe it was the VCR that marked the beginning of the end. Anyone remember video cassette recorders?[3] They achieved mass distribution in the 1970s, and for the first time allowed time shifting. Viewers no longer had to live their lives according to the networks' schedules. They could record programs for playback later. Consumers could reconstruct the networks' schedules to conform to their needs, rather than vice versa. What's more, during playback the customer could fast-forward through the pod of ads, further derailing the "program audience equals ad audience" assumption.

In practice, VCRs were fiendishly difficult to program, and most consumers never did figure it out. So time shifting was probably minimal. But VCRs also introduced a new competitor: pre-recorded materials. Once the movie studios lost their fight in the early 1980s to suppress VCRs as infringing copyright (sound familiar to anyone?), pre-recorded tapes of movies became widely available. Instead of watching network television, the consumer could now watch a pre-recorded tape (most likely rented) and see (almost) no advertising at all.

The advent of consumer DVD (digital video disk, or if you like the cutesy, digital versatile disk) players led to pre-recorded DVDs becoming available. This, and the emerging high definition (HD) DVD players (and their pre-recorded content), simply improved video and audio quality, and made watching pre-recorded content even more appealing.

Cable and Satellite

Or maybe it was the growth of cable and satellite television that began the disintegration of the broadcast television model. As cable and satellite television developed in many countries, viewers had vastly wider choices. They could bypass the networks completely and watch cable/satellite content. The array of channels was so dizzyingly great that simply trying to figure out what was on became a hobby!

Although some cable/satellite content was ad-supported, other content contained no ads and was funded by monthly subscription or on a pay-per-view basis. Some estimates put the so-called "pay TV" market at $120 billion worldwide by 2006.[4] The net result? The broadcast television audience was shrinking, fragmenting, and less locked into watching advertising in order to see programs.

Digital Video Recorders

Or just maybe the television model was okay until the advent of digital video recorders (DVRs, also known as personal video recorders, PVRs), which many know as TiVos after the path-breaking brand. First launched to the mass market in 1999, DVRs made time shifting – and a few other tricks – a reality.

Technologically, the DVR is fairly simple. It is a computer hard drive connected to your cable or satellite box. Instead of running directly into the television, the digital signal from the box runs into this hard drive. This allows you to either view the television programs in "real time," as you have been doing for decades, or "time shift" programs.

Not only are DVRs much simpler to program than VCRs (or maybe the market has got a bit more savvy at such things) but DVRs, particularly TiVo, incorporated some neat new features. It was possible to pause live television. When paused, the DVR simply recorded the live program (digitally) to the hard drive. When the user was ready to resume playing, the "live" (well really slightly delayed) program played, now from the hard drive, while the true live feed continued to be recorded.

Most of the DVRs also provide fast-forwarding in convenient increments of 30 seconds, nicely using that rigid format of television ad units to avoid the ads completely! What's more, in some countries DVRs can access a searchable database of television programming. So it is possible, for example, to set the device to record all broadcasts of ballets that would occur over the next week; or for that matter, all the unique episodes of *The Simpsons*! Then, when users wanted, they could have a cultural feast of ballet, or of *The Simpsons* (according to taste), watching uninterrupted hours of their favorite type of program.

The TiVo, in particular, is also a little smarter than previous technologies. It will try to learn viewers' preferences from what they chose to record. It will then spontaneously record programs that it thinks are similar to those viewers themselves have chosen. Viewers can rate programs and help teach the device – a precursor of our smart agents of chapter 3. Of course, this feature is not always perfect. *The Wall Street Journal* in 2002[5] ran a piece about an executive whose TiVo thought he was gay, and spontaneously recorded gay-themed programs! The interesting thing about this humorous article is the recognition that, only three years after launch, the TiVo was sufficiently well-known that it could be joked about in mass media.

Software solutions are also available (for example, Sage TV, www.sagetv.com) which effectively converts your computer into a DVR.

In any event, wherever it started, it seems pretty clear that the traditional model of television programming and advertising doesn't have much time left! But let's be careful, that brings us to our next topic.

TV is Dead, Long-Live TV

Despite all the trends listed above that seem to have destroyed the television model, in early 2007 (in the US market), the most popular types of pre-recorded video materials are television programs!

Seven of the top 25 DVDs on Amazon, and 20% of the seven million DVDs rented every week through Netflix[6] (www. netflix.com, which describes itself as "the world's largest online *movie* rental service"[7]), were television shows, and over 50 million television shows have been downloaded as video podcasts from iTunes[8].

All the gloom and doom we report above involves the traditional television model. This does not necessarily relate to consumers' interest in watching content-formerly-known-as-TV! The point is that what we have traditionally termed *television* programming is really merely *video* programming. That is, the content – which apparently people still like – is device independent.

Consumers are still paying to watch video content that used to be shown on televisions. Many are still watching the material on televisions, although some are not. Consumers are buying the DVDs and the video podcasts of television programs. It has been suggested that this phenomenon be called *buy shifting*, the logical extension of time shifting (originated with the VCR), and place shifting, discussed next.[9]

Personal Broadcasting Devices

Launched mid-2004, personal broadcasting devices are the logical next step in consumer-created content: it's consumer-created television stations! If you're not familiar with these devices, take a look at Slingbox (www.slingmedia.com) or at Sony's Location Free (www.sony.com/locationfree).

The content itself may or may not be consumer-created: it's up to you. The programming – what you show, the schedule

– when you show what, and the device on which you watch it, are also totally up to you.

Personal broadcasting devices stream whatever is playing on a television (or on a game console, or a handheld game console, or a computer – depending on the particular personal broadcasting device you use) over a broadband internet connection. The user can then view that same content from a computer (or mobile device, or PDA, or game console) with a broadband internet connection, anywhere in the world. The user can even change channel, or video source (for example, switch from the cable television to the DVD player to the iPod) from the remote location. This phenomenon is also known as *place shifting*, analogous to the time shifting of the VCR and the TiVo. This gives television content – let's just call it *video content* from here forward – truly anytime, anywhere.

Although the original user was envisioned as the executive away from home who misses the local sports game, or the latest episode of their favorite show, the actual applications are enormous. Even television stations are using these devices to monitor traffic and weather. Slingbox even builds a community of users (www.slingcommunity.com) to help each other in the often complex task of configuring their Slingboxes.

As well as the hardware solutions of Slingbox, Sony Location Free and others, there are software solutions to let your computer do the same thing. At least one is free: Orb, www.orb.com, now known as Orb2.0, uses Web 2.0 technologies (see chapter 3) to allow you to stream any content on your computer (files, images, audio, video, and so on) to just about any internet-connected device.

Orb uses the very descriptive term MyCast for the web applications that help users set up their personal streaming media. As they put it so well: "With Orb and the advent of personal broadcasting, we put you in charge of the programming decisions. You choose what goes into your channels – no more need to channel surf. You can tune into your channels wherever you have an internet connection – no longer constrained by the broadcaster's (or Steve Jobs's) choice of technology."[10]

That's exactly what these personal broadcasters do. They allow each user to create their very own "cast." The user becomes the programmer, selecting the images, the video and the music that they want to see, when they want to see, where they want to see it.

The technology beneath all these devices is the same: internet protocol television (IPTV). Television programming becomes digital and is just one more data stream sent over the internet. IPTV usually encompasses video-on-demand (VOD) whereby customers browse content, select a video stream to see, and that video stream is served to their location.

IPTV is already the fastest expanding segment of the pay television market, with revenues in 2005 at almost $700 million, expected to rise to over $20 billion in 2010.[11] Global IPTV subscribers will reach 14.5 million in 2007: almost three times the subscriber base for 2006, and by 2010 worldwide IPTV subscribers are expected to exceed 60 million.[12]

Multiple Platforms

This means, as we have already seen, that viewing video is no longer the exclusive province of the television set. And it is worth remembering that viewing downloaded digital content is no longer the exclusive province of the computer: up until a very few years ago, digital files had to be viewed on a computer (or transferred to DVD). Now I can view downloaded content (which as we have seen is usually video, and often originated as a television program) on an iPod, or a game console, or on an Apple TV. In the future, consumers are likely to watch video content on many new types of hardware that sit somewhere between the classical television set and the computer.

DIGIMARKETING BEST PRACTICES

Internet protocol television is evolving so quickly that DigiMarketing best practice is scarcely established. However, as we have discussed, "television' as it describes content (not the device on which that content is watched) is no more or less than video. And much of our prior discussion on DigiMarketing best practice with respect to video on other channels is relevant here. In particular, we will summarize the best practices that seem most relevant, and urge you to return to re-read those sections. It would be very pertinent to review the section on successful viral marketing in chapter 6.

Collaborative Personalization

As we saw in chapter 3 on the web, consumers are increasingly asking for producer tools. They want to be active prosumers: producers and consumers. The couch potato wants to sprout!

The big mindshift that marketers have to make from traditional television to digital television is the move from linear programming – watching what someone has created – to more random access of video content. Successful DigiMarketers will make IPTV viewers IPTV participants. In the world of IPTV, this means being able to stop the program in progress at any point to have an extended sidebar of information, perhaps a biography of the presenter, or more details about the products being shown in the program.

What's more, television participants will be able to add their own content to the program. DigiMarketers will need to provide tools to allow participation: to encourage reviewing, blogging, voting, adding content, answering quizzes, and so on, all in real time, in an involving, brand-laden context that will excite and enable those motivated amateurs and turn IPTV into a dynamic, do-it-ourselves resource, which participants can mold into the shape that suits them best.

As we saw in chapter 1, Current TV (www.currenttV.com) allows participants to submit their own videos, and vote on what gets shown.

The other big shift of outlook that is required is that this mass media, once it is digital, will be addressable right down to individual users. And, the address of that user can potentially be linked to his or her browsing and searching behavior, and in fact the entire contents of his or her computer!

Contextual Relevance

In chapter 4, in discussing search, we noted the importance of contextual relevance. As noted, the success of AdWords owes much to the unobtrusiveness of its advertising coupled with the relevance of that advertising. As we already know from experiments with advertising in web-based video, tomorrow's video advertising will be far less intrusive than today's television advertising. The norm for ad duration is likely to be under 15 seconds. What's more, there is absolutely no reason for ad duration to follow fixed 15-second increments. Length will be driven by participant interest, which in turn is based on participant relevance.

As video search tools improve, so IPTV participants will expect overwhelmingly relevant advertising content. Indeed it may well be that the advertising is not itself video. Rather, the ads may be text based, perhaps clickable for interested viewers to see a video.

It's worth noting again that one of the attractions of digital channels, of which IPTV will be one, is addressability. That means that you, on your channel of IPTV, see ads which are especially relevant for you. That relevance is established not only by the video you are currently watching on IPTV, but by the totality of your behavior across all digital channels. Or at least, as much of that totality as you have chosen to share with the DigiMarketer.

Customer in Control

As we have pointed out again and again, in the world of DigiMarketing the customer really is in control. If you thought that channel surfing with a remote control was a problem, IPTV will put the full array of digital assets (websites, television shows, movies, music, news, blogs, podcasts, games, and so on) all one click (or maybe two) away. Any marketing that is intrusive, seems irrelevant or is out of place will be avoided in a moment.

Authenticity and Fit

To be effective, DigiMarketing has to sound authentic and really enhance the customer's experience. If DigiMarketers are to fit in, they must sound authentic and harmonize with the true voice of the customer. The last thing consumers want, on their own IPTV programs, is a hard-sell marketer.

FUTURE TRENDS – WHERE IT'S HEADING

More than half of Europe's incumbent telcos have launched IPTV. However, at this stage they don't have many IPTV subscribers. Only three of the 11 incumbents with live IPTV services have published any subscriber numbers – a sign, perhaps, of a very immature market and many startup problems. While these subscriber numbers are currently still very low, it's projected that a quarter of all European DSL broadband users will watch IPTV by 2015.

In many ways the state of IPTV resembles that of the web 10 years ago; there is a mass of activity, however much of it will be destined for failure. Do you remember that website, from the early days of the internet, with the cows in the field? Visitors clicked on a cow and it fell over. That was the height of cool in its day – a meaningless demonstration of interactivity. But it was the leading edge at the time. Well that's where most of IPTV is now.

At this stage, there seem to be three types of IPTV development. We will look at each in turn[13]:

- IPTV *Trend* 1: Internet Television Portals
- IPTV *Trend* 2: My IPTV
- IPTV *Trend* 3: Radical IPTV

IPTV Trend 1: Internet Television Portals

Just like the origins of the web, most IPTV seems to be organizing initially around IPTV portals. There are probably thousands of channels of internet television currently available. The portal sites seem to be trying to retain the familiar look-and-feel of watching a DVD on a television. They provide a path to IPTV for traditional broadcasters and for their traditional audience – not too much of a shock to the system for either group.

As well as the established portals entering IPTV (for example, Yahoo! TV, in beta-testing, at tv.yahoo.com), there are specialist portals like View TV from the UK (www.viewtv.co.uk, now owned by Med1a). View TV is a portal of 900-plus streaming channels offering free-to-air IPTV content both on the web and to 3G-enabled mobile devices. View TV is designed to mimic standard television, and seems to be targeting traditional television stations that want to test the web waters.

And, of course, most television broadcasters are getting into this space either with their own IPTV "stations" or as part of subscriber-based consolidated offers (for example, www.mobitv.com from AT&T offering FOX News Channel).

There are even consolidated IPTV guide listings starting to emerge. So Find Internet TV (www.findinternettv.com) recently launched an online guide to live television streaming over the internet. Not only do they list programs, but mouse-overs provide further information about the program, and a "watch" button lets you launch that channel in a separate window. We can expect the smart agents of the future to internalize these sorts of listings so as to find exactly the program you want, when you want it.

There are several adaptations of the straight IPTV portal model, all still in beta testing, which promise to push the envelope a little. Zattoo (www.zattoo.com) delivers live streaming video of existing over-the-air and cable television channels to your computer. The idea is that multi-tasking users will have one eye on the Zattoo feed(s) while using other applications to chat, browse, or whatever.

LiveStation (www.livestation.com) promises particularly the ability to interact with ads, bringing the web's clickable advertising to IPTV.[14] This product is being developed by a UK company, Skinkers, and is in part based on technology licensed from Microsoft Research.[15] Skinkers is pursuing the interesting idea of integrating information transmission across media channels. Seen that way, whether you receive content via LiveStation, SMS, podcast or whatever will be determined by the urgency of the communication and the consumer's choice of device. At the time of writing, LiveStation had only one piece of content, and no time shifting, or even pausing abilities.[16]

Webcasts as un-TV Stations

We are also seeing video webcasts emerging as un-TV stations. These are effectively broadcasting content, but technically tend not to come under the regulation of current television stations.

For example, in the UK, YourKindaTV presents a more structured view of consumer-created content than that carried on sites like YouTube. It "broadcasts" on a daily basis and has even bought time on satellite television to showcase its offerings.[17] Also from the UK, 8 Doughty Street presents political broadcasts, news and opinions, and what some have called *controversial attack adverts*. Although effectively television station, these do not operate under the Ofcom Broadcasting Code.

For DigiMarketers, advertising on these portal sites, or in the programming they offer, is an easy step from existing television advertising. But remember that the format is more flexible (duration need not be fixed by 15-second intervals), and anything that adds interactivity is desirable.

IPTV Trend 2: My IPTV

Another set of IPTV applications are intensely personal. In part, My IPTV, means my choice of programming – as chosen from IPTV portals, or selected from video hosting sites. This is really an extension of the idea of personal broadcasting devices discussed above – simply accessing a wide range of content – from which each customer can create their very own station.

For example, Kyte.tv (www.kyte.tv) calls itself "an interactive personal broadcasting platform" and allows users to instantly share pictures and video with family and friends. Its tagline is "TV out of the box," aiming to combine what we have already seen as two key trends on the web: online video and social networking. Kyte.tv lets you upload content (photos, video, music or text) and then broadcast your "channel," all from a mobile device or computer. Viewers can log on and contribute to each other's channels, chat, and take part in opinion polls.[18] Some are using Kyte to promote their music, some to share video of locations with clients. Although there don't seem to be ads at the moment, these could easily be accommodated on the site, or in the video player, or embedded in the videos themselves.

But we are also seeing other aspects of My IPTV – an extension of the consumer-created content boom discussed in chapter 8. This is an IPTV that stars me, my family, and my friends. For example, Justin.tv (www.justin.tv) features the life of one Justin Kan, as seen through the eye of a mobile camera attached to his cap, 24/7. The peak simultaneous viewership of the site supposedly reached 19,000 viewers.[19] Aside from watching what Justin can see, visitors can chat to each other on the site. It's hard to see Justin TV as a major force on the media scene, although his television channel does illustrate some of the possibilities of IPTV.

Already, parents are using IPTV to watch their children in school. Home-owners are surveilling their properties while they are absent. Employers are monitoring employees. Perhaps this application of IPTV sounds mundane, but one thing the web has taught us is that people will use digital technology for the things they want and need most.

IPTV Trend 3: Radical IPTV

There are several developers attempting to reframe the entire television experience. How they will finally end up is hard to guess. At present, these are generally in semi-stable beta forms. But these bear watching for DigiMarketer use in the future.

Joost TV (www.joost.com) is founded by the people who were behind Kazaa (www.kazaa.com, the file-sharing service), and Skype (www.skype.com, the voice over IP leader, see chapter 3). Joost is losing no time in exploiting its first-mover advantage, having signed content deals with MTV, Comedy Central, CNN, Sony Pictures television, CBS, and National Geographic. Joost is currently ad supported, and there are already postings complaining about the intrusive feel of the ads.[20] Joost gives an interesting perspective on how the post-television experience might feel. Joost goes for a full-screen IPTV feel – the program takes over the entire PC screen – and bundles built-in "widgets," including a channel-based chatroom, an instant messaging system, and an RSS news ticker. The end result is like a social-networking site on the television screen, rather than a television mini-screen on a social networking site (as YouTube offers).

Babelgum (www.babelgum.com) similarly "aims to combine the 'lean-back experience' of television with the interactivity and social elements of the web."[21] Again a full-screen experience, but of necessity (fewer content deals than Joost) more focused on connecting niche content with its audiences. It is also reportedly still lacking in some social content widgets.[22]

Vuze (www.vuze.com) is a search, browse and download engine that describes itself as "open entertainment." Vuze uses BitTorrent, a fast file sharing protocol, to find and download high-definition television content. The company is pitching the platform as a way for independent video and film producers to distribute content. Vuze will also be offering paid-for content, via rental and purchase, from the BBC, A&E, and Showtime.[23]

VeohTV (www.veoh.com) presents itself as a "DVR for the web,"[24] claiming to be more open than other IPTV systems, playing all types of video, and allowing viewers to download and save almost any DRM-free (digital rights management free) online video. You can even browse channels representing the major video portals (YouTube and the like), and there are a smattering of widgets.

Jalipo (www.jalipo.com) offers on-demand television shows and movies, and live broadcasts, charged in some cases on a minute-by-minute basis, paid for by "J:Credits" – Jalipo's own online currency.

Some of the seemingly great ideas in IPTV are sure to fall by the wayside. It will be important to look at facts and figures and not get seduced by the hype. At the same time, experimentation in this new field is likely to offer marketers options that are currently hard to evaluate.

SUMMARY: TELEVISION REINVENTED

The evolution of television will mean that what the channel marketers and consumers have known for generations will take on a number of new characteristics:

- IPTV will merge video-based programming and the interactivity of the internet to create a more participatory medium.
- Consumer-created content will play a major role in future "television."
- Personal broadcasting devices and evolving forms of DVRs will liberate video content from the hardware we've known as a television. Accordingly, marketers will need to think about liquid video content that will be viewed on multiple screens at the time consumers choose.
- Marketers should watch the development of new IPTV and radical IPTV portals as emerging players in the television business.

As with all things related to the digital channels we have covered, change will be continuous as marketers and media providers experiment with new, participant-friendly formats.

END NOTES
1   www.zenith.com/sub_about/about_remote.html
2   www.phrases.org.uk/meanings/surfing.html
3   *Variety* announced November 14, 2006 that the VCR had died "of loneliness", www.variety.com/article/VR1117953955.html?categoryid=20&cs=1
4   www.isuppli.com/catalog/detail.asp?id=8194
5   online.wsj.com/article_email/SB1038261936872356908.html
6   www.hackingnetflix.com/2007/01/20_of_netflix_r.html
7   www.netflix.com/MediaCenter?id=5379
8   www.engadget.com/2007/05/04/ins-and-outs-is-buyshifting-the-future-of-television-part-1/
9   *ibid*.
10 www.orb.com/help/index.overviewMyCast.html
11 www.isuppli.com/catalog/detail.asp?id=8194
12 blogs.zdnet.com/ITFacts/?p=12447
13 This section benefited from the detailed reviews of IPTV offered at www.readwriteweb.com/archives/8_internet_tv_apps_in_8_weeks.php
14 www.livestation.com

15 www.techcrunch.com/2007/07/06/first-look-at-livestation-not-much-to-report
16 www.iht.com/articles/2006/11/12/business/webtv.php
17 www.sfgate.com/cgi-bin/article.cgi?file=/c/a/2007/04/23/BUG02PCM7C1.
      DTL&type=tech
18 www.en.wikipedia.org/wiki/Justin.tv#_note-1
19 For example, franticindustries.com/blog/2007/01/16/joost-beta-reviewed-tv-just-
      got-a-little-smarter/
20 www.readwriteweb.com/archives/8_internet_tv_apps_in_8_weeks.php
21 www.techcrunch.com/2007/06/09/hands-on-with-babelgum-a-poor-mans-joost
22 www.techcrunch.com/2007/06/21/vuze-bittorrent-with-a-friendly-legal-face
23 www.veoh.com/veohTV/getStarted.html

A DigiMarketing
Planning Framework

Having reviewed the digital channels at your disposal, and seen examples of what DigiMarketers are already doing in those channels, it's time to turn to how *you* can develop your DigiMarketing plan. Some marketers may be perplexed about where to start. How does DigiMarketing planning differ from traditional marketing planning? Should you start with specific technologies? How can you create an effective plan when things are changing so rapidly? How will you know if your plan is a success?

To help you organize the decisions you'll have to make, we will follow a simple DigiMarketing Planning framework. The framework is broken into four main phases and covers 12 steps. These steps relate directly back to the 12 **DigiMarketing Tenets** that we reviewed in the first section of this book. Indeed, the steps will help ensure that your plans adhere to those tenets. As we go, you will see how these steps integrate into a unified process.

Briefly, here's an overview of the framework, which will be explained in detail in this section of the book:

DigiMarketing Tenet	DigiMarketing Planning Step
PHASE 1	
Tenet 1: Consumers as Participants	Participant Print and Goals
PHASE 2	
Tenet 2: Involvement/Interaction	Platform Proposition
Tenet 3: Addressable Channels	Channel Mix and Creative Concept
Tenet 4: Time Shifted	Content Outline (Company-Provided)
Tenet 5: Consumer Created	Content Outline (Consumer-Created)
PHASE 3	
Tenet 6: Opt-In and Share Marketing	Messaging and Viral Plan
Tenet 7: New Media Planning	Digital Awareness Plan
Tenet 8: Digital Influence	Digital Influence Plan
Tenet 9: Unified Marketing	Channel Unification Plan
PHASE 4	
Tenet 10: Data-enabled	Data Plan
Tenet 11: Real-Time Measurement	Analytics Plan
Tenet 12: Optimization	Optimization Plan

12 **DigiMarketing Tenets** with Related Planning Steps

Chapter 11

Phase 1 – Defining a Participant Print and Goals

The first phase of planning starts with a focus on the consumers or customers with whom you will interact through DigiMarketing. This differs from traditional planning in requiring much more emphasis on how consumers interact with you as participants. From the start, you should also establish goals for your DigiMarketing (Figure 11.1). By the end of the first phase, you should be able to answer the key questions, "What are the key insights about my participants?" and "What are my main goals?"

Figure 11.1: DigiMarketing Planning, Phase I

DigiMarketing Tenet 1: Consumers and customers must be actively engaged as participants – creators, contributors, and commentators – not treated as passive viewers or targets.

PARTICIPANT PRINT

Good marketing always begins with the consumer or customer, and that's where DigiMarketing planning begins too. We call it a *Participant Print*. Whether your DigiMarketing is intended to appeal to millions of consumers or a select business-to-business audience, you will need a clear understanding of the people at the other end.

Most marketers do some form of planning to define their target audience. You might feel this is sufficient and wonder why a Participant Print is required. This isn't a shallow semantic issue. There are deep implications inherent in the shift from targeting to the broader exercise of participant planning. You will need to anticipate how consumers will act

A DigiMarketing Planning Framework

as respondents, participants, and even initiators. Recognizing this from the start is a key mindshift required for successful DigiMarketing.

Frankly, it's time to retire the word *target* from the marketing lexicon. It's an outdated term which doesn't reflect that people now interact with the multiplicity of channels around them. What's required is a more contemporary and holistic way to think about your consumers and how to generate sustained engagement with them. This is where the Participant Print comes in.

How to Develop a Participant Print

A Participant Print, which is modeled upon Ogilvy & Mather's Customer Print[1], is intended to capture the essence of the group of people who comprise your customers. The Participant Print should build upon any existing Customer Print or target audience definitions you have by adding information and insights about your customers in relation to digital channels. Your Participant Print should straddle both existing and new customers.

Key elements of a Participant Print are:
1. General Profile
2. Digital Profile
    a. Digital Usage Habits
    b. Content Consumption Preferences
    c. Consumer Content Creation Profile
3. Individual Profiles

Participant Print 1: General Profile

The first section of the print includes basic information about your customers. This might include demographics, transactional behavior information (for example, purchasing patterns), and response rates to previous promotions and marketing activities. This will certainly be useful when it comes time to decide your DigiMarketing content, messaging, and activation strategies.

You should also have "lifestyle" data to help you understand the deeper psychographic aspects of your participant base. This is vital, since consumer attitudes and tendencies today do not follow lock-step with demographic data. For example, a Harley-Davidson enthusiast could be 16 or 60 years-old. Knowing more about the psychographic profile of your current and prospective participants will help you when you craft the themes and materials to use in your digital marketing.

Participants' own words are important too. How do participants talk about your product category and about your brand? What are the actual words they use? This information will be vital later when you define your search marketing strategies (SEO and SEM, refer back to chapter 4).

While you will already know a fair amount about your consumers, writing your Participant Print affords you the opportunity to update and reassess your assumptions. You might collect data from prospective consumers or your competitors' consumers, as well as from your existing consumers.

Participant Print 2: Digital Profile

The next portion of your print will focus on your customers/ prospects as users of digital media.

Digital Usage Habits

What digital channels do your customers currently use and in what proportion? What sites do they surf? What kind of digital devices do they own? Which do they use most often? Are there any digital trends among your participant group (for example, an increase in their desire to receive podcasts) that are particularly worthy of note? Any insights you can gain about your customers' attitudes towards digital channels and devices will prove invaluable later when you make channel and content decisions. Digital usage habits can change rapidly so current data is critical.

Content Consumption Preferences

As content becomes liberated from channels, understanding participants' content preferences becomes essential. Participants' loyalty will be to the content not to the delivery mechanism. If you haven't done the important spade work to really know what content is likely to interest your participants, you run the risk of being ignored and overlooked when you go live with your DigiMarketing plans.

Two things are especially important. First, what are your participants' favored sources of information? What influences them? What do they consider the best single source of information they can tap? Insights here will be used when you create your influence plan, consider potential partners for affiliate marketing, and select digital media.

Second, what are your participants' attitudes to your competitors' content? Competitors are only a click away, so it's worth identifying what they are doing well, and where they are failing to deliver. These gaps or unmet needs can prompt valuable ideas.

Consumer Content Creation Profile

The final area in the digital section of your Participant Print covers what your customers (or prospective customers) are creating at the moment. This should yield some important insights about participants as active creators. What type of contests do they participate in? What photo sites do they upload pictures to? What kind of blogs do they create? Are they already engaged in blogs about your product category or your competitors' brands – or your brands? In the planning process, you might consider contacting a handful of top bloggers to see if you can gain any insights from them. As we'll see when we build your Digital Influence Plan (in chapter 13), tracking blogs should be a standard operating procedure, giving you some first-hand knowledge of what people are saying about you and your competition.

Participant Print 3: Individual Profiles

You will need to know all you can about individual customers. You may find this data in your existing customer databases or through tracking customers' current web activity. Of course, your profiling should include some segmentation. How you segment will depend upon the type of data you have on hand. Ideally, you will have consumer purchase data and share of wallet data, so you can identify high lifetime value customers. These customers should be on the top of your list for alerts and interactions when you eventually launch your DigiMarketing program. Ideally you will have some behavioral or psychographic segmentation data too, so you can identify the psychographic attributes of your existing customers.

Of course, the goal of DigiMarketing is to take your marketing beyond general segmentations. You will want to get down to interacting in a tailored manner with each and every individual participant. This will come with time. As participants interact with you individually, and you analyze those interactions, the individual database will start to form. However, at the initial planning stage, you will probably be forced to rely on your existing segmentations.

Sources of Information

You may wonder where you'll get all this information. As noted above, you're likely to have some of it in your organization already in the form of existing customer prints and customer databases. To get the information you don't have, here are a number of options to consider:

- You could modify an existing tracking study, or other market research instrument, to include questions that will fill some gaps.
- You could commission research among current and prospective consumers to look for general insights about your products and specific insights about participants' digital habits and preferences.
- You could better use existing digital channels to gain new insights. Many marketers don't get enough value out of their websites as a means of garnering consumer feedback, particularly from brand loyalists. Start to solicit, read and analyze customer feedback.
- You could use digital tracking tools to glean information about your participants' current online behaviors.
- You could buy information from media owners, agencies, and research companies, who have online data.

Investing in good data at the start of the planning process will yield enormous benefits by placing all the decisions you make in your DigiMarketing planning on a sound footing. Unfortunately, marketers are sometimes so eager to get started that they are unwilling to spend the proper time or money to establish the solid factual foundation that will more than pay for itself in the end.

A Working Example:
Eagle Athletic* – Participant Print

To help bring the DigiMarketing framework to life, we will use a composite company – Eagle Athletic, a top-end maker of sports shoes and apparel – as an example throughout each of the planning steps. For the purposes of this case, assume Eagle has in the past only used traditional mass media (selected television, print, and billboards). However, in order to stay relevant to their customers and prospects, they have decided to shift their marketing budget to digital and now need a DigiMarketing plan.

Here's an excerpt of what Eagle's Participant Print might look like:

Area	Focus	Key Highlights or Insights
General Profile	Overall user base and prospect trends	The Eagle user base has a high participation rate in amateur sporting events. Eagle consumers react positively to sales but say in research they'd rather have sports experiences than just price reductions.
	Participant psychographics	The typical Eagle consumer is a challenger who is always looking to do his or her best. Eagle users like extreme sports as well as more conventional sporting activities.
Digital Profile	Digital usage habits	The current Eagle participants are very internet savvy; 90% of them use the internet and email daily; 95% of them have a mobile phone; 75% own an mp3 player; and interestingly, 79% of them say they read a blog every day.
	Content consumption preferences	Eagle participants enjoy sports programming and attend more live sporting events than average adult consumers. Online, they favor key sports sites, but also enjoy EA sports games. Plus, over half of them say they follow a regular sports blog. 20% regularly visit a competitor's website for information.
	Consumer content creation profile	56% participate in sports fantasy leagues. Additionally, 30% have sports-related avatars in *Second Life*. 35% of Eagle participants have their own blog.
Individual Profiles	Current High-value consumers	Of 1.5 million customers in their database, 300,000 consumers purchased Eagle gear within the last six months. Eagle has identified 100K users who contribute 76% of sales. They have a list of email addresses they will refer to when it comes time to launch digital messaging.

Figure 11.2: Eagle Athletic – Participant Print

* This is a fictitious company and name.

What to Do with Your Participant Print

Your completed Participant Print should give you a good contextual background, rooted in fact, as the starting point of your planning. It will provide a composite snapshot that will enable you to anticipate some of your participants' needs and desires. You cannot foretell everything that people will want or do. As you interact with your participants via digital channels, you will learn more about what they actually want and do. However, the more you can establish about your participants at the start, the more guesswork you can take out of the process.

A good Participant Print will help inform a number of your DigiMarketing decisions:

- Knowing your participants' digital destinations and digital media usage habits will help in your channel(s) selection process.
- Understanding your participants' current content habits and psychographics will give you insights when deciding the type of content you will create, and encourage participants to create.
- Knowing how consumers and prospects talk about your product category and your brand will help you select key phrases both for your search engine optimizations (getting to the top of the search engine listings) and for your search engine marketing (deciding which key phrases to buy for your ads).
- Knowing where your participants turn to for information and opinions will be vital when you put together your Digital Influence Plan.
- Insights about which websites, networking sites, podcasts, and other digital destinations they use most will help inform your digital media, affiliate marketing, and sponsorship choices.

- The response patterns of your consumers as a whole, as well as for individuals, will help when you set your messaging strategy.
- Understanding their current habits will help you develop effective activation strategies that should be part of generating awareness and influence.

GOALS

Right from the start you need to establish clear goals for your DigiMarketing. This obvious point is ignored by too many marketers, who often lack well-articulated expectations of what they hope to accomplish. As a result, they are lost when it comes time to assess if they have been successful or determine whether their approach is making a reasonable return on investment and merits further investment. You should set goals. These will serve as key performance indicators (KPIs) for your DigiMarketing. We will return to these goals later in the planning framework when we discuss analytics and measurement.

Most probably, your goals will stem from two main things. First, effective DigiMarketing can drive hard business results, such as acquiring new customers, increasing sales, and building customer loyalty. So, some of your DigiMarketing goals will mirror your overall business goals. You may well apportion some (or all) of your customer acquisition or sales targets to your DigiMarketing plan.

Second, in the process of putting together your Participant Print, you will have identified some qualitative issues that you will want to address via your DigiMarketing. This might involve changing existing consumer perceptions or habits or addressing unmet consumer needs. This will really depend upon what you uncover in the process of putting together your Participant Print.

The following are a number of broad areas that you might consider as you set goals. Of course, the specific metrics of the goals will need to reflect your particular situation and ambitions.

Customer Acquisition/Registration

It is vital that DigiMarketing generates responses. Otherwise, the key benefits of one-to-one communication can't be realized. For this reason, most marketers gear their efforts to some goal for customer acquisition or registration.

Brand Exposure

While DigiMarketing delivers sales or specific customer leads, it also builds basic brand exposure, just like other forms of marketing communication. There are times when a DigiMarketing effort contributes to awareness and interest, even if the customer doesn't immediately click through to registration and sales. You should set some goals for increasing brand interest and likeability.

Product Knowledge/Education

Digital channels provide an excellent way to deliver extended educational or product information. If used properly, videos on the web or mobile phone can add depth to consumers' understanding of a company's products and services, or the context for the use of that product. For example, in Italy, Buitoni Pasta[2] provides video cooking lessons via its website. You might set specific goals for the number of people you reach with educational material via digital channels.

New Product Introductions

While traditional channels are often used to generate awareness for a new product, they usually don't lend themselves to telling the extended story of that new product. Digital channels, on the other hand, can be ideal for extended product information, demonstrations, background test details, or any other information that helps substantiate the benefits of a new product. So, your goals might include reaching a certain number of people about a new product or service.

Enhanced Customer Service

Some marketers are using digital channels to improve their customer experience and/or reduce their customer servicing costs. A website can provide customers with information and 24 x 7 access; teleweb services (allowing call centers to be phoned from websites) can deal quickly with customer queries and complaints. Your DigiMarketing goals might include specific increases in customer satisfaction, the number of customers serviced via digital channels, and targets for customer servicing cost reductions.

Detailed Participant Database

As we have seen, DigiMarketing provides a feasible way to build detailed customer profiles. Therefore, your goals might include some specific KPIs in relation to deepening your databases.

Company PR Coverage and Influence

Innovative DigiMarketing often leads to significant PR coverage. Some companies set goals for what they expect to achieve in terms of exposure and influence. We will cover the topic of Digital Influence in detail in the third phase of the DigiMarketing planning.

Consumer Insights and Feedback

DigiMarketing is an effective way to get consumer feedback. Smart companies use the interactivity of digital channels to listen to their customers, which acts as an early warning system about new products or other issues. You can set goals in this area too.

Activation

DigiMarketing is playing an increasingly important role at points of purchase, where the vast majority of purchase decisions are actually made today. Good digital activation strategies will help your products get noticed and trialed. Therefore, you should consider setting goals for reaching consumers via activation at relevant points of consideration or purchase.

Sales

We mention this last, rather than first, since not every DigiMarketer will necessarily be conducting e-commerce. However, it's a no-brainer that if you are selling on the web, you'll have sales targets as part of your goals.

There are other areas that could be part of your goal setting. This brief list merely serves to prompt your thinking about the many options you have in setting DigiMarketing goals.

- Via DigiMarketing, acquire 300,000 first-time Eagle participants over the first two years.
- Expand by 25% the base of existing Eagle customers who attend an Eagle-sponsored event within a 12-month period.
- Increase by 30% Eagle's brand attribute tracking scores for "innovative," "youthful," and "the coolest in the category," versus main competitors.

Once you've finished your Participant Print and set some goals, you'll need to turn your attention to deciding what you and your participants will create or build – our next topic.

END NOTES
1 Customer Prints is a trademark protected term registered by Ogilvy & Mather.
2 www.buitoni.it/content/school/milano_index.asp

Chapter 12

Phase 2 – Creating Your Digital Platform

T he next planning steps focus on your Digital Platform. A platform is the totality of the digital assets (and related content) through which you and participants will have ongoing engagement (Figure 12.1). For some marketers, this might simply mean a website or mobile site. For others, such as Coke, who created iCoke (www.iCoke.com), it might involve developing an integrated, interactive marketing program involving a digital destination for a particular audience (in this case, youth), integrated with game environments (iCoke recreated *World of Warcraft* scenes in China[1]), and on-pack codes that earn credits to enter online competitions.[2]

There are a number of key decisions you will need to make about your digital platform, such as its proposition (which defines the key consumer benefits of the platform), the channel mix you will use in your platform, the creative concept that will make it appealing, and the content that participants will both find at and contribute to the platform. By the end of this phase of the planning process, you should have the answers to the key questions, "What will I build and how will participants interact with and contribute to it?"

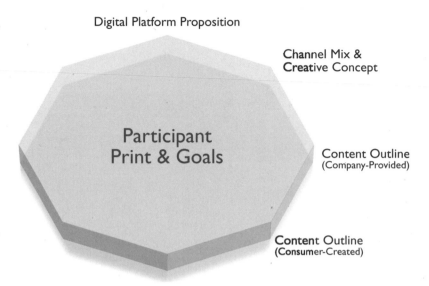

Figure 12.1: DigiMarketing Planning, Phase 2

DigiMarketing Tenet 2: Marketers must move beyond the traditional metrics of reach and frequency. Successful DigiMarketing engages people on a sustained basis. This requires better planning and a clear proposition of why you merit participants' time and attention.

DIGITAL PLATFORM PROPOSITION

People today have a vast array of digital options. Therefore, you will need a Digital Platform Proposition to articulate why people should engage with you, via your platform, on a regular basis. This Digital Platform Proposition isn't about what *you* want to achieve; that should have been adequately addressed in your goals. Instead, the Proposition defines the consumer benefit of engagement. It makes clear what participants will see or experience or be able to do when they interact with your platform.

Your Digital Platform Proposition also serves to position your platform. Generally, your Digital Platform Proposition extends from your current brand positioning to articulate how your DigiMarketing will amplify your brand in new ways. The Platform Proposition should be a clear, written description of a sustained direction for your Digital Platform. Having a clear Proposition will ensure consistency in your approach, even as underlying technologies evolve.

How to Develop Your Digital Platform Proposition

Your Digital Platform Proposition should be simple. It might be only a sentence or two, though it can be longer if you choose. The complex part is not writing the Platform Proposition; what takes time and effort is the consideration process that leads to it. Here are some of the key elements you will need to think through:

Competitive Differentiation

There's a lot of competition out there today. Anything you create will have multiple competitors. So it's important to be clear about *how* your DigiMarketing Platform is distinctive and *why* customers will care.

For example, as a pharmaceutical marketer, you might write your Digital Platform Proposition as: "To provide online advice to patients with the most updated medical information possible." However, there are thousands of sites that consumers can visit for medical information. What will make *your* site better and more worthy of consumers' time? Why should consumers seek information from you instead of others? You'll have to stretch to ensure you're not me-too. And stay realistic: your Proposition must reflect what you can actually deliver. Perhaps you should sharpen your Proposition to be: "Provide the only medical destination that offers consumers two alternative medical views on any medical query, so patients can see their options."

Contextual Relevance

Hard-selling generally doesn't work in digital channels. What's usually more pertinent, especially if you want to engage consumers on an ongoing basis, is to focus on how people are using your products and services in their lives. As an example, let's consider a company that makes diapers. That marketer will probably be more successful focusing on the context of use of the diapers – baby care – than on the diapers themselves. The resulting proposition for their DigiMarketing could be to "help parents take care of their babies with age-appropriate advice from birth to the time they stop wearing diapers."

A tire manufacturer might focus on providing good driving advice, or tips on car travel, rather than a narrow focus on tires. As you take a wider contextual approach, you will be challenged to provide information and content you may not have to hand. Very shortly, we will address this topic.

Personalization

Next you will need to decide what degree of personalization you intend to offer. Will individual participants log on to individual accounts? Will they receive personalized products or services? At this stage, you should not be addressing the specifics of the site design or functionality. Rather, you should be establishing the broad parameters of what you will do.

Transactional Role

How much do you intend for your DigiMarketing effort to focus around sales, as compared to building awareness and engagement for your brand? If you have a sales focus, will it include online sales? Again you don't need to get into site design specifics yet.

Where Technology Fits In

In writing your Digital Platform Proposition, you must separate the technology and the strategic issues. Some marketers get fixated on cutting-edge technology and confuse this with strategy. We fully applaud using innovative technologies to bring your proposition to life. However, technologies tend to be short-lived. A marketer who doesn't have a strategy to ensure consistency often bounces from one innovative technology to another in a purely tactical way, and risks terminally confusing consumers.

As an example, let's go back to you as a pharmaceutical marketer. You might have started in a fairly low-tech way offering two medical opinions via text on a website. However, as broadband develops, you might add instructional videos. As 3G rolls out, you might extend your offer to short videos delivered to mobile phones. Your Proposition stays the same, although the technology that delivers it evolves. Technology should not lead; it should simply enable you to reach your goals in delivering your Proposition.

Market Application

You may wonder how this can be done given the maddening difference of technologies between markets and constant technological upgrades. How can you come up with a proposition that could apply to many different markets, all in different stages of technological development? The answer is to make the benefit the centerpiece and then choose the technology according to what's available.

Again, let's use the example of our pharmaceutical marketer. In Japan, you might deliver two medical opinions via an i-mode site (the Japanese mobile web). However, in the US, you might deliver opinions in shortened format via SMS or email. While technology varies by market, marketers can stay true to their Propositions.

A Working Example: Eagle Athletic – Digital Platform Proposition

From their Participant Print, Eagle gained useful insights about the psychographics of their participants, particularly in regard to the type of information they seek and the events in which they participate. Subsequently, they have articulated their proposition as follows:

To create a platform dedicated to helping athletes improve their athletic performance by providing exercise information and tools that help them monitor their individual progress. This platform will be the definitive destination for those athletes who are committed to being their best at their chosen sport.

What to Do with Your Digital Platform Proposition

Your Platform Proposition is your long-term roadmap. You won't necessarily look at it every month or even half-yearly. However, when it comes time to review your future direction, you will want to refer to it.

In the immediate term, you will use the Platform Proposition in the next few steps as you define your creative approach and your content plans. Sometimes, when you get to these steps, the true impact of your Proposition becomes apparent. In some cases, you may realize that delivering on the Proposition is simply unrealistic – perhaps requiring huge amounts of content. When that happens, you have to go back and further sharpen your Proposition.

DigiMarketing Tenet 3: Marketers need to determine which mix of channels is right for their marketing needs. Engaging digital creative should encourage participants to adapt your digital marketing around their personal preferences and desires.

CHANNEL MIX PLAN AND CREATIVE CONCEPT

The next step in the planning process involves some important decisions about which digital channels you will use to engage your participants (your Channel Mix Plan) and what unique ideas you will convey through those channels (your Creative Concept).

In digital channels, the line between channel selection (Channel Mix Plan) and Creative Concept can be blurred. Sometimes, channel selection is the essence of the creative idea, particularly when a marketer creates a new channel or uses a particular channel in an innovative manner. A case in point is Bacardi's B-Live radio station, a company-branded, customizable radio station (www.barcardibliveradio.com), Sprite Yard – a mobile-based social networking site created by Coca-Cola – is another example. In both cases, the companies had to design the layout and an interface for what they created. However, the idea was essentially the use of channels in new ways.

Let's look at channel selection first. This can be daunting for some marketers, as they must choose from so many changing options. However, it's specifically *because* there are so many options that you need a well-considered Channel Mix Plan. Gone are the days when you could simply buy your way into reaching a particular audience. Instead, you'll need to carefully determine which combination of channels is most likely to reach a sufficient number of your participants.

At a minimum, your Channel Mix Plan will force you to prioritize the channels you will use. However, a top-notch plan can help you identify the optimal mix of channels – namely, which channels, in what proportion, and with what linkages. The channel planning process should go beyond digital channels and incorporate traditional channels too. However, we will cover that topic later when we consider integration.

At this stage, the most important thing is that your channel selection defines the broad parameters of what you will create – websites, mobile sites, podcasts, custom music portals, and so on. A natural follow on from channel selection is to consider the creative concepts that will breathe life into your chosen channels.

How to Develop a Channel Mix Plan

Channel Insights

Your Participant Print will quickly prove its worth, as the first step in the channel planning process is to review your customers' digital media habits. Your channel selection should not be dictated simply by what your participants currently do. However, their current digital habits should yield some insights and help you start to identify channel priorities.

Do your participants have a strong preference for mobile devices versus fixed line internet? Do they spend a lot of time in online chat rooms? Are they avid gamers? In reviewing channel habits, some marketers discover that they have incorrect notions about what their consumers do or don't do. The channel planning process often forces reappraisal. It should also stretch the limits of what you have traditionally considered in terms of channel selection.

Channel Data

You will want to substantiate your insights with specific media data. Does the data confirm that your participants use mobile phones more than other participant groups? Do they play online games at a higher rate than other groups? Grounding your plan in solid data will be important later when you commit funds and may need to validate your plan. However, data alone can't guarantee a good plan. You will always have to apply some judgment as you start to decide which channels make the most sense for you, given your goals.

Participant Journey[3]

The next step is to identify not only which channels you want to use but also how and where they will fit within your consumer journey. This step grounds the planning in *your* business.

A Participant Journey (as we saw in chapter 2) is a mapping of the most common path (or journey) by which your customers or consumers get to know about, consider, and perhaps purchase your product. For example, the participant journey for a car buyer might involve checking consumer reports websites, reading car blogs, visiting a dealer, talking to a sales rep, and going for a test drive. Journeys can vary dramatically by product category and by participant. The participant journey to buy a car would differ substantially from, say, the journey for buying shampoo – which might be shorter and have more in-store focus. So, you will need to plot out the steps and touchpoints that typify your participant journey.

Different participant journeys will suggest different applications of the same digital channel. For example, the car marketer might decide to use the mobile device primarily to stay in touch with people once they've purchased a car, while the shampoo marketer might use the mobile device primarily to incentivize consumers through m-coupons to buy the product. Digital channels are versatile enough to serve many applications. It's important not to be vague about what you want to accomplish with each channel. This leads to the next topic: identifying the core metrics for each of the selected channels.

Channel Metrics

Strange as it sounds, many marketers don't think through the role of the channels they chose. They assume they "need a website" because "everyone has one," or they want to do something on *Second Life* because "everyone else is in there." The point is that if they really do need these digital channels, they also need to identify just what each channel should deliver in their DigiMarketing plans. The best way to force articulation of goals is to specify measures of success. So, the fourth element in the channel planning process is to identify specific metrics for each of the channels on your selection list.

At this point, where and how your channels fit into your participant journey should link directly to what you expect those channels to achieve. In the car marketer example above, mobile was selected as a channel to help stay in touch with customers post-purchase. The role of the mobile channel is to promote loyalty and provide customer service. Consequently, the car marketer might set goals for improving customer care scores or for increasing responses to after-sales offers via mobiles.

A Working Example:
Eagle Athletic – Channel Mix Plan

After reviewing their Participant Print and reviewing available media data, Eagle has decided upon the following channel mix selection, with corresponding metrics. A simple table can capture the key decisions:

Channel Type	Purpose in the Customer Cycle	Metrics
Website	Acquisition and ongoing customer contact, particularly in regard to participants' own sports activities	Brand Awareness, new customer data capture (live profiles), and number of users who register to track their personal athletic activities
Mobile Devices	Activation of Eagle participants	Response and participation rates in Eagle-sponsored sports events
Blogs (Sports Related)	New customer acquisition and existing customer retention	Percentage of participants reading links to Eagle blogs

Figure 12.2: Eagle Athletic – Channel Mix Plan

What to Do with a Channel Mix Plan

There are numerous ways to express your Channel Mix Plan. So, we believe it's important to have a fairly flexible view of how you articulate your plan. However, it is essential to capture the key facts about the channels that make it onto your selection list, clearly articulate the role of each channel, and describe the corresponding metrics for each channel. Some marketers might take a more creative approach to the channel plan and treat it as the start point of the creative development process.

CREATIVE CONCEPT

Following your channel selection, you will need to decide what it is you will actually create, including theme, creative layout, and functionality. The scope of your creative decisions will depend on the digital media you've decided to use. If you decide to build a website or mobile site, you will need to settle the site architecture. However, nothing dictates that you will default to building a website. If you decide to use viral videos, they will involve a different set of creative decisions. Or you might decide to use innovative podcasts to build your brand. Or, perhaps you will build a branded advergame as your key DigiMarketing platform. Each of these choices will involve their own types of creative decisions.

In our example, Eagle Athletic has decided to build a website, use mobile devices, and to create a company-run blog. Now they have to determine what creative shape those things will take to ensure that they are interesting and appealing to consumers. Eagle will face the tough question that all marketers face: how to stand out among the millions of alternatives consumers can choose instead. There are no right answers, particularly since you could wind up in so many different places with your channel selection. However, irrespective of your selection of digital channels, the Box Insert below (Digital Creative Guidelines) summarizes some of the key hallmarks of good digital creative work.

Digital Creative Guidelines

Strong Creative Idea

DigiMarketing is like all other marketing: great ideas matter. Interesting ideas intrigue people and are key to gaining their attention and holding their interest. Just like television commercials, websites should have a creative idea to them. It's the creative ideas that will bring your Digital Platform Proposition to life.

Reflective of the Brand

Digital channels give marketers a new creative palette to work with. Media richness and interactivity can be combined in ways that traditional one-way channels can't match. However, digital communication is still brand communication. The fact that you're creating a podcast or mobile site or email campaign doesn't somehow remove it from your overall brand parameters. You can be experimental in digital channels, but you should never be off-brand.

Engaging in Style and Tone

A key part of being on-brand is to reflect the tone of your brand. Your digital creative concepts can have wit, a human touch, authority, and intimacy. A well-written SMS can communicate in an engaging tone, not the functional sales pitches commonly used. Too many websites default to bland, brochure-style corporate-speak. Don't let them! Be brave with your DigiMarketing. Consistently question whether participants will enjoy what you are creating and find it interesting on a sustained basis.

Intuitive in Use

In creating interactive digital assets – websites, mobile sites, games – you are creating things that people will interact with rather than simply watch with folded arms. The layout and design of these assets need to ensure they are intuitive to use. If potential customers are perplexed or confused, they are likely to click away from your DigiMarketing. Good architecture and usability planning are vital

Functionality

This differs from usability: usability is about architecture, functionality relates to download times and intelligent uses of technology to enhance the creative idea. A simple rule of thumb is that the technology should *never* get in the way of the user experience. Your creative idea should always be at the fore.

Great design, site architecture, and the other issues in the digital creative process are major topics in their own right. Since our primary purpose here is to focus on the planning process, we won't go into details. However, these are important topics, and you will need to work with an appropriate agency or partner to help you address them. In the meantime, we suggest you go to www.DigiMarketingNow.com/GreatCreative for links to see a selection of award-winning creative work.

DigiMarketing Tenet 4: In DigiMarketing, content will increasingly be freed from specific delivery mechanisms, the limitations of media units, and physical boundaries. All DigiMarketers will need to make relevant, quality content their focus in order to generate sustained participant interest.

CONTENT OUTLINE (COMPANY-PROVIDED)

Your channel choices will involve some form of content; therefore, a Content Outline is vital. As we have seen in this book, content now comes in two (hopefully harmonious) flavors: company-provided and consumer-created. In this section we focus on outlining the portion of content that the company will provide. The next section turns to the content you will hopefully stimulate consumers to create.

Marketers are often overwhelmed by the demands placed upon them to supply content for the channels they have chosen. Those that don't plan ahead realize after the digital launch just how big – and continuing – the content demands really are.

Maintaining a content-rich site is a bit like buying an elephant (yes, an odd analogy, but bear with us)! When you bring the elephant home, all your friends and neighbors are excited and come to have a look. After a bit, the excitement dies down. But the elephant is still there. And you start to realize that day-in and day-out, you have to feed it – a lot. After a point, you will despair of having to feed this elephant, and turn your thoughts to how you can rid yourself of this burden.

This doesn't have to be the case for your DigiMarketing, not if you're realistic from the start in estimating what content you will provide and what your participants can be encouraged to provide. The purpose of the Content Outline is to start to describe what content you will have, where you will obtain it, and how you will update it on an ongoing basis.

Your Content Outline should not be solely focused on your desires as a marketer — not just about what you want to tell participants. Rather, your guiding principle must be that only content that will truly appeal to your participants should be included.

How to Develop Your Content Outline (Company-Provided)

A Content Outline is not a specific editorial schedule of what will be on your website, mobile site, or blog. Rather, as the name implies, it should be an outline of the main content types that must be supplied to support your Platform Proposition. It is intended to be an outline. Of course, later in the implementation process, you'll have to get to the more granular level of creating a specific content schedule. At this stage, there are several things you will want to consider in putting together your Content Outline.

Key Content Type(s)

Many marketers start with their company information when they consider content. This was particularly true in the early days of the internet, leading to boring "brochureware." While you no doubt will want to include some information about your company, it should not dominate your company-provided content.

There is a lot of text-based information that you can include: news, opinions, white papers, comparative reviews, how-to's, edutainment, and so on. But why stick with text? Today, given the growth of broadband, there's a wealth of rich content options: photos, videos, archive footage, dynamic graphs, satellite photos, location finders, maps. Think broadly about the types of things you might include to add exciting new dimensions to what you are creating.

Purpose/Benefit

As you identify content types, be sure that each has a clear purpose and makes your Proposition more compelling. Simply dumping tons of information into a site or blog won't make it better; it's more likely to make it unfocussed and cumbersome.

The content must satisfy and involve participants to keep them coming back. The hard part is deciding which of all the mound of content available is the right content. For example, in the music business, simply deciding that you will have music information is too vague. That could include new artists, tour information, entertainer news, entertainer profiles, or backstage information. It behooves you to truly think through and define the purpose of your content. Later, through analysis of your DigiMarketing, you will be able to see which content is generating the highest consumer interest. You can then use this learning to fine-tune your Content Outline.

Dynamic or Static

A key aspect of content is whether it is to be dynamic or static. For most marketers, product descriptions change relatively infrequently, so they generally constitute static content. News, on the other hand, changes daily, and is therefore dynamic. But there are also some types of content that might be both static and dynamic. For example, basic medical information doesn't change daily, but you may have dynamic content as new clinical studies are released. Dynamic content also includes content that doesn't exist until it is requested. Many sites display pages of content that are generated dynamically to tailor to individuals' specific needs or profiles.

As part of your Content Outline, you'll need to identify the frequency with which content will need to be updated. Even if your site is going to have a large amount of static content, you should still think through how you can rotate or refresh it. Otherwise, your platform will become stale and participants won't engage or return again.

Source(s) of Content and Upkeep

You may well already have a raft of useful content. Of course, your content has to fit your Platform Proposition. If, for example, you are a pharmaceutical marketer with a proposition to provide medical information online, you are likely to have at least some of that content already. However, if you are a beverage company with the proposition to provide participants with the latest from the music scene, you will probably need to turn to third parties to get that information.

There are numerous potential sources of content, including: government organizations, academic institutions, private foundations, leading experts in the field, and non-competing companies. Be sure to give some thought to this last source – non-competing companies. In the digital world, new and innovative alliances are being forged all the time. If your Participant Profile is similar to another company's, or if they have content that's relevant to your Platform Proposition, you might be able to work out an affiliate partnership or other reciprocal agreement. After all, working together could provide you both with valuable exposure and links to more prospective participants. Also, give some thought to what publicly available digital tools or sources you could incorporate into your content. Remember the power of mash-ups (chapter 3): many marketers are figuring out how Google Earth images (http://earth.google.com) could work in conjunction with their DigiMarketing...or maybe Google Sky would fit better for you.[4]

If you will be sourcing content outside of your company, is it a regular and reliable source? Will the content be credible? How will you vet or edit the content to fit your needs? How will you ensure copyright protection? You need to make sure you have all the necessary disclaimers and legal protections in place. You will also need to monitor the internet for people "borrowing" your content without permission. If it's your participants, you might want to encourage this. If it's your competitors, you might be less tolerant.

If you're in it for the long haul – as any serious DigiMarketer should be – you will need a process to regularly update and manage your content. Many companies finish up with multiple websites, a range of digital media, and traditional media (brochures, and so on). Keeping all this information updated, and in sync, can be a challenge. This is often handled by making all digital media database-driven. That way a master version of the latest information resides in one place, and all the digital media – and the traditional media – take the data from that one place. That means one point of update, vastly simplifying content management.

> ### A Working Example: Eagle Athletic – Content Outline (Company-Provided)
>
> As a key part of supporting their Platform Proposition to "help athletes improve their athletic performance by providing exercise information, and to appeal to consumers' desire to participate in local sporting events," Eagle has decided to focus on content in two areas: local sports

events and exercise and sports performance information. Their Content Outline is as follows:

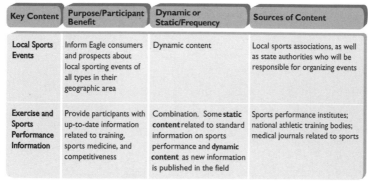

Key Content	Purpose/Participant Benefit	Dynamic or Static/Frequency	Sources of Content
Local Sports Events	Inform Eagle consumers and prospects about local sporting events of all types in their geographic area	Dynamic content	Local sports associations, as well as state authorities who will be responsible for organizing events
Exercise and Sports Performance Information	Provide participants with up-to-date information related to training, sports medicine, and competitiveness	Combination. Some **static content** related to standard information on sports performance and **dynamic content** as new information is published in the field	Sports performance institutes; national athletic training bodies; medical journals related to sports

Figure 12.3: Eagle Athletic – Content Outline

Since Eagle's channel plans focus around a website and a mobile site, it will be important for Eagle to determine how to adapt web content to mobile devices.

What to Do with a Content Outline

You will use your Content Outline as you implement your DigiMarketing Plan. Specifically, when you and your agency partner start to work on using your chosen digital channels – designing your website, developing your advergame, or whatever – you will refer to your Content Outline.

DigiMarketing Tenet 5: Consumers will initiate and direct more of the participant–marketer interchange. A large portion of content will come from consumers themselves. Marketers will play a role in this by encouraging and rewarding consumer content creation in a manner that is relevant to their brand(s).

CONTENT OUTLINE (CONSUMER-CREATED)

Only a few years ago, consumer-created content was not a factor in digital planning. At that time, most digital marketers were building websites with one-way content. When consumers were prompted to participate, it was very limited, perhaps taking part in an online game – an approach that many digital marketers thought would make their sites "sticky."

However, as we've seen in earlier chapters, consumer-created content has exploded in the past few years. We now live in a cut-and-paste era when mash-ups and consumer content origination are common. Marketers need to adjust their plans to reflect this trend. You need a clear plan for how to harness your participants' creative energies. We call this the Content Outline (Consumer-Created).

How to Develop Your Content Outline (Consumer-Created)

If content is consumer created, you may wonder how a marketer can outline it. Consumers can create almost anything they wish using the open forum of digital media. However, marketers can prompt and steer this participation by the tools they provide and the promotions they run. Here are some of the key things to consider in developing an outline for consumer-created content.

Content Type

As noted in chapter 8, there are many types of content that participants can create. Which content types do you want to encourage? Do you want participants to customize content relative to your brands? As you start identifying the key types of content you will prompt users to create, think broadly about your options. Related to the type of content is the next issue: what tools will you provide to help participants create things?

Tools

This might be as simple as encouraging participants to share home videos by providing an easy video upload function. Or you might think about more complex tools that could lead to more involving interaction. For example, an auto brand offered tools for participants to do virtual car detailing, save the car as they worked on it, and to share the final result with their friends.

You will need to think through not only what you would like participants to create but also how they will do it. Consumers today are indeed creative, so they often find ingenious ways to get things done on their own. However, providing them with the right means to get things done will undoubtedly boost their participation. This could include providing them with logos, visuals, and video clips which they can use in their creative processes. For example, the Adobe site for designers, kuler.adobe.com, gives tools to mix and share new color combinations.

Think about how your tools will help peer-to-peer sharing of the content your participants create. People don't derive satisfaction from creating in isolation; they want to share what they have created. The best way to maximize the value of your DigiMarketing is through viral pass-on, not only of messages you create, but also of content your consumers create. So think about developing digital forums that encourage peer-to-peer sharing.

Prompts and Promotions

Even if you provide useful tools on a website, it doesn't guarantee consumer participation. In some cases, you will need to prompt users to create content via promotions or other activities. In chapter 8 we discussed Doritos' US web promotion, held in conjunction with Yahoo! Video, which put a winning consumer-generated TVC for the brand on the 2007 Super Bowl – the most expensive 30 seconds available globally on commercial television. But there are much simpler methods you can use too. For example, you might consider having a section of your website or mobile site dedicated to consumer tips relating to your brand or category. This is a good way to prompt consumer-created content.

Consumer creation isn't just about fun or humor. It can also be an extremely effective way to get customer insights. If you are about to launch a new product, you might use your DigiMarketing platform to capture consumers' ideas about product features. In addition to asking them questions, you can prompt them to send you photos, videos, or other types of multimedia content to express their views. Brand loyalists are often willing to go to great lengths to share their views, which can be highly insightful and useful to you. Virtual detailing of those trucks (example above) provides a great source of insight into how customers really want their trucks to look.

Linkage to Platform Proposition

Finally, there's a basic question you should ask yourself about your intended plans: "If people participate, will it reinforce our proposition?" This question serves as an important acid test to make sure you don't fall into the trap of simply trying to get people to participate, but without that participation having any real, meaningful link to your bigger goals. Too many marketers have made the mistake of thinking that all time logged on their site is of value, even if participants are playing a game completely unrelated to the brand's Platform Proposition.

Relate Back to the Platform Proposition: That's Why It's There

It's critical that the elements of your plan link back to your Platform Proposition (see Figure 12.4). Otherwise, your DigiMarketing will feel disjointed.

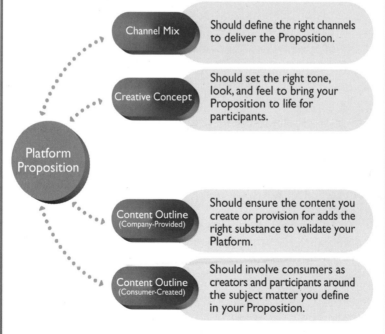

Channel Mix — Should define the right channels to deliver the Proposition.

Creative Concept — Should set the right tone, look, and feel to bring your Proposition to life for participants.

Platform Proposition

Content Outline (Company-Provided) — Should ensure the content you create or provision for adds the right substance to validate your Platform.

Content Outline (Consumer-Created) — Should involve consumers as creators and participants around the subject matter you define in your Proposition.

Figure 12.4: Links to Platform Proposition

A Working Example: Eagle Athletic – Content Outline (Consumer-Created)

Eagle has decided to encourage participants to create content in three primary areas that link to their Platform Proposition:

Content Type	Tools	Prompts and Promotions	Linkage to Platform Proposition
I. Individual exercise profile (log)	Exercise tracker software	Both mobile and website-based section on daily exercise tracking	Enables individual participants to chart and improve their personal performance
2. User videos of their participation in events	Easy upload software of participant videos	"When I'm at My Best" section, with "best of the month" promotion to reward participants and encourage their contribution	Will encourage participants to show others how they participate in sports events
3. Participant performance tips (individual blogs)	Blog tools on the site and via mobile	"Share Your Secrets of Performance" section that encourages participants to share what they do to boost their athletic performance in a given sport	This section will help ensure that Eagle users are getting the best advice possible by having other athletes share their "tips" for training and competing

Figure 12.5: Eagle Athletic – Content Outline (Consumer-Created)

What to Do with a Content Outline (Consumer-Created)

As you execute your DigiMarketing plans, you'll want to monitor what consumers actually create to see how they are responding. This is not to imply that you should edit or censor what consumers do, though you will need to decide how you'll deal with content that is vulgar, illegal, or gets into subjects like politics in your country. These are real issues. Once you hand over the digital car keys to consumers, anything can happen.

Your content monitoring should include: participation rates (are people participating in the numbers you expected?); best/worse performing items (which promotions or prompts are generating the highest and lowest participation rates?); and qualitative learning from what your participants say or create. Some of them will amaze you! You should take advantage of this learning to modify and optimize your Content Outline as appropriate.

A Brief Note About the Planning Process

As we end this section, we want to point out something very fundamental about the planning process. While we are presenting your plan in a very linear sequence, your DigiMarketing planning won't always be so linear. You might well have media ideas or influence ideas from the start, which you should capture and consider. The key is to ensure that, in the end, you have a well-considered plan that fits together.

We'll now move onto Phase 3 of the planning framework that covers how you can ensure that people are aware of what you've created.

END NOTES
1   www.worldofwarcraft.com/community/chinaicoke.html
2   www.icoke.ca/help/pins
3   Participant Journey is an Ogilvy proprietary technique.
4   earth.google.com/sky/skyedu.html

Chapter 13

Phase 3 – Generating Awareness and Influence

There are millions of websites out there, so your work isn't done once you've created your Digital Platform. You'll need a plan to ensure that people know it exists! Decisions at this stage include selecting your digital media and sponsorship options, developing a search marketing strategy, and integrating offline marketing activities with your DigiMarketing activities. By the end of this phase of the planning process, you should have the main answers to the question, "How will people know about what I've created?" (see Figure 13.1).

Figure 13.1: DigiMarketing Planning, Phase 3

DigiMarketing Tenet 6: Messaging with participants must be on an opt-in basis only and tailored to each participant's indicated preferences. Companies will increasingly seek the exponential payback that comes from having consumers share information through social networking sites and virally with each other.

MESSAGING AND VIRAL PLAN

A starting point for building awareness is to reach out to your participants through messaging. In this age of consumer-created content, some marketers might think they should stay away from this seemingly old-fashion, direct approach. However, nothing could be further from the truth. Provided your participants have opted-in for some form of relationship, email and SMS can provide the backbone of a rich digital dialogue with them.

At the same time, however, marketers must come to grips with the fact that marketing is no longer a one-way street. The shift from a push world to a truly two-way world

A DigiMarketing Planning Framework

means that participants frequently become aware of brands from friends or colleagues via viral marketing, rather than by advertising or direct communication. However, this doesn't mean that marketers should simply surrender to random luck to get their brands known. Rather, they will need to encourage people who receive something virally to visit the brand website and see more. Ultimately, the "push" tactics of messaging and the "pull" effect of interested participants connect via the natural tendency of people to share. We will briefly cover this push–pull–share dynamic below.

How to Develop Your Messaging and Viral Plan

Messaging

Digital messaging, predominantly via email and SMS, generally follows the principles of direct marketing, which marketers have followed for years. These guiding principles include:

Opted-in: As we've said repeatedly in this book, you should only send messages to participants after they have indicated a desire or willingness to receive those messages. So, as you plan your messaging, you should evaluate how many of your consumers have opted-in. If you feel it's too few, you might first need some sort of promotional activity to get more opted-in participants. This may be frustrating to you, particularly as you're eager to get started communicating directly with your participants. However, it's a necessary investment in your DigiMarketing. And even those companies that have an adequate base of opted-in participants will need to continue to build their base of opted-in consumers.

Purpose of the messaging: The key to all good messaging is to ensure that the benefit for the recipient is clear. This may seem like an obvious point. However, there are scores of emails and other marketing messages where the wants and needs of recipients are all but ignored.

What types of things can you do with your messaging? Messaging should serve to highlight timely or targeted information that's useful to consumers. If you're a food marketer and your Platform Proposition is to be the key source of information about nutrition and healthy eating, food alerts – rather than general information – constitute useful, timely information. Alerts to opted-in participants are what they want from you. Remember though that in this world of consumer choice and control, participants should be able to select to pull that information via an RSS feed from your site if they wish. We suggest you refer back to the Best Practices – Permission section of chapter 5.

Segmentation: Having decided the main reasons for your messaging, the next question is how to tailor your messages to different segments of your participant base. There's a great irony that today we have access to the most powerful personalization tools in the history of marketing, however many of us are still doing mass emailings rather than personalized messaging. This is a waste.

Email and SMS should be tailored to different users – and we're not referring to simply inserting a name in a mass email. Depending upon your business, you will want to tailor your offers, invitations, rewards, information, and anything else your messaging might contain. Using digital technology, it's relatively cheap and easy to personalize.

Frequency: As we discussed in chapter 5, frequency is one of the key characteristics of messaging and all too often it doesn't get adequate attention. Messages that are too frequent are annoying; those that are not frequent enough seem sporadic or disconnected. Getting it just right is the key.

However, *just right* can vary a great deal and relates back to your Platform Proposition. If the key reason participants have opted-in to your messages is to get information about events, the optimal frequency of your messaging might be fortnightly or monthly. However, if your Platform Proposition involves alerts about health issues, messaging might be daily.

How can you know what's right? The best way is to both ask your participants directly and monitor their usage patterns. You should allow participants to select messaging frequency right from the start. Some might choose a daily message, while others might prefer a monthly summary. Opt-in marketers must make it easy to opt-out. But, you don't want participants to have to tell you you're getting annoying or that your content is irrelevant. Once they vote with their digital feet and leave, it's too late. You're better off getting it right from the start. Plus, you can give participants the tools to indicate or adjust the frequency of the messaging, making them partners in fine-tuning your engagement with them. You should also be tracking participants' reactions to your messages on a regular basis. You can automatically monitor whether they follow links to detailed material – a good gauge of their interest. Lastly, again, they might pull the information via RSS feeds, which gives them complete control over the frequency.

Digital Channel Preferences: Consumers use multiple devices in their lives. So it's worth finding which channel(s) a participant prefers. As with most things in digital, the best way to determine this is to let participants choose.

A Working Example: Eagle Athletic – Messaging Plan

Eagle has reviewed their Platform Proposition and Content Outline and decided upon the following Messaging Plan to help drive participation in Eagle events and encourage consumers/prospects to receive regular information about sports and performance improvements:

Segment	Purpose	Content	Frequency
High value customers *(who have not yet attended an Eagle-sponsored event)*	Make customers aware of upcoming Eagle-sponsored events. Prompt first-time participation	E-mail invitation to upcoming events. Offer special event area with lucky draw for product	As events occur
High value customers *(who have attended at least 1 Eagle-sponsored event in the past 12 month)*	Further bond high value customers by encouraging them to take part in Eagle events	E-mail invitation to upcoming events. Special offer for first 100 people to sign-up for event.	As events occur
New registrant on site (within past 3 months)	Welcome new registrants and begin to engage them in events and tips for sports performance	Welcoming e-mail highlighting opt-in for alerts on Eagle-sponsored events.	Within 1 week of registration
All opted-in participants who selected to receive information about training and sports medicine	Deliver on platform promise to help participants improve athletic performance by providing information	Sports medicine alerts, with links to longer pieces on sports medicine	As information is available, unless participants opt-in for monthly synopsis

Figure 13.2: Eagle Athletic – Messaging Plan

VIRAL

As we noted earlier, viralness is out of marketers' direct control. Participants are the ones who determine what they want to pass on, and to whom. But while it's hard to predict, and impossible to guarantee, which content will ultimately be passed most from one consumer to the next, there are indeed some basic principles that can dramatically improve your chances for success.

Our suggestion is that you refer back to the key points in chapter 5, which covered email and viral marketing. In particular, you should note the discussion on compelling content. These issues will be key factors in determining your Viral Plan, which you should be able to articulate in a very simple format, as we've done in the following working example for Eagle Athletic.

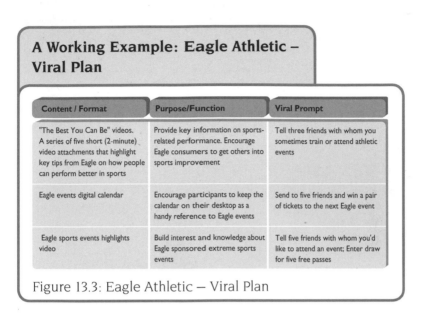

A Working Example: Eagle Athletic – Viral Plan

Content / Format	Purpose/Function	Viral Prompt
"The Best You Can Be" videos. A series of five short (2-minute) video attachments that highlight key tips from Eagle on how people can perform better in sports	Provide key information on sports-related performance. Encourage Eagle consumers to get others into sports improvement	Tell three friends with whom you sometimes train or attend athletic events
Eagle events digital calendar	Encourage participants to keep the calendar on their desktop as a handy reference to Eagle events	Send to five friends and win a pair of tickets to the next Eagle event
Eagle sports events highlights video	Build interest and knowledge about Eagle sponsored extreme sports events	Tell five friends with whom you'd like to attend an event; Enter draw for five free passes

Figure 13.3: Eagle Athletic — Viral Plan

What to Do with Your Messaging and Viral Plan: The Push–Pull–Share Value Chain

The goal of your Messaging and Viral Plan is to have the elements of your program integrate to create a value chain in your relationship with your participants. This happens when interesting content is highlighted in (or attached to) messages to your participants, who then choose to send the content to others; the others are interested enough to find out more from you and to pass on the content further.

For example, a DigiMarketer in the automobile business might send out email to opted-in prospects (primary participants) with a short video attachment highlighting a new model car and a special test drive offer. Interested primary participants would click through to the marketer's website and register for a test drive. To prompt viral pass-on of the video clip, the marketer might further sweeten the test drive offer to include a free automobile-related gift if the primary recipient brings along three friends.

The reach of the original messaging is extended as primary participants email the video clip to their friends (secondary participants). Interested secondary participants, who weren't on the DigiMarketer's database, then visit the website. They can register for a test drive too, and possibly download further information about the car. If there's a good reason to do so, they might even pass that information on to others (tertiary participants). In this way, the marketer expands their database of potential buyers and starts to reap the multiplicative effect of viral marketing (see Figure 13.4).

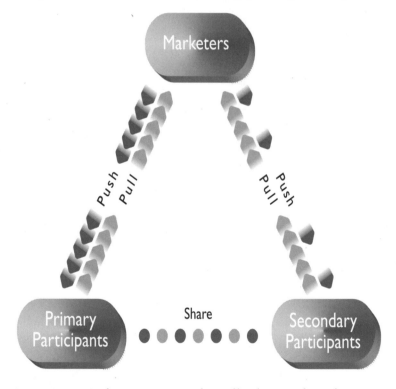

Figure 13.4: Viral Content – Push–Pull–Share Value Chain

DigiMarketing Tenet 7: Marketers will need to understand a wide variety of new media options, many of which have pay-for-performance metrics. Search will play a key role in companies' DigiMarketing plans too.

A DigiMarketing Planning Framework

DIGITAL AWARENESS PLAN

One of the key lessons from the past decade of digital marketing is that marketers cannot simply rely upon a "build it and they will come" mentality. Digital consumers have literally tens of millions of options on the web, all of which are equidistant – just a mouse click or two away. In the dotcom days, there were young companies that recognized the importance of building some form of "drive-to-web." However, they resorted to outrageous gimmicks (ironically, most often on television) to get their names known. Today, a well-considered program is essential.

DigiMarketing has come a long way. Marketers have more digital media options than ever before, and a lot of awareness building happens via digital media. While viral marketing can certainly create buzz, it generally isn't sufficient on its own for serious DigiMarketers. What's required, in addition, is some form of purchased digital media, and that's the topic of your Digital Awareness Plan. We will use the term *digital media* loosely as some of what you may choose to buy for awareness building is not "media" in the traditional sense. Awareness building may include sponsorships, advertorials, and product placement in negotiated space. The point is that instead of buying fully defined units, a greater proportion of DigiMarketers' budgets are going to space that is created.

Earlier, we considered how you develop your Channel Mix Plan. It's important to clarify that your Awareness Plan is different from this. The Channel Mix Plan identifies which channels you will use to engage and interact with your participants. Your Digital Awareness Plan will identify the channels you will use to highlight and promote your Platform. Of course, the two often work in some coordination. For example, you might have decided to use mobile phones for your marketing and consequently developed a mobile site. A logical choice would be to use the mobile channel for your advertising too to create awareness for your mobile site.

How to Develop Your Digital Awareness Plan

As most marketers know, there are two sides to the media coin – planning and buying. The two used to be relatively separate in media agencies. One group created the plan, using a battery of data and an agreed strategy. Another group then went out and negotiated for that space, generally aggregating the requirements of a variety of clients in order to create volume deals.

This process with digital media is different for several reasons. First, there is a lot of non-standard media placement in digital. So, whether something gets included in the plan is dependent on whether – and at what price – a non-standard placement can be negotiated. Second, the area of digital media metrics is much more complex, so the process of determining what is effective requires even greater interconnection of planning and buying. We will cover this topic of performance metrics shortly. Third, given the way viral marketing works, the purpose of some of your placements will be to "seed" digital material into certain locations, from which it will be passed on by participants.

Developing your Digital Awareness Plan will involve lots of data, syndicated research, and a series of decisions and trade-offs to arrive at an ideal plan. Frankly, it requires a professional partner, rather than a do-it-yourself approach. So, our intention here is to highlight the key building blocks of a Digital Awareness Plan, rather than an in-depth explanation of the planning process. At this point, we suggest you refer back to chapter 4 to review the main digital media options and best practices.

As you work through the various potential digital media options, you will make decisions about apportioning your funds to the different areas of digital media. In the end, you should get to an overview that might look a bit like the following example from our Eagle Athletic case:

A Working Example: Eagle Athletic – Digital Awareness Plan

Eagle has decided to go with a plan that will cover various forms of display, search, and sponsorship.

Type	Site or Digital Channel	Role	Key Metric(s)
Display	ESPN.com ad network - variety of sites	Rich media banners to build on Eagle's image in extreme sports	Click-throughs to Eagle site registration
Search	Key words on Google and selected European and Asian search engines	Build traffic for sales at the holidays -- 50% of annual sales (noted in Participant Print)	Click-throughs to sale
Affiliate	Extremesports.com	Key partner relationships both online and with in-market events	Click-throughs to Eagle site
Sponsorship/ Negotiated Space	New Electronics Art Game dedicated to extreme sports	Title sponsorship, with Eagle-branded signage and special in-game promotion	Click-throughs to participation in promotions -- cost per registration

Figure 13.5: Eagle Athletic – Digital Awareness Plan

What to Do with Your Digital Awareness Plan

The elements you include in your Digital Awareness Plan will have implications for the types of commitments you must make in buying media. An in-game sponsorship, for example, will require a longer commitment period than banners or key search words. In fact, one of the things marketers like about search is the ability to buy keywords for a very focused period of time. So, as you create your Digital Awareness Plan, you not only want to look at the types of elements you want in your mix, you also need to decide upon the time horizon that suits your plans.

The time horizon issue relates directly to how much flexibility you do, or do not, have to optimize your plans. Many DigiMarketers want the flexibility to dynamically re-allocate their funds to those media elements which provide the best return. And what constitutes *best return* is not always obvious:

the measure is not simply the cost of the media space; it's the efficiency of that space in generating a desired action.

There are many metrics that can be used for determining which sites are giving the best return on your money. We will cover the issue of performance in more detail when we address data, analytics, and optimization. But, at the stage of media planning you must already have a clear picture of what metrics you will use to measure your performance, both in terms of the media buy and in the wider context of your DigiMarketing performance. It's also an important issue at this stage since the metrics you agree to will impact how much you pay for media.

DigiMarketing Tenet 8: It is impossible to manage news in a digital world where consumers are faster than companies. Instead, DigiMarketers will have to adapt their approach to be a meaningful part of the public conversation, using all the digital tools available to them to influence – not dictate – the debate.

DIGITAL INFLUENCE PLAN

While a Digital Media Plan is essential to creating awareness, the story doesn't stop there. As you've seen throughout this book, participatory media have changed how people relate to each other, to marketers, and to the traditional media. DigiMarketers must look beyond paid awareness to consider how the public dialogue in digital channels influences people.

The shift from the "Age of Deference" – influence emanating from authorities – to the "Age of Reference" – influence emanating from peer opinion – is important for companies to harness.[1] Consumers' recommendations can be an amazing force for those brands that are recommended. In fact, Frank Reichheld, a loyalty expert at Bain & Company, argues that a positive recommendation is the key differentiator between market leaders and market followers.

He postulates that companies with the most "net promoters" – namely, companies who have a majority of their consumers highly recommending them – are invariably market leaders in their category.[2]

Therefore, a Digital Influence Plan is as necessary as a Digital Awareness Plan. It helps marketers determine how they can be a credible part of this 24x7 dialogue, shaping the views and recommendations for their brands. We stress both *credible* and *part*. As we have seen (refer to Flogs and Flogging in chapter 8), some marketers have found out the hard way that trying to dominate or manage the conversation can have a disastrous effect. Consumers in the virtual world are particularly harsh on companies they see as attempting to encroach on their digital space, particularly via stealth. So, a credible plan must include how to embed your brand in the digital discussion in a natural, accepted way.

How to Develop a Digital Influence Plan

A Digital Influence Plan is more than a list of things to do; it must also reflect how you will do them. As just noted, this is particularly important when you want to engage participants in the blogosphere. Therefore, we'll first cover three essential elements that should apply to everything you do in building digital influence. This is followed by some specific components you will need to incorporate into your Influence Plan.

The Three Essentials of Digital Influence

Essential 1 – Speed: Social media moves faster than your company does, or possibly can. News today zips around the world, spreading through countless social networks at light speed. Therefore, it's impossible to manage the digital discussion in the same way PR used to be managed through traditional channels. While you cannot control the message in this environment, you must be prepared to keep up with the debate. Once the digital chain reaction starts around a piece of news, you must be speedy if you hope to influence opinion as it forms.

Essential 2 – Conversational Tone: The tone of direct-to-consumer communication is very important; it's not just *what* you say, it's *how* you say it. The public can quickly smell insincerity or spin, and they are indeed harsh if they feel you are making a sales pitch. Therefore, it's critical that you maintain an open and informal tone. Remember also that this is a two-way conversation. So, your response to participants needs to maintain the same tone as your outbound message. After all, influence is created by conversation, not domination.

Essential 3 – Transparency: Organizations generally don't like criticism. However, consumers equally don't like companies that won't admit mistakes or listen to criticism. So, along with creating a conversational tone, your company must be prepared to be transparent and honest in your communications. If basic honesty disappears, and the "false face" of the corporation takes over, trust will quickly wane. Take note of the Box Insert, Transparency, below.

Transparency

There are some key things you should keep in mind to ensure transparency:

- Disclose conflicts of interest at once. If you don't, people will find out anyway.
- Be prepared to answer all questions posed to you, particularly the thorny ones, since answering a tough question well wins the most respect.
- Censorship doesn't work in the digital democracy. Never attempt to delete criticism from your digital interaction with consumers. If you do, they will simply generate more.

A DigiMarketing Planning Framework

- Engage critics and try to understand their viewpoint. If they have genuine complaints, you must admit them and fix them. If there is a misunderstanding or misinformation, you must correct it.
- Remember: everything digital is on-the-record, forever.

Critical Components of Digital Influence Plans

Keeping these three essentials in mind, there are a number of key components that your Digital Influence Plan should include:

Identification of Key Influence Channels and Actions: As you develop your Digital Influence Plan, you will want to refer back to your Participant Print. The investment you made upfront will again pay off as you have already identified the channels that are most important to your participants. You may wish to revisit the Participant Print and develop more specific details on which blogs, websites, chatrooms, and other digital destinations are important to your participants. These are where your Digital Influence Plan should start.

Company Communication and Blogging Policy: You will need to decide who will provide the voice/face of your company. Generally, interaction on blogs comes from individuals, each with a singular, individual voice, not from PR departments who represent the corporation. This might mean having a company executive start a company blog via which you openly share information or address consumer issues. This could be in video blog (vlog) format or you could use podcasts to share your information. Or, if you're more adventuresome and it fits the digital media habits of your participants, you could establish a virtual customer care center in a virtual world such as *Second Life*. As with all other aspects of your DigiMarketing, the only limit is your imagination.

You should enter the digital conversation with an upfront acknowledgement of who you are and your capacity with the company. People can – and will – find out anyway, so best to tell them from the start. As part of the conversation, you might address gossip or misinformation head-on. Or, you might represent your company point-of-view on a given issue as part of the conversation.

One Caveat: many companies have been too slow to establish clear corporate blogging guidelines. While you want corporate transparency, this doesn't mean letting every employee in the company say what they wish, particularly if it becomes a way for them to vent personal frustrations or – worse – to share confidential information. If you do decide to allow employees to blog – with corporate backing – you'll need to establish company guidelines. If you don't allow employees to blog…they may well anyway! Your Digital Monitoring Plan (see below) should pick this up. Executives responsible for any blogging must adhere to the three essentials outlined above.

Brand Fans: Influence doesn't always come directly from the company. There are times when a brand fan can be a better influencing advocate. Of course, the brand fan must keep an open, honest tone; otherwise, you might as well do it yourself. Brand fans could share their experiences about your product, mentioning your brands only occasionally. For example, using our Eagle Athletic case, you might consider having a few extreme sports fans write a blog about extreme sports competitions, with occasional mentions of Eagle products. Provided that the blog – or other format – stays focused on the topic of sports, and provides relevant, useful information to other participants, this can be a perfectly acceptable way to gain positive exposure.

Digital Influence Material: At the core of influence are usually some facts, information, or key opinions that make the difference. Sometimes, a body of clear information builds a persuasive case. Other times, there is one, specific piece of evidence – a statement, an action, or a photograph or a video (what PR people sometimes refer to as a *mind bomb*) – that is the key to swaying people's views. Therefore, it's important to determine what material will be critical to your reputation management efforts.

The benefit of digital channels is that they give you a chance to amplify your key information in a way that traditional channels don't. Your influence materials can be shared in rich formats, interspersing video, audio, text, and links to in-depth material. You can add graphs, charts, and so on that you'd be unlikely to share in detail via traditional PR channels. The web is the most efficient two-way distribution system the world has ever known. You can share information around the world, and get opinions back. You'll need to determine what you want to say and which digital formats you'll use for influencing the public discussion.

Digital Monitoring Plan: According to Chris Graves, President of Ogilvy PR in Asia, the blogosphere can serve as an "early warning system" for your brand. Because of the speed of digital media, consumer complaints often show up first in blogs or other consumer-created content. However, you will not know about the public debate unless you are monitoring it – all the time. Your Digital Influence Plan needs to include a definition of what you want to monitor and how you will monitor it:

You will probably monitor a range of topics directly, or tangentially, involving your brand and product category. A beer brand, for example, might want to monitor the discussions of beer lovers but also keep an ear on the issue of drunk driving, which could potentially influence the public's opinion of beer drinking.

You will monitor the digital discussion via digital tools. There are a range of powerful tools today that go all the way from monitoring keyword mentions to sophisticated qualitative analyses about who is saying what. You should talk with your agency about which monitoring tools best suit your needs, as well as what range of topics are the most relevant to monitor.

The Crisis Plan: Unfortunately, crises are inevitable. These may be company-specific, brand-specific, or involve the entire product category. For example, if you are in the food business, a company-specific crisis would be a quality problem in one of your factories, while a product category issue would be a food contamination scare, which would temporarily make consumers nervous about all food manufacturers.

Crises can vary a great deal depending upon your business. And it's impossible to foresee every potential eventuality. However, you should know from previous experience the type of topics with which your company or industry may have to deal. For example, an airline is always at the ready in case one of its planes goes down. The liquor and tobacco industries are very familiar with the various social issues that are frequently raised in relation to their products. Therefore, you will need to think through what type of issues you are most likely to have to address in a crisis and have key company information at the ready.

Lastly, your Crisis Plan should include a list of priority digital influencers (individual blogs, website, or agencies) that you should contact first in the case of an emergency. Your Crisis Plan must identify clearly who in your organization will be responsible for responding in the case of a crisis.

Influence Channel/ Audience	Content	Frequency
Selected extreme sports and sports performance blogs	VP of Eagle events to join key discussions on these blogs	Daily
Eagle Blog – The Running Man	Provide insights on life inside the company and behind the scenes information about extreme sports events that Eagle sponsors	Daily
Brand Fan V-blogs	Video blogs by three extreme sport enthusiasts who use Eagle products	Weekly
Monitoring Plan	Various topics and keywords on extreme sports, performance improvement, and sports medicine	Ongoing
Crisis Plan	Key Eagle material on their commitment to sports safety plus their stance on only legal performance enhancement techniques	Ready when required

Figure 13.6: Eagle Athletic – Digital Influence Plan

What to Do with Your Digital Influence Plan

Your Digital Influence Plan is part activity print, part guideline. Given the fluid nature of the public debate, set-piece public relations won't be sufficient. Sure, you will still instigate influence activities and create initiatives. However, there will be things you need to address dynamically. Some of them you won't be able to foresee, and it will require you to act promptly. However, having your Influence Plan – and materials – at the ready will help you as you engage your participants.

DigiMarketing Tenet 9: The current approaches to integration of marketing communications generally aren't sufficient. Marketers will need to use more sophisticated approaches to connect digital and physical touchpoints. Plus, they will shift their focus from the integration of brand image to the unification of each customer's experience. The

use of individual customer data will enable a continuous customer dialogue.

CHANNEL UNIFICATION PLAN

Faced with so many digital and non-digital channels, marketers must not only choose channels carefully; they must also interconnect the channels they choose. Many companies talk about integrated marketing, but in truth their integration efforts amount to little more than coordination of visuals across multiple touchpoints. Even achieving consistent use of visuals is difficult for some marketers as distributors or sales departments run off in different directions.

What integration should be delivering is greater marketing impact as a result of using all the customer touchpoints together to amplify the brand message. Unfortunately, some marketers still address their digital and their physical marketing separately. During the early hype of the internet, pundits said the internet was "completely different." This slowed integration of digital into marketing plans. In fact, some companies still have their IT department managing their digital marketing, rather than their marketing department. What insanity!

Physical and digital touchpoints should be in a symbiotic relationship, reinforcing each other in their different ways. That is the point of integration. As digital marketing becomes the centerpiece of marketing efforts, companies must move past integration to Unification. As we have argued throughout this book, marketers will need to think about consumers and ensure that their brand experiences are unified, continuous and connected.

How to Develop Your Channel Unification Plan

Here are key steps to first integrate your channels, and then move towards a more unified customer experience.

A DigiMarketing Planning Framework

Level 1 – Physical-Digital Channels Integration

Marketing has most impact when digital and traditional channels work together. For a start, physical touchpoints should link directly with digital activities. When physical touchpoints direct customers to digital channels, you close the loop of consumer information. The digital channel can gather specific customer data – and offer interactivity – which traditional channels can't.

Every physical interaction can be leveraged into a digital relationship, if you apply enough ingenuity. For example, your customer care center or call center can encourage callers to visit your website for more information about the topic they called about. Product packaging can be a drive-to-web vehicle. Don't just mention the website URL – that's not a reason for participants to visit. Provide unique identifier codes on or in the packs to give buyers some benefit (points, or a chance to win) when they go online. Promotions and in-market events can deploy kiosks or hand-held readers to enable consumers to sign up, digitally, on the spot. This streamlines data capture from shopping malls, bars, or sports venues. As we have seen (chapter 6), mobiles can photograph QR codes, prompting participants to connect to mobile sites from in-market locations and register for a promotion.

At this step in the planning process, there are some basic things you should do:

- List out all the touchpoints in your marketing and customer care efforts.
- For each touchpoint, identify how the activity in that channel could be amplified, extended, or improved by connection with your digital platform.
- Decide what drive-to-web elements you will use to connect each physical touchpoint to your digital platform (as summarized in Figure 13.7).

Drive from/to Physical Channels

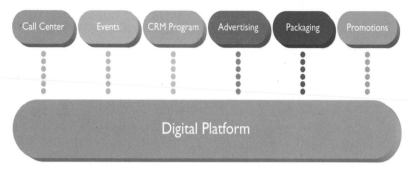

Figure 13.7: Physical Touchpoints Integration

Level 2 – *Content Integration*

Marketers are also experimenting with new ways to integrate content across traditional and digital channels. Well-known media properties, mascots, or even stars promoted by traditional media can heighten interest in watching, participating, and then interacting via digital channels.

Pirates

A good example of content integration was Volvo's tie-in with *Pirates of the Caribbean – World's End*. In keeping with the movie theme, Volvo created a treasure hunt in which consumers could win a treasure chest full of gold, plus a new Volvo car. The connection to the Volvo Platform Proposition was "Volvo is the only car safe enough to drive the gold home in."

Volvo's "Hunt" website (www.volvocars.us/thehunt) was the centerpiece of the promotion. By directing consumers to the website to register, Volvo was able to capture data on prospects they wouldn't normally have identified. Plus, Volvo included two elements to bolster a sales connection. First, they tied one of the steps in the online treasure hunt to car dealerships, requiring participants to visit a Volvo showroom to get an additional clue. Second, consumers had the opportunity to earn points during the hunt that could be redeemed after the purchase of a new Volvo.

Traditional media played a largely supportive role. Television commercials highlighted the movie, building consumer traffic to both the website and theatres to see *Pirates*.

A way to express this integration of digital channels and traditional media, with a media property or star connecting them, is the triangle in Figure 13.8.

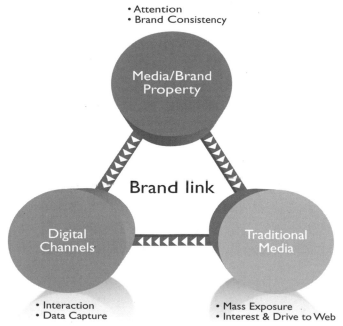

Figure 13.8: Channels Integration Around Key Marketing Property

As you think through how you will integrate digital and traditional media, try to make this diagram work for your brand. You need to know:

- What key brand property will you use?
- How can this brand property be extended meaningfully to your digital media?
- What specifically will your participants do through digital that adds a new layer of engagement to this property?
- What specific new data will you capture through the digital channels?
- Are there logical extensions to other digital media (mobile, podcasts, consumer-created content, and so on)?

Level 3 – From Integration to Unification

To a consumer, marketing too often feels like a series of discrete activities. Worse, customer information from one touchpoint is often not used in another. So, despite having a long history and established personal preferences with a company, a consumer might be treated like a new customer when he or she participates in a promotion or interacts with the company online. This is a truly underwhelming user experience. What's required is a way to create a continuous and seamless participant journey with your company: that's the aim of your Unification Plan.

You can start moving towards unified marketing by ensuring that your digital channels are fully interconnected with each customer's individual data. This means identifying *digital unifiers* – the elements that act as the glue between your digital channels. As you add digital channels in the future, they too can incorporate those unifiers and be fully informed of the customer's data.

An example of a unifier, using our Eagle Athletic case, would be each person's personal exercise profile. This element is central to Eagle in delivering its Digital Platform Proposition to "help athletes improve their personal performance." So, via every digital touchpoint, it will be important for Eagle to utilize each participant's personalized training profile, either making that training profile readily available to the participant or using data from the profile to tailor material to each participant. In unified marketing, information on individual consumers is held at the center and used to inform every channel. This knowledge can be instantly distributed to every touchpoint. As a result, there is continuity of personal preferences and configuration.

Digital marketers frequently use some form of membership or sign-in on their website or other digital media as the starting point of a customer interaction. Some use a loyalty program, or club with special access privileges, to incentivize participants to register and sign in. Usually, basic customer profile data is connected to the sign in. This might include opt-in preferences or other individual information. If you don't have this already, you should consider the type of unique customer identification process you will include in your DigiMarketing. If you do already have this, ask how you can take it further to improve the customer experience. For example, participants' customizations should show up on all the digital channels so each customer touch feels consistent and reflects the customer's preferences.

There are, of course, technology issues that you'll need to address as you ensure that real-time customer data is available at every touchpoint. And, to be honest, it may take you some time to get there. But every day, as our world becomes more digital, marketers – including your competition – are moving in this direction.

Here are some key questions you can ask as you define appropriate digital unifiers:

- What elements of DigiMarketing might participants find useful at every digital touchpoint?
- How can each participant interaction be used to capture data relative to these unifiers?

- What needs to be done operationally to collect consistent data around the unifying elements of your DigiMarketing?

A Working Example: Eagle Athletic – Channel Unification Plan

Eagle has developed a comprehensive plan at all three levels – physical touchpoints, content integration, and digital unification. The following are some highlights of their plan:

1. Physical–Digital Channels Integration

- *Promotions*: During the Eagle promotional period at Christmas/New Year, for every purchase, participants can log onto the Eagle site to redeem special gifts.
- *Packaging*: Year-round, Eagle shoe boxes contain a special code with a unique member identifier to be used on the Eagle website and mobile site. Existing Eagle members can accrue points that are tracked on the site. These points can be redeemed for tickets to Eagle-sponsored extreme sports events.

2. Content Integration

Eagle Athletic will be the title sponsor to a new global extreme sports championship. This will be the content centerpiece for their activities. A special Eagle-branded site will be created for the competition. The site provides in-depth profiles of all the athletes, featuring their sports performance tips. Also included on the site are key scores, so participants can track their performance versus top athletes. This information can be accessed via mobile phones for when they work out. Lastly, the site includes the world championship schedule, facilitating consumer viewing of the championships.

3. Digital Unification
Eagle's digital unifier is the individual exercise profile of each member. Via all digital touchpoints, participants can update their exercise profile. Plus, each time they receive information, it is tailored to their profile and level of exercise.

What to Do with Your Channel Unification Plan

As with other components in this DigiMarketing framework, the Channel Unification Plan is not set in stone. Rather, it should serve as a dynamic blueprint for your marketing. It will need to be constantly reviewed and updated as you gain feedback from what is, and is not, working in the marketplace. Over time you will no doubt want to reassess the various touchpoints as new channel developments provide fresh opportunities.

NIKE+: A Real-Life Case Study

Our working example is a fictitious athletic company. However, this doesn't mean that real companies aren't doing innovative things with their DigiMarketing. Nike, a marketer known for doing new, inventive things, is a terrific example of the leading edge of DigiMarketing.

Nike's joint effort with Apple, another innovative marketer, can be seen at the Nike+ site (www.nike.com/nikeplus). Nike+ integrates the physical and virtual worlds. It does this through harnessing technology to amplify the essence of the brand – physical activity. A sensor in the

Nike shoes records each person's speed and distance when they run. This is connected to an Apple iPod, which saves the data. This data is then uploaded to the Nike+ site, which acts as the Digital Platform through which Nike and runners connect on an ongoing basis.

Nike's proposition seems very similar to Eagle's — to help individuals improve their performance by providing them with useful tools. So when you go to the Nike+ site, you see a variety of tools that enable participants to set individual goals, track their data, monitor performance over time, and stretch their personal performance.

Another interesting aspect of the site is the way it creates social connections. Runners can challenge each other, even if they're not in the same physical location, since the scores from their runs can be posted publicly. This literally connects running enthusiasts from Belfast to Bangkok, who might never have a chance to meet in person, but who can enjoy competing and comparing performance via this digital relationship platform.

At this stage, we have worked through the first three phases of the DigiMarketing framework. You have defined a Participant Print and Goals, decided what to create as your Platform, and how you can go about building Awareness and Influence.

Before we move onto the final DigiMarketing steps — covering data, analytics, and DigiMarketing optimization — it's important to note something about the planning steps you've gone through so far. As we've highlighted throughout this book, the democratization of digital media means that your consumers will be participants in your marketing process like never before. It's vital to recognize that the steps we've covered have many elements in which participants will play a key role.

Marketers must decide what platform to create. But participants – perhaps prompted by the marketer – will be very active in generating content; passing on viral material; providing their votes, views, and opinions; building awareness; making recommendations; and influencing others, as they interact with your marketing. At the end of the day, it is your consumers' interest and willingness to be ongoing participants that will determine your success. So, despite all the planning, you must be prepared to modify everything in your plans, based upon what consumers tell you directly and what you infer from their behavior.

Now, in the final section of our DigiMarketing framework, we will review the use of data and analytic tools to monitor customer behavior and modify your marketing accordingly.

END NOTES

1   Chime, UK, is credited with coining the terms "from Age of Deference to Age of Reference".
2   www.theultimatequestion.com

Chapter 14

Phase 4 – Harnessing Data, Analytics, and Optimization

T he fourth and final phase of DigiMarketing planning relates back to the data and analytic disciplines of direct marketing, the antecedent of DigiMarketing (see Figure 14.1). DigiMarketing both utilizes and generates data. Therefore, a clear data plan is vital. Further, you will need a disciplined process for analyzing your data and your DigiMarketing efforts. This analysis will ensure that you learn from what consumers actually do so you can make continuous improvements based upon specific findings, not guesswork. By the end of this final phase of the planning process, you should be able to answer, "How will I measure my DigiMarketing and ensure it improves continuously?"

Data, analysis, and optimization underpin all the previous steps. For this reason, our DigiMarketing model takes on a three-dimensional quality. You'll notice too that you move back to the starting point – the Participant Print and Goals. The aim of optimization is to help you become even more appealing to the participants you aimed to engage from the start. The process of measuring and optimizing your work provides a natural opportunity to assess whether you are achieving your goals.

Figure 14.1: DigiMarketing Planning, Phase 4

DigiMarketing Tenet 10: Data will be recognized as the lifeblood of marketing. Data is the key to using addressable channels effectively. A good data plan will be the centerpiece of DigiMarketing. Marketers will use this data for more detailed psychographic and behavioral profiling of consumers.

DATA PLAN

Data has been at the heart of direct marketing for years and, indeed, it is at the very center of DigiMarketing too. Data is the currency of the digital age. Everything that happens in

A DigiMarketing Planning Framework

digital channels either relies upon or generates data. Data is both the fuel and the byproduct of DigiMarketing.

This is the good news. The bad news is that there are a host of data issues to deal with. Consumers are increasingly guarded about sharing data (see following Box Insert, Cautionary Tale) and know what their data is worth. Meanwhile, many marketers struggle to make sense out of all the data they now have. For all these reasons, it's important to have a Data Plan.

We address the Data Plan relatively late in the planning framework. In practical applications, you may need to begin identifying required data at an earlier stage. For example, if Eagle Athletics – our case study company – has the proposition to focus on helping individuals improve their athletic performance, they will need data about individuals' sports performance. Even the Platform Proposition has significant implications for the data a marketer will need.

How to Develop Your Data Plan

There are a number of steps in a Data Plan. However, before we cover those steps, let's first examine the key data types that you will be working with.

Data Types

All data is not the same. Some data relates to individuals, other data relates to groups. Some data may be required by your registration system while other data may be volunteered. Some data (such as the individual's name) is relatively static, while other data (such as his or her bank balance) might be highly variable. Some data you get directly from people, while other data – so-called *behavioral data* – is gleaned indirectly by studying participants' actions. As you plan out your DigiMarketing, you are likely to use all these types of data.

Let's focus though on four classifications of data that will be most prominent in the process of interacting with your participants and performing analytics (covered in the next section).

Participant-Provided Data (Individuals): This is what your participants tell you about themselves. It might be factual, such as street address, date of birth, and so on. Or, it might be preference-based data, such as their interests or personal choices from a list of options.

Behavioral Data (Individuals): This is what participants show you about their individual behaviors. Participants leave a trail of digital crumbs behind them every time they use digital media. Although this relates directly to them, they are usually unaware of leaving this trace.

Participant-Provided Data (Aggregated): This is data on participants that you aggregate (for example, users' total responses to polls). In addition to using this data, you may well want to share it with your participants. People love to see poll results.

Behavioral Data (Aggregated): This is data about what participants show you as a group. This will include response rates to promotions and may be measured over subgroups of participants. This gives you an indication of which part of your DigiMarketing participants spend most time on, where they tend to leave you, and so on.

All this data is important to your DigiMarketing. We will come back to the behavioral data later in this chapter. For now, however, our primary focus will be on the data that will guide your interactions with your participants.

Creating a Data Plan

Key Data Set: A Data Plan starts with identifying exactly which data you will need and how you will use it. The important point here is that you need a vision of what you will do with the data, before you even collect it. Are you asking a consumer for his or her birthday so that you can verify that he or she can legally enter your site? Or is it because you want to send an age-appropriate promotional offer? Or will you send a birthday greeting as part of your loyalty program? Or do you plan to track the demographics of your participants? Perhaps it's all of the above.

Companies almost always collect more data than they can actually use, or they collect the wrong data. Data is a bit like fruit. It is perishable. It goes bad over time as people change addresses, get new phones, switch jobs, and get married. As a result, a portion of your data is always becoming invalid. When companies collect data during a promotion, and then decide months or years later to finally use it, they are often naively surprised that a large proportion of it is useless. Always limit yourself to the data you will actually need and use on a timely basis.

Permission Data: Opt-in data is the essential information you will need to maintain a dialogue with participants. As well as permission, opt-in data might include consumers' mobile phone numbers, email addresses, and so on. Over the years, we have seen many companies who wish to engage in mobile marketing, but realize that they've either forgotten to collect participants' mobile phone numbers or have failed to ask for opt-in for mobile messages. You can't simply assume that because a consumer has provided their mobile phone number they are open to receiving mobile messages. You need to plan ahead and ask consumers for permission to contact them in different ways, and get the frequency with which they are prepared to receive messages from you, plus any other limitations on their permissions.

Personalization Data: Another component of the Data Plan is to identify data that you will need to personalize your communications. If, for example, you have music on your site, a key piece of personalization data will be each participant's favorite music. This will allow you to tailor music offers to each person.

Data Collection Mechanisms: Determining how you will collect your key data is vital. We're not referring here to the literal process of porting data into a database or the construction of the database, though that will need to be addressed too. Rather, the question is what consumer-friendly mechanisms will be used in the interaction process to (painlessly) extract the necessary data.

In the early days of digital marketing, companies used long registration processes as a prerequisite for entering their sites. Most marketers learned the hard way that consumers won't spend time registering unless they truly see a benefit. As companies saw massive drop-off rates during the registration process, they started to limit registration to just a few, necessary fields of data. Marketers now often deploy a multi-stage process of data collection, asking for just a little data at any one time. As we saw in chapter 6, these benefits are the sugar on the data-provision pill. As long as you have the digital unifiers in place (see the last chapter) you can collate the data fragments and gradually build detailed profiles.

One of the most effective ways to collect data is to leverage the thing that most fascinates consumers: themselves! You do this by providing configurators, self-tests, and other tools that help consumers know more about themselves or more about their needs in relation to your products. For example, a food company had difficulty getting moms to answer questionnaires about how they feed their children. However, once the company provided a self-quiz on the topic of whether they were feeding their children properly, they were able to get data that consumers were previously reluctant to share. The reason was that consumers weren't thinking about giving data to a marketer; consumers were focused on the benefit that they would gain through the quiz.

Business-to-business marketers can also use this approach. A computer company, for example, could help small businesses determine their computing needs. An online configurator could recommend computing packages in response to participants' inputs on their business growth rates. Respondents receive useful information in relation to their businesses. At the same time, the respondents have effectively done all the pre-qualification work, making it easy for the company to follow-up with some form of sales call.

An important byproduct of this approach is that you tend to get more accurate data than when you ask consumers to fill in a survey or questionnaire. The reason is that participants don't want to cheat themselves, as their input directly impacts the output of the test or configurator. This leads to our next topic: data accuracy.

Data Accuracy: As we've seen, data can become obsolete very quickly. You will need a plan for revalidating data on a periodic basis. The impact of inaccurate data will vary. At minimum it's inefficient as emails sent to old addresses are bounced back. At worst, the results can be detrimental to the brand as consumers receive inappropriate information. Even the US Army has botched the use of its databases. In a truly embarrassing incident, the families of some troops killed in Iraq received letters asking the deceased soldiers to return to active service![1] While most brands aren't a matter of life and death, inaccurate data can derail marketing.

Keeping data current is easier for some companies than others. Businesses such as credit card issuers require individual data to complete every transaction. And, since your credit card issuer sends you a monthly bill, and will shut off your card if you don't pay, consumers are motivated to keep their data accurate and alert the credit card company to changes.

Other businesses, particularly consumer goods companies, don't have data as a natural part of their transaction process. For years, customers have walked in and out of grocery stores, buying products, without the manufacturer even knowing their names. One of the main appeals of DigiMarketing for these types of companies is that they can finally identify individual consumers. However, they still have the challenge of determining how to create enough interaction with participants via digital channels so they can keep their customer data accurate. This is where creative data collection mechanisms come into play.

There are several things DigiMarketers can do to keep data current. Periodic promotions can revalidate data. Incentives could prompt participants to review and reconfirm their data. Every customer service interaction should routinely reconfirm different data items. The most effective way, however, is to architect your DigiMarketing in a manner that every consumer interaction involves data in some form.

You will want to review your Platform Proposition and find ways to leverage it to yield timely, relevant data. In our Eagle Athletic example, the digital tools they provide to help participants track and monitor their athletic performance become a natural way to stay current with those participants. Also, the ability to customize products and buy online will help Eagle keep customer information up-to-date.

Data Privacy: The last topic is data privacy. This issue could take an entire book on its own. Data privacy is now quite complex and laws vary across the world. Not only that – data laws are changing as more governments grapple with the issues of determining what data can and should be captured, how (if at all) it can be used, how it can be stored and secured, and how it can be shared. Our advice, as you work through your DigiMarketing plan, is to seek the guidance of experts who can help you ensure that you're complying with any data restrictions in your country. You should also develop a clear, stated privacy policy, so that participants, and the general public, have confidence that you will treat their data carefully.

There may be no specific data laws in your country (yet). However, there is always the basic "law of the consumer" that should be respected. That is a law of logic rather than statute. And what that law dictates is that anything you do that frustrates, compromises, or angers a consumer isn't going to be a good thing. Temporary gains you might make by ignoring this law of the consumer will certainly be negated by the long-term bad will – and bad publicity – that will result. So, our advice is to use common sense. And, if you really don't know what to do, ask yourself the simple question "How would you feel if you were on the receiving end?." Would that be something that would please and interest you, or would it frustrate and anger you? It's amazing how often the golden rule can be a guide.

More on Privacy: A Cautionary Tale

The most pressing issues for DigiMarketers will surely be identity and privacy. Already the internet is massively exacerbating the once almost unknown crime of identity theft. The term "identity theft" only seems to have occurred post-1980s, yet by 2006 identity theft losses surpassed $50 billion in the US alone.

Privacy protection is already making headlines. The AOL data spill of 2006 alerted many to just how much the search engines know about them. On August 4, 2006 AOL released the records of all searches conducted on AOL over a three-month period by some 650,000 of their customers[2] (in fact AOL search is powered by Google). This was apparently aimed at assisting the academic research community by providing real search data.[3] Records were identified only by an ID number.

By August 7, AOL recognized its mistake and pulled the data off the web. Unfortunately, in those three days, the data had been mirrored around the world, and is still readily available.[4] By August 9, reporters at *The New York Times*, using only the search records, had successfully identified customer #4417749 and had interviewed her at her home![5] Many bloggers focused on user 17556639 and his apparent interest in killing his wife.[6]

By August 14, The Electronic Frontier Foundation – a non-profit consumer privacy advocate group – had filed a complaint to the US Federal Trade Commission (FTC) that release of this data violated AOL's privacy policy and the *Federal Trade Commission Act* and should be investigated.[7]

By August 22, it was reported that AOL's Chief Technology Officer had resigned and two employees had been fired.[8] By September 3, AOL members had sued AOL and were attempting a class action suit.[9]

Google has agreed to make users' search data anonymous after 18 months.[10] But this has caused more privacy uproar because of its proposed DoubleClick takeover. DoubleClick has a massive amount of data on individuals' browsing and click-stream activities, using cookies left on users' computers to allow their activity to be linked across websites. This could now be integrated with their search histories and even email. Google claims that only "non-personally identifiable data" will be merged to better target ads.

Yet for the offer to be tailored to the customer, the DigiMarketer needs to know the customer in detail. Somehow DigiMarketers and consumers need to negotiate just how much benefit in terms of customization the consumer will get at the cost of how much privacy they will lose. This will be one of the key marketing imperatives of this century. The smart agent will only be smart if the users let the agent know their secrets. The DigiMarketer can only personalize the offer if the customer reveals their preferences. Trust will be at the heart of successful DigiMarketing relationships. Building trust with the consumer is not something that traditional marketing has been good at!

A Working Example: Eagle Athletic – Data Plan

Topic	Data or Data Source
Key Data Set	- Name - Favorite extreme sport - Membership details - Product customization and purchase history
Permission Data	- E-mail and mobile phone number - Opt-in agreement for messaging - Preference for frequency of messaging - Preference for messaging platform -- mobile or e-mail
Participant Segmentation and Personalization Data	- Favorite extreme sport - Sports performance interests - Attendance record at Eagle-sponsored sports events
Data Collection	- Membership registration - Personal exercise profile - Performance improvement tools
Data Accuracy	- Self-updating exercise profile - Data revalidation at each product customization or e-commerce interaction

Figure 14.2: Eagle Athletic — Data Plan

What to Do with Your Data Plan

As noted, your Data Plan will inform many aspects of your overall DigiMarketing plan. You'll use it as you design the functionality of whatever you build, perhaps having a registration process on the landing page of your site (that might allow single sign-on). It will inform the architecture of your DigiMarketing as well as your messaging plans. So, along with your Participant Print, your Data Plan is likely to be one of the most used portions of your DigiMarketing plan. Your Data Plan will also tie into the analytics process, the next topic.

DigiMarketing Tenet 11: The "rear view" approach to marketing, which bases decisions primarily on historical information, is insufficient. Marketers will deploy real-time analysis of data to make quick, constant, and fact-based modifications to their DigiMarketing activities.

ANALTYTICS PLAN

The essence of digital channels is that they are learning media – or at least they have the potential to be. We stress *potential*, because having the data doesn't by itself provide learning. Marketers need to have a clear framework and process for extracting learning from that data. Unfortunately, many marketers still don't. They have reams of data, but they often fail to devote the proper resources or sufficient time to actually learn from it.

Perhaps what's most daunting for DigiMarketers is the sheer volume of data. E*very* interaction with any digital media yields data. This benefit creates an immediate challenge: how can you analyze millions or billions of clicks and decipher what they actually mean? This opportunity/challenge of analyzing data to gain insights is really the essence of analytics: converting the raw data of click streams to the information needed to make informed marketing decisions.

Some marketers' eyes start to glaze over when you get into the subject of analytics. They prefer the sexier parts of DigiMarketing – briefing the agency or reviewing creative work. However, data analysis is where the extra value of your efforts can be unlocked: it's the road to the pot of DigiMarketing gold, so it should be sexy for every marketer!

In a digital world, technology deals with technology. As digital media spawn data, technology can be applied to track, aggregate and display that data in usable formats As digital marketing grows, the variety of tracking tools is increasing. These include sophisticated relational databases, with analytical processing modules, to help sort and compare billions of pieces of data. However, if you don't use the results of the analysis to make material decisions, you've lost the real advantage of the analytics. It's a bit like a coach simply watching the scoreboard without altering his strategy.

Ideally, your analytics should yield insights which you then use to make improvements and gradually optimize your work. Analytics and optimization go hand-in-hand. When we cover optimization, you'll see how it follows on from the analytics process quite naturally.

How to Develop Your Analytics Plan

KPIs *Linked to Your Goals*

Having data makes digital measurable. However, you must still determine which things to measure. You will need to set some key performance indicators (KPIs) that will reflect the Goals you set in Phase I. If you set out to acquire new customers, then the new customer acquisition rate will be a key performance indicator. If, on the other hand, your goal was to get more existing customers to your company events, then the event participation rate will naturally be a KPI.

In our example case of Eagle Athletics, the company set goals for both new customer acquisition and for the number of existing customers who attend Eagle-sponsored events In the analytics process, they will use both these KPIs.

The areas we have covered so far in the planning process – viral and messaging, consumer-generated content, digital awareness, and so on – will translate into KPIs. You will want to know if participants are responding to your messaging, passing on your content virally, participating in content-creation, and so forth. So you will most likely have multiple KPIs that relate to your key goals.

Measures

A key performance indicator is generally a top level indicator. But it alone won't provide enough information for you to truly understand what's going on. Within one KPI, there might be a number of measures that help you see the richer substrata of customer behavior. Therefore, it is also important to identify the various measures that will make up each KPI.

Let's use as an example the KPI mentioned above: Eagle Athletics' customer base growth rate. One key measure of this KPI will be the growth rate by time period (week, month, year), so Eagle can see when customer acquisition is accelerating or declining. However, this number doesn't tell Eagle anything about whether they are succeeding with female participants while utterly failing with male participants. Therefore, a second measure could track sign-up rates by gender. Eagle has a seasonally skewed business (50% of sales during holidays), so another measure might be the total customer acquisition rate during this high season versus previous high seasons. Marketers have to exert some judgment to ensure they won't drown in measures and yet have enough to truly understand the complexion of the KPI.

It's important to note that the interval for measurement is part of establishing the measure. While a consumer goods marketer might want to look at key data on a monthly basis, an online computer vendor might look at their KPIs on a daily basis. We are also moving towards real-time analysis and optimization, when data will be parsed and analyzed continuously, automatically driving micro adjustments to gain efficiency. Whatever time period you choose, it's important that your measures are quantifiable and enable you to observe changes at regular intervals.

Analytics

Analytics is the study of the measures you've selected. The purpose is to understand just what is happening to your measures, and why: to understand cause and effect – the essence of insight.

To illustrate these points, let's return to our example measure of Eagle's weekly new customer growth rate. This can be affected by many things. In particular, a change in the digital media mix, perhaps using banners on a better portal site or buying better search key phrases, can lead to a spike in new participant activity. Equally, Eagle might see an immediate decrease, if they've chosen some duds. So, one analysis would be to look at customer growth rate when we change media placement, to see if traffic from one (or all) of the media changes. This type of analysis should yield tangible learning that can then be used to improve media placements.

A Working Example:
Eagle Athletic – Analytics Plan

The following illustration summarizes the direct connection of KPIs, measures, and analytics. It shows how our example Eagle KPI (the growth rate of new customer) will have three measures and then three analytic points corresponding to each of these measures.

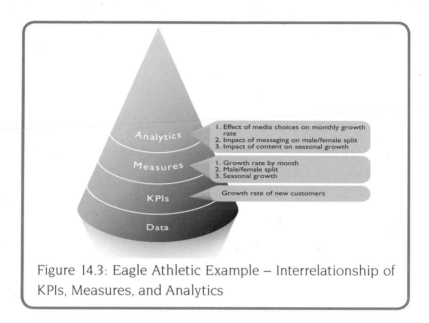

Figure 14.3: Eagle Athletic Example – Interrelationship of KPIs, Measures, and Analytics

Analytics can be applied to your overall participant base, or to individual participants. The latter is particularly relevant if a goal of your DigiMarketing is to improve customer management. In this case, you might look at KPIs that serve as milestones for how individual participants interact with you. These might include specific transactions (value and volume), measures of how recently and frequently participants have visited your site, responded to an email offer, and so on. You might also include psychographic measures as you try to profile your participant base.

What to Do with Your Analytics Plan

Your analytics plan will quickly fall by the wayside if you don't put in place the proper resources to carry it through. Analytics takes you deep into the bowels of the science of DigiMarketing, so you'll need experts. Who will they be? What technology will they use? How often will you review the results?

The whole point of analytics is to change your actions. However, it's amazing how many companies have information – and have analytics – but don't translate it into meaningful actions. This brings us to our final step: optimization.

DigiMarketing Tenet 12: Via addressable channels, everything in the marketing mix will be measured and optimized to ensure continuous improvement. DigiMarketing is the future evolution of more accountable marketing.

OPTIMIZATION PLAN

"Performance marketing" is a buzz phrase today. This term is sometimes used to describe compensation schemes for new media, such as affiliate marketing, which are based upon specific results. But it is also being used to describe the use of technology, and real-time data, to analyze and optimize performance. As data comes in, sophisticated software tracks and compares customer responses, then reallocates funds to those things which are providing the best results (look at Omniture, www.omniture.com). Decisions are enabled by technology, focusing on setting decision parameters ahead of time, not simply making decisions after the fact. This is the DigiMarketing future.

Everything Digital Can Be Optimized

A brief reminder is perhaps in order here. In our example, we have been referring primarily to a website. However, any and every digital channel can be optimized. So, if you are conducting mobile marketing or are sponsoring an online game, you should be looking at the same issues of how you learn from the data in order to improve your performance through specific actions that make your DigiMarketing more easy to use, more appealing, and more impactful.

Even if you don't use the full technological capabilities associated with performance marketing, there are things you can and *should* do to optimize your DigiMarketing. Optimization is not theoretical or academic: it's about having a plan to take practical steps to change things so they work better. This could mean optimizing a specific portion of your DigiMarketing, such as your registration process or your email layouts. Or it might mean taking a more holistic approach to optimizing your overall campaign. The extent of your optimizations will depend upon your company's ability and willingness to make changes based upon what the data shows.

By the way, optimizing doesn't mean simply fixing things that are broken. You certainly should change something that isn't performing well so it performs acceptably. But you can also optimize something that is performing well by making it even better. In today's highly competitive marketing environment, every incremental gain is useful.

How to Develop Your Optimization Plan

There are different types of optimizations and performance improvement approaches. We will briefly outline some of the most common approaches. The easiest place to start though is to go back to the Eagle example we discussed under Analytics, and show how it is completed with optimization.

A Working Example: Eagle Athletic – Optimization Plan

In our Eagle case, there were three analytic steps used to track growth of the customer base: 1) effect of media choices on monthly growth rate; 2) the impact of messaging on male/female split, and 3) the impact of content on seasonal growth. Analytics will yield insights that can then be used to optimize performance in each of these three areas.

For example, to optimize analytic step 1, resources will be shifted away from media that do less well in producing new customers and re-allocated to media that deliver better results. This could mean moving banner ads from one portal to another that performs better or moving resources from banner ads to search engine marketing (buying more search key phrases) – or even moving resources from web marketing to in-game marketing.

Remember the KPI Eagle uses is "growth of new customers." Don't get distracted by traffic to your media. High traffic media will not necessarily be those that produce new customers. That will depend (as we saw in chapter 4) on the conversion rates (that is, what proportion of traffic actually becomes customers). The appropriate optimization will drop media that have the lowest new participant acquisition yield, even if that media option appears to be driving a lot of traffic. Big doesn't always mean *effective*.

Looking at analytic step 2, Eagle might test different messaging layouts, and creative, to find which performs best for males and for females. An experimental design, tested on a small sample, can help Eagle see which match of layout and offer is most likely to yield the best results for their male and for their female participants.

Finally, for analytic step 3, Eagle could test different seasonal offers and the channels used to deliver them. For example, in the high season when participants are out doing holiday shopping, (opted-in) mobile messaging might be very effective. In the low season, Eagle might find that it takes e-coupons delivered via email to stimulate purchase.

Effective DigiMarketers need to have a scientific streak and be willing to trust the results of their analytics. The illustration below shows how the optimizations just mentioned follow through on the analytics process we covered in the last section.

Figure 14.4: Eagle Athletic Example – Link of Optimizations to KPIs and Analytics

Typical Optimizations

Here are some of the most common ways in which DigiMarketers are optimizing their marketing:

Search Engine Optimization (SEO): As we saw in chapter 4, search engine optimization makes your websites more search engine friendly and makes sure pages get a good place in search engine results for relevant search phrases.

Paid Placement Optimization (SEM): This focuses on getting the best return on your search phrase buys. You might want to review the section on Getting the Most Out of Paid Search Placement (again discussed in chapter 4).

Behavioral Targeting: The aim of behavioral targeting is to tailor your messaging to match the behavior of the participants flowing to you. (Yet another topic from chapter 4.)

Creative and Messaging Pre-Testing Optimizations: Pre-testing allows small scale experimentation in message design and content. The most successful options can then be rolled out to your participants. You might want to review the material on email messaging in chapter 5 and SMS messaging in chapter 6.

Site Optimizations: Sometimes there are mechanical issues on a website that need to be fixed. For example, low new customer registrations could indicate an overly long or intrusive registration process. You will want to look especially at where participants leave your site. This is a guide to where things are boring, frustrating or confusing – or even malfunctioning.

Campaign Performance Optimization: Don't forget while you are optimizing individual aspects of your marketing, it's the effectiveness of the entire campaign that's important. You will also need to take a holistic view of the entire campaign. Really you are trying to optimize the entire Participant Journey.

What to Do with Your Optimization Plan

A simple way to track your overall success in optimizing is to use a scorecard system. This will give you an easy overview of how you are tracking against your goals. The scorecard can be used in key management meetings as you decide what to do next with your DigiMarketing. It also will prove useful when you talk about one of the topics that is on every marketer's agenda – return on investment (ROI).

ROI is a much abused term. However, it is a critical topic as marketers are under more pressure than ever to demonstrate specific results and justify the money they spend. Fortunately, this is where DigiMarketing truly shines: digital provides the most measurable form of marketing available today. In a sense, DigiMarketing is the fulfillment of the promise that direct marketing has made for years to be measurable marketing. You will want to use the data you have to quantify the business case for your DigiMarketing. If you do it well, the numbers will speak for themselves.

The key to getting a good ROI is to translate knowledge into definitive action. Insights are frequently not turned into optimizations. Why? Sometimes companies take the view that DigiMarketing is still primarily an IT function, and expect the IT department to "fix the website." They simply don't understand the wider applications of DigiMarketing, so they don't apply many of the points of learning. In other cases, DigiMarketing is seen as a marketing function, but it is overseen by just a few marketing managers. Unfortunately, the culture in many companies doesn't encourage managers to identify where they can improve. So, marketers prefer to talk about the positive numbers rather than drilling down to find potential optimization points. What's required is better alignment of the people who are tasked and the incentivized to act upon insights in order to make efficiency improvements and thereby drive better return on your investment.

THE DIGIMARKETING PAYOFF

DigiMarketing represents an evolution of marketing that is characterized by a number of key benefits we've noted throughout this book:

- Digital channels generate information that can be used for more dynamic brand management. The immediacy of DigiMarketing enables companies to be more responsive to consumers and the marketplace.
- The viral aspect of new media enables companies deploying DigiMarketing to reach audiences faster and more efficiently than ever before.
- This viral aspect also means digital reach is not necessarily correlated with spending. Marketers with interesting content can interact with far more customers than they could afford to reach through traditional media.
- Direct dialogues with consumers via digital channels yield more and better information about consumer needs and preferences.
- The engagement of consumers as participants provides a powerful way to harness brand enthusiasm.
- Analytics and optimization reduces latency and inefficiencies In marketing programs.

All of these points drive results. In the final analysis, the payoff of DigiMarketing is improved marketing effectiveness. DigiMarketing can improve your ability to generate, convert, and sustain more business from customers. While some marketers are still feeling their way with their digital marketing, there are more and more examples of DigiMarketing delivering for companies today:

- A global computer company developed a compelling campaign integrating video embedded in email, games on its website, and a persuasive presence in social networks. Their campaign outperformed conventional media campaigns by over 6 to 1, with people opening each email on average three times.[11]
- The communications company Cingular Wireless secured all ad inventory for one day in Windows Live Hotmail, creating a "roadblock" which reportedly yielded increases in branding metrics, in a single day, which were at or above the average for entire campaigns. Unaided brand awareness increased 23% among those in market to purchase in the next three months, and by 9.1% among users of other cellular brands. What's more, association between the Cingular brand and the Motorola L2 (the primary offer of the campaign) increased by 6.7%.[12]
- A magazine found that an opt-in email boosted subscription renewal rates by over 25% compared to a control group receiving no emails.
- Diageo created a 3-minute viral ad (*Tea Partay*) for their brand Smirnoff Raw Tea in the US, reportedly for a total budget of $100,000. The viral, aired only on www.youtube.com, as of April 2007 has been seen by 3.1 million viewers – and is estimated to have gained 48 million impressions online, in print and on television. The product was originally launched only in the Northeast of the US. But the viral communication went national, and as Rob Malcolm, President, Global Marketing, Sales and Innovation put it, "certainly had some global implications." The viral ad prompted consumers to ask when the product was going to reach their region, creating an exceptionally easy sell-in to retailers and prompting a swift roll-out of the product.[13]

The list can go on. And as DigiMarketing increases, there will be more and varied examples of success. The key will be to continue to evolve your approach as new digital options become available.

SUMMARY – DIGIMARKETING PLANNING FRAMEWORK

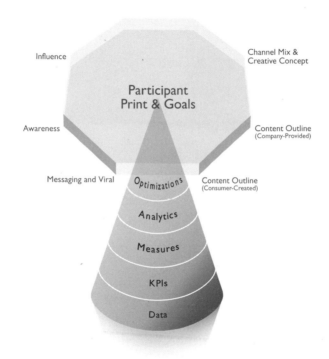

Figure 14.5: DigiMarketing Planning Framework – All Steps

DigiMarketing is an iterative process. As you gain better insights into your participants, so your DigiMarketing strategy will evolve. As we warned in chapter 2, as a DigiMarketer you will be in a perpetual beta test, constantly improving upon and modifying your marketing. This is not a result of a failure in planning; rather, it's the way things *should* be done in digital channels.

The key is to build value as you go. This happens by ensuring that the most important part of DigiMarketing – the participant engagement – constantly improves. That means watching how your participants behave, and listening to what they tell you. If you do this well, participants will want to stay connected with you. And the results will be what all marketers seek: faster, better, and continued success. (The DigiMarketing planning framework is summarized in Figure 14.5.)

DigiMarketing – The 10 Deadly Sins

Having covered the components of an effective DigiMarketing plan, it's worth reminding you of some of the most common mistakes that DigiMarketers make. Hopefully, having read this book, it will be obvious why these are DigiMarketing deadly sins that you must avoid:

1. Long Registrations
Despite all we have learned over the past decade, some companies are still creating barriers to interaction in the form of cumbersome registration processes. Do you enjoy long registrations (a rhetorical question)? If you take up too much of the participant's time right at the start, you will fail.

2. No Data Plan
Sad but true: companies (even good companies) collect data but don't have a clear plan for what they will do with

A DigiMarketing Planning Framework

it. This is often linked to the first sin noted above – long registrations. Companies that ask for data but lack a plan to turn it into information are wasting participants' time.

3. Data but No Analysis

In other cases, companies have data but lack the discipline to analyze it and glean any learning from it. You will need a clear plan for how you will regularly analyze and apply your data. Remember: the aim is optimization, not data collection.

4. Going for Gimmicks

A while ago, many DigiMarketers insisted that adding games to their sites made them "sticky." What resulted was a bunch of cyber loiters who were more interested in the games than the brands. Using gimmicks in your DigiMarketing will give you short-lived success at best.

5. Ignoring an Awareness Plan

The notion that you can "build it and they will come" is so wrong. There are millions of digital destinations out there today. If you don't have a smart plan to build traffic to what you've created, your DigiMarketing will wither unnoticed.

6. Omitting Search

After reading this book, this shouldn't require any explanation. Failing to have a search marketing strategy is a major no-no for DigiMarketers. If you don't think it's worth the money, then don't be surprised if you rank 2,250,743 in the search results.

7. Poor Usability

Remember, time is relative: ten seconds waiting in a bank queue means great service, while ten seconds waiting for a webpage to load often results in participants clicking onto something else. Be mindful of how user-friendly your DigiMarketing is.

8. Spamming

Perhaps more than anything spam is the sign of a marketer that doesn't "get" DigiMarketing. Don't be a spammer.

9. Failing to Involve Your Participants

Many marketers would still prefer to talk *at* their consumers rather than discuss *with* their participants. Brochureware and other types of one-way marketing still plague the internet. This represents a major opportunity lost. Self-centered corporate marketing will fail to produce results.

10. One-size Fits All DigiMarketing

Digital provides you with the greatest personalization power in the history of marketing. It's plain stupid to treat it like mass marketing without any customization to individual participants.

END NOTES
1 www.msnbc.msn.com/id/16493727/
2 en.wikipedia.org/wiki/AOL_search_data_scandal Excite had apparently released similar records, less publically, in 2000. informationr.net/ir/6-1/paper90.html
3 blog.searchenginewatch.com/blog/060807-105252
4 www.gregsadetsky.com/aol-data/
5 www.nytimes.com/2006/08/09/technology/09aol.html?ex=1312776000en=f6f619 49c6da4d38ei=5090
6 www.aolpsycho.com/user/17556639
7 www.eff.org/Privacy/AOL/
8 online.wsj.com/article/SB115618361010241207.html, seattletimes.nwsource.com/html/businesstechnology/2003216030_aol22.html
9 www.computerworld.com/action/article.do?command=viewArticleBasic&articleI d=9003619&intsrc=news_ts_head

10 news.wired.com/dynamic/stories/E/EU_GOOGLE_PRIVACY_PROBE?SITE=WIR
   E&SECTION=HOME&TEMPLATE=DEFAULT
11 Effectiveness examples 1 and 3 from Jeanniey Mullen of the e-mail marketing
   practice at Ogilvy & Mather New York.
12 advertising.microsoft.com/research/cingular-case-study
13 Diageo, 2007 Investor Conference April 2007, www.diageo.com/NR/rdonlyres/
   12ADEFBD-5676-4B73-8516-5F3C837BA619/0/MarketingTrendsTranscriptandQA.
   pdf

Conclusion

Stay Connected

We're now at the end of this book. As we finish, there are some last items that merit a mention.

We *didn't* cover everything related to digital in this book. For example, we didn't cover the actual process of building, and usability-testing, websites. We didn't cover the important issue of site architecture, or the decisions you'll need to make about technologies, content management systems, and the like. We didn't outline how to manage technology vendors, or set timelines for digital production. All of these issues are important. However, they are topics which are best addressed working with an agency partner or vendor. We suggest you not attempt to do everything in-house. Advice from the right partners will more than pay for itself in the long run as you execute your DigiMarketing plans.

In the introduction of this book, we covered the need for marketers to bring a new mentality and flexibility to marketing. In particular, we noted the need to be willing to take risks, to try something new. In fact, if you hope to stay ahead of your competition, DigiMarketing will require you not just to take one risk, but rather experiment continuously. Given the speed with which digital is changing marketing, there are no safe or certain routes. The key DigiMarketing steps and best practices outlined should serve as guideposts, but they're not a static formula. Nothing guarantees success. You will need to have the guts to apply these best practices in new ways and be prepared to learn from your mistakes. But isn't that the case already?

As with all DigiMarketing, the conversation continues. If you have thoughts or comments, we invite you to share them with us and our other participants. You can do that by posting your comments on www.DigiMarketingNow.com. Additionally, that site has links to a variety of destinations noted throughout this book.

Best of luck with your DigiMarketing, and stay connected.

Index